Study Guide
for Howell, Fox, and Morehead's

Curriculum-Based Evaluation
Teaching and Decision Making

Second Edition

Sheila L. Fox
Western Washington University

Kenneth W. Howell
Western Washington University

Mada Kay Morehead
Kyrene School District
Tempe, Arizona

Stanley H. Zucker

Brooks/Cole Publishing Company
Pacific Grove, California

Brooks/Cole Publishing Company
A Division of Wadsworth, Inc.

Printed in the United States of America

10 9 8 7 6 5 4 3 2 1

ISBN 0-534-16429-3

Sponsoring Editor: Vicki Knight
Editorial Assistant: Lauri Banks-Wothe
Production Coordinator: Dorothy Bell
Cover Design: Roy R. Neuhaus
Cover Art: Ron Grauer
Printing and Binding: Malloy Lithographing, Inc.

PREFACE

This study guide was written to provide you with some opportunities to test your understanding of the concepts and some opportunities to practice procedures that were presented in the text, <u>Curriculum-Based Evaluation, Teaching and Decision Making</u>. It was designed with the intent of helping learners to establish ownership of the information in the text. We want students to become so comfortable with using evaluation information and making teaching decisions, that data gathering will become their first step in teaching.

Each chapter in the study guide contains some questions that will require <u>identification</u> of important concepts and <u>production</u> of responses that will test understanding of the text material. The recommended procedure is to read a chapter in the text then complete the questions in the study guide. Next, check the answers in the study guide key, and if your response or understanding of the material is incompatible with the key, return to the text to re-read the relevant section. In some cases, you will be asked to base your response to a question on what you answered in the previous question. When that situation arises, check your answer to the first question with the key before proceeding to the second question.

The study guide also contains directions for writing probes and reproducible copies of selected exhibits, including some tests, from the text.

The purpose of the study guide is to serve as a supportive tool that will help ease students through critically important (but sometimes complex) material. We hope it serves that function for you.

CONTENTS

PART A: GUIDE TO TEXT

SECTION ONE   CHAPTER EXERCISES

SECTION TWO   ANSWER KEYS

SECTION THREE SUPPLEMENTARY MATERIALS

PART B: EVALUATION MATERIALS

CHAPTER ONE

TEACHER THOUGHT PROCESS

In this section you will learn:

...how to think about curriculum;

...the difference between placement and teaching decisions;

...how to match assessment information to the type of decision to be made;

...the concept of alterable vs. unalterable variables;

...the task-student-instruction relationship; and

...the role of judgment in decision making.

1. Conceptualization of curriculum
    In order to understand the authors' suggestions for making decisions about curriculum, it is important to know how they think about curriculum. Which of the following best represents the textbook's definition of curriculum?

    a. Published materials adopted by a school district.

    b. Learning outcomes expected to result from instruction.

    c. A set of organized activities that keep students actively engaged during the school day.

2. Expected rate of performance
    On the chart below, a) draw a line that represents a student progressing at expected rates through 8th grade; b) add a second line representing a student who falls two years behind expected performance by fifth grade; and then c) draw in a vertical line at sixth grade to represent the beginning of successful changes in educational programs that bring the second student back to grade level by the eighth grade.

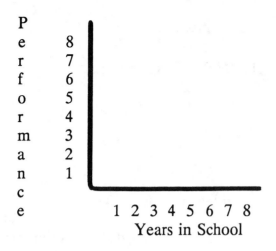

```
P
e    8
r    7
f    6
o    5
r    4
m    3
a    2
n    1
c
e       1 2 3 4 5 6 7 8
           Years in School
```

3. Placement and teaching decisions

    Educational decisions serve two functions: to guide placement and to guide teaching. Consider each of the following and identify whether it is a placement decision or a teaching decision. The first item is completed as an example.

    a. __t__   Sally's teacher has decided to teach her the periodic table of elements.

    b. _____   Brad has been assigned to work with the Chapter 1 remedial reading teacher.

    c. _____   Juan will learn to use a specific learning strategy to improve his reading comprehension.

    d. _____   Willard's teacher suggests that he use a number line to help solve arithmetic problems.

    e. _____   Kathleen will work with a cooperative learning group as a strategy to help her learn to write a report.

    f. _____   Debbie scored low on her achievement test, so she will work with the lowest reading group.

4. **Select the right type of assessment information to make placement and teaching decisions.**
    No single assessment can be used for all the decisions teachers have to make. Different types of tests are used for different purposes. Which of the following statements best represents the textbook authors' analysis of how assessment data should be used?

    a. All important decisions are made with incomplete data, therefore it's not necessary to waste time gathering assessment information.

    b. The only information that is useful in school settings is gathered directly from student performance on classroom assignments.

    c. Normative comparisons are most often used for placement decisions; measurement of prerequisite skills and criterion-referenced performance are best used for teaching decisions.

5. **Task-student-instruction interaction**
    The ease or difficulty a student has in learning is influenced by the interaction between a) the nature of the task the student is asked to complete, b) the characteristics of the student, and c) the quality of the instruction. Many of the characteristics of the student will be **unalterable** variables. Task and instruction characteristics are more easily changed. For each of the following, label the item **T** for task variable, **S** for student variable, or **I** for instructional variable. After labeling, state whether it is an **unalterable** or an **alterable** variable within the context of a teacher's role.

		Alterable	Unalterable
a) S	Chemically dependent parents.		X
b) ____	Assignments given directly from a textbook that is two grade levels above the student's reading level.		
c) ____	The teacher uses a "hands off" approach to reading instruction.		

d) ____   The student is a tough looking 6-foot 5-inch 13-year-old.

e) ____   The teacher maintains a 50% engagement rate with students during group lessons.

6.   <u>Interaction between task-student-instruction should guide teacher decisions.</u> The following two paragraphs give examples of teacher decisions that would affect either task or instruction. As already noted, teachers generally do not control the variables necessary to change student variables, so no examples of social agency or drug treatment programs are included; but note that student-related factors are important, when the critical characteristic is the lack of a skill or knowledge base the student needs to learn. Teachers <u>should</u> attempt to change nonreaders to readers and students without study skills to organized learners.

Read these two examples, then add your own suggestions for the last scenario.

<u>Example 1:</u>   Milton J. has terrible handwriting. All jokes about his promising career in the medical profession aside, his handwriting prevents him from being understood by his teachers when assignments require written responses. One of his teachers has suggested that he be allowed to use the classroom computer to type them. <u>Task</u>

<u>Example 2:</u>   Another teacher said that unless all students have access to word processing, Milton J. shouldn't be allowed to use the computer. Instead, the teacher suggested that Milton J.'s handwriting be evaluated to see if his errors were in formation of the letters, the slant of the letters, or their spacing. Once the problem is isolated, Milton could receive daily instruction to remedy the problem and be given feedback on key letters from his classroom work. <u>Instruction</u>

<u>Your turn:</u>   Lynn is not passing history. To pass history, the teacher says it is important to remember 1) the sequence of events surrounding significant periods of change; 2) which events were catalysts for change; 3) specific people who were central figures in creating change; and 4) typical life styles of "average people" during a given period. Lynn just can't seem to get all that together. Even though the lectures are entertaining and the text has interesting stories and illustrations, Lynn doesn't know what information to write down in notes. Without good notes, it is difficult to recall everything before a test. Help!

      a)   Make a <u>task</u>-related suggestion for change:

      b)   Make an <u>instruction</u>-related suggestion for change:

7.   <u>Student progress is increased when evaluation information is related to the interaction between task, student, and instructional variables.</u>
Teachers should seek evaluation information that is relevant. This includes information about the appropriateness of the task, the student's prior knowledge, or the teacher's instructional methods.

Match the evaluation information to the decision that logically follows from it.

Teacher Decision	Evaluation Information
1. ___ Teach the student to generate a list of adjectives and adverbs to modify a word. (Instruction: <u>how</u> to do it.)	a. Barbara's I.Q. is 95. b. When asked to write an essay in English Lit., Bill wrote in sentence fragments.

2. ___ Allow the student to write PENS on the top of the paper as a reminder to vary sentence structure. (Instruction: how to remember to do it.)

3. ___ Teach the student the prerequisite skill of writing complete sentences. (Student: teach prior knowledge.)

4. ___ Tell the student to write a three-sentence paragraph that contains one main idea and two supporting sentences. (Task: how much to do.)

c. Chuck scored in the 40th percentile on the TOWL (Test of Written Lang.)

d. Debbie's writing is boring. If she uses modifiers at all, she repeats the same one over and over again.

e. Marie writes letters at one third the rate of her peers because she has broken her preferred writing arm. Therefore, written assignments take her three times as long to complete as her average classmate. The standard assignment for in-class essays is to write one page in fifteen minutes of "write time."

f. Jack has demonstrated that he can use a learning strategy designed to vary sentence structure, but he is not using the strategy outside of the study skills lab.

8. Expert teachers follow effective decision-making procedures and exercise good judgment.
Sione is a new student in Ms. Easton's classroom. The first day he walked through the door he appeared shy, small for his age, and gave only one- or two-word answers to Ms. Easton's questions. She quickly sized him up as a student with poor language skills who was less than eager.

Which of the following is the most accurate statement about her judgment?

a) Teachers with experience don't need a road map or elaborate assessment tests to tell them a student is likely to have a learning deficit. Her judgment is likely to be correct.

b) She made her judgment too quickly. The sample size of information is too small and she should seek more information before coming to conclusions that will affect instructional and task-related decisions.

c) She hasn't made any decisions yet. It's too soon to criticize Ms. Easton.

d) Ms. Easton has wrapped this case up efficiently. Even violent criminals are sometimes convicted on circumstantial evidence.

9. <u>Effective decision-making procedures require good judgment.</u>
Which of the following provides the best analogy for the role of teachers' decision making?

a) Teachers are like orchestra leaders. They need to get the group playing the same note, in tempo, all together.

b) Teachers are like detectives trying to solve a case. They gather information, form a possible explanation, and then test the accuracy of their assumptions by gathering more evidence.

c) Teachers are like pilots. They file a flight plan and take off facing weather, wind velocity, and the chatter of their passengers as they wing their way across a three-dimensional landscape. Sigh. (Occasionally, they crash.)

d) Teachers are like artists. They may be spontaneously inspired by theme, attitude, or other characteristics of the moment. Their medium is the classroom.

10. <u>Effective decision making requires good judgment.</u>
Imagine that you made a decision that did not result in the desired change in a student's learning. Identify: 1) a possible reason for the judgment error, 2) a plan of action, and 3) what type of decisions you will be required to make next. The first item is completed as an example.

a)   Because Anna said she could add decimals, you put her in the group working on multiplication of decimals. Her performance indicates that she doesn't even know what a decimal is, let alone how to add them together.

1.   I failed to define the problem before I made a placement decision.

2.   Now I need to gather information about her skill level and

3.   make placement, teaching, and task decisions.

b) Linda reminds you of Connie, another student you taught last year. They both entered fifth grade with reading deficits, spelling problems, and shallow vocabularies. Last year, you used Direct Instruction Reading, Morphographic Spelling, and Direct Instruction Language programs with Connie and she learned very quickly. By the time she moved on to sixth grade, she was at grade level in all of her language arts skills. Linda, however, hasn't responded in the same way at all. She seems bored with instruction and resists participating in the lessons even though pretests indicate that she has the prerequisite skills necessary to be successful.

1.   Reason for your judgment error:

2.   Plan of action:

3.   Decisions required:

c)   Poor Ralph. When he began taking study skills to help organize his own brand of chaos, you showed him how to outline when taking notes. In spite of your instruction, he is still disorganized. This term he has failed to hand in a completed assignment or earn a grade higher than a "C-."

1.   Reason for your judgment error:

2.   Plan of action:

3.   Decisions required:

~~~~   ~~~~   ~~~~   ~~~~   ~~~~   ~~~~   ~~~~   ~~~~

CHAPTER TWO

THINKING ABOUT LEARNING AND STUDENTS

In this section you will learn:

...to recognize some commonly held educational myths;

...about the components of information-processing theory;

...the difference between performance and learning;

...how students use short-term and long-term memory; and

...the function of automaticity in tasks.

1.   This chapter identified seven myths about learning. Identify the myth statements with an "M" and the true statements with a "T."

   a. ____   The best way to motivate a student to work is to provide easy tasks that s/he can do fairly effortlessly.

   b. ____   Learning occurs almost instantaneously. Proficiency may develop gradually.

c. ____   What a student learns and how s/he learns is determined by a fixed capacity to learn.

d. ____   Students cannot be taught to attend by removing distractions from the room.

e. ____   Students who are different from each other <u>can</u> be taught together.

2. Information-processing theory suggests that it is not capacity, but rather attention, memory, and motivation that determine how receptive students are to instruction.

Does information-processing theory differ from modality-learning theory?

a. No. They may use new vocabulary, but conceptually the theories do not differ much from one another.

b. Yes. Information-processing theory suggests that the way the brain responds to information is not by coding and responding through sensory modalities, but by selecting strategies to fit the demands of the task.

c. No. Information-processing theory accepts the assumptions of learning style and then assumes that students will select whatever strategy best suits their preferences.

d. Yes. The two theories aren't in competition because they are concerned with different sets of problems.

3. Information-processing theory implies that if executive control function is limited to just a few strategies or a collection of not very useful strategies, the student will:

a. be mentally retarded.

b. have definite limits on her or his capacity to learn.

c. need to receive medication to improve neurological health.

d. benefit from instruction to improve attention and memory.

4. The waitress came rushing over to the table and said, "I've got something to show you." She began, "Johnnie's mother had three children." She laid a penny on the table and said, "She named the first one Penny." Next, she laid a nickel on the table and said, "She named the second one Nicole." Then she laid a dime on the table and asked, "What did she name the third one?"

What was that third child's name, and which of the big three (attention, memory or motivation) is important in solving this question?

5. Motivation is sticking to a task even though it may be difficult.
Which of the following students is the most motivated?

   a. Willie believes that his "personal best" time at the swim meet was the result of poor competitors and that he will never be able to replicate it.
   b. Waylen gave a poor performance at the talent show, but he refuses to be embarrassed about it. He simply won't play the accordion again.
   c. Dolly isn't such a great musician either, but she intends to add back-up rhythm to her vocal and try it again at the junior class Karoke night next week.
   d. Garth has difficulty following the coach's rules about attending extra study sessions if any grade drops below a "C." He wants to play ball, however, so he pays his twin brother to attend study hall for him.

6. The activities teachers ask students to do might lead to performance and/or learning. The two concepts are independent of each other. A student can perform (complete a task) without learning, or s/he can learn (improve) without finishing the assignment.
Circle the word that indicates what each teacher is asking the student to do:

a. Ms. Jensen assigned each student to write answers to the six questions at the end of the chapter. Each student must have the questions completed before they may go to recess.

       Performance   Learning

b.   Each time a student responds incorrectly to an algebra problem, Mr. Berry has the student orally explain the procedure that was followed in the attempt to solve the problem. When the source of the error is identified, Mr. Berry provides the correct component and then has the student orally repeat the entire sequence, this time including the corrected step.

Performance   Learning

c.   Michael has become very clever at taking multiple-choice tests. He has learned to avoid absolutes like "never" and "always"; he monitors to see if other questions on the test have the answers to questions he doesn't know; he knows that the longest choice is often the correct choice; and he eliminates options he knows are wrong choices, then selects from the remaining choices. By being alert, he can usually earn at least a "C" grade on tests. His teacher insists that he must average 65% on the weekly quizzes in order to pass the class.

Performance   Learning

d.   Ms. Hankinson takes a two-minute "brain storming" timed sample at the end of each science lesson. Students are asked to write down "things they know" related to the current unit. Each day students count their own "write idea" rate and chart it, comparing the day's count to the previous day's count. Since each unit lasts several weeks, students watch the "idea" count grow day to day and monitor for a relationship between fluency in the daily timed samples and the weekly test scores.

Performance   Learning

7.   Keeping in mind the subject matter you teach, write three statements a teacher might make to a student that would promote a <u>learning orientation</u> rather than a performance orientation.

a.

b.

c.

12

8. Self-monitoring is another executive function. It alerts us to the need for extra effort. It can be promoted by encouraging students to judge the difficulty of a task, to check their own work, and to be accountable for their own decisions.

    Rank the following teacher behaviors in order from most likely to least likely to promote self-monitoring.

    Most likely:____   Somewhat likely____   Least likely:____

    a. Ms. Lopez gives her students the choice of either correcting their own work or having her correct it. A correction key is always available at the back counter, but if a student chooses to have Ms. Lopez correct the assignment, he or she places it in a tray on the teacher's desk.

    b. Before Mr. Lovitt's students begin an assignment, he asks them to predict how many responses they will make and how accurate they will be. When the work is complete, students correct their own work and compute the difference between what they predicted and what they actually did.

    c. Students in Ms. Follett's class can always count on receiving corrected assignments with 24-hour express service. She makes it a point to return every assignment with either a "C" for correct or an "X" for error by every response. Students can tell at a glance how well they did.

9. When a task requires thoughtful attention, the thinker is using the short-term memory function. There, conscious intention is required to solve a problem or remember a sequence of strategic steps. When a person performs without conscious thought, even in the presence of distractors, the long-term memory is using information that has been learned to an automatic level.

    Consider the following challenges and circle the appropriate descriptor that indicates which memory function you would use to complete the task described.

                        Programming your VCR

    Long-term memory   Short-term memory

Singing "Happy Birthday"

Long-term memory   Short-term memory

Reciting the Gettysburg Address

Long-term memory   Short-term memory

Filling out an itemized income tax form

Long-term memory   Short-term memory

10.   What criterion should be used to determine whether a task should be learned to the automaticity level or not?

a.   Time allocated to teach that particular task in the teaching day (week, month, year).

b.   The student's capacity to learn.

c.   How critical the task is to future performance and how frequently the student will be called upon to use it again.

d.   How easily the student responds to instruction.

11.   Fill in the blanks:

a.   Self-monitoring allows students to be mindful. This is important because students can become automatic at doing tasks _____.
                                                (too well) (wrong) (without thinking)

b.   It is a waste of time to take students to automaticity on skills they will use_____.
            (later)   (repeatedly)   (infrequently)

14

c. Information-processing theory suggests that the most important variable in learning is:

_____.

    (prior knowledge) (capacity) (learning style)

d. Special and remedial students do not make good use of

_____.

    (their time) (practice) (executive control)

e. Prior knowledge and use of strategies can both be altered through

_____.

    (instruction) (drill) (surgery)

~~~~ ~~~~ ~~~~ ~~~~ ~~~~ ~~~~ ~~~~

CHAPTER THREE

THINKING ABOUT CURRICULUM

In this section you will learn:

...the purpose of goals and objectives in curriculum;

...about task, concept and error analysis;

...the authors' definition of literacy;

...the importance of enabling skills and conceptual knowledge;

...characteristics of goals and objectives; and

...important vocabulary and background knowledge regarding curriculum.

1.   Which of the following describes curriculum?

    a.   Instructional techniques used to improve learning.

b.   The content of what is taught, often described in goals and objectives.

c.   Published materials which are field tested and validated as effective.

d.   The sum total of the behaviors students engage in between 9:00 and 3:30 of the school day.

2.   Students need to gain skills, knowledge, and strategies for learning if they are to successfully move through increasingly difficult learning challenges. Identify each of the following as **SK**ill, **KN**owledge, or **ST**rategy.

____   Write digit

____   Study for test by paraphrasing key concepts

____   Measure object

____   In science class, recognize the need to test the properties of an unknown compound.

____   Keep track of assignment due dates by using a calendar and task completion time line.

____   Explain how to use basic meteorological information to predict the weather.

3.   Should curriculum for remedial and special-education students placed in general education classes differ from that of their typical peers? Justify your response.

_____Yes   _____No

Justification:

16

4.   Please fill in the blank: The value of an instructional method is determined by how well the curriculum is learned. When learning does not occur, it is _____ _____ that should be changed.

5.   When a student is having difficulty learning, which of the following is <u>most likely</u> to be the source of the problem? (Yes, we know there are no sure things, but we're fishing for <u>probabilities</u> here.)

   a.   The task

   b.   The student's capability

   c.   The student's prior knowledge

   d.   The curriculum

6.   If a student has trouble learning, a teacher should use a task analysis, concept analysis, and/or an error analysis to identify what the student does and does not know. Try your hand at each of the three by responding to the following scenarios:

   <u>TASK ANALYSIS</u>   List at least three skills that the student would have to perform in order to add 2 and 2/3 to 12/9.

   1.

   2.

   3.

   <u>CONCEPT ANALYSIS</u>   Identify at least three concepts that a student must understand in order to complete the problem described in the task analysis section above.

   1.

   2.

3.

ERROR ANALYSIS When working addition of mixed and improper fractions, three different students gave the following patterns as they worked the problems. For each student, identify the error he or she is making.

Student A Error Pattern: $8/5 + 3/10 = 11/15$

Student B Error Pattern: $8/5 + 3/10 = 16/10 + 3/10 = 19/10$

Student C Error Pattern: $8/5 + 3/10 = 16/10 + 3/10 = 17/10 = 17/10$

Correct Pattern: $8/5 + 3/10 = 16/10 + 3/10 = 19/10 = 19/10$

7.   Teaching students to be literate is the major mission of schools. The concept of literacy might be best understood by thinking of it as communication. A student is a literate reader when he or she receives the message the author meant to communicate. A writer is literate when the mechanics of writing do not interfere with the content he or she intended to communicate. Speakers might be considered literate when the intended audience understands the ideas the speaker meant to send. Social behavior and body language also send messages, so social literacy may be defined by how closely the form of behavior matches its function.

Are the following examples of literacy? Respond "Yes" or "No" and then justify your answer.

a. _____ Carol ordered a play swing set for her children. When the kit arrived (some assembly required), she read the assembly instructions but could not even understand the kind of tools that would be required, let alone what thinga-ma-bob should be attached to the numerous do-hickies.

     Justification:

18

b. _____ Rudy needed to get an extension on a due date for a report he had to write. He approached his teacher, said her name, looked right at her, then stated what he wanted and the reason he had to ask. He offered a new due date, then apologized for having to ask for the extension.

Justification:

c. _____ After completing his play rehearsal at the park stage, Raymond needed a ride home from his mother. He left her a note on the kitchen table with information about when he would be finished and where he would be waiting, but he omitted a few words and misspelled some others. She thought he wanted pork chops without sage for dinner. By 7:00, they were both cranky.

Justification:

d. _____ Lupita was on her way to the store when a stranger asked her for directions to the library. She thought for a minute, chose the most direct route, then gave verbal directions that included details about major landmarks that would indicate where to turn. The directions were clear enough that the stranger found the library without making any wrong turns.

Justification:

8. To be literate, a student needs both enabling skills and a conceptual grasp of when to apply strategies like planning, transcribing, reviewing, revising, etc. Consider these scenarios and identify what component is missing, Enabling skill, Conceptual understanding, or Both; then name the skill or concept that should be taught.

a. ___ Uwanda was an English as a Second Language kindergarten student, but the truth is he didn't speak any English other than "good bye," "yes," and "no." He desperately wanted to know where the bathroom was located. He had been shown on his first day of class, but because his kindergarten class met only every-other day, he hadn't been to school since Thursday of last week, and now he couldn't remember how to get there. Oops.

What should be taught? _____

b. ___ Arthur looked at the teacher while he lectured. Although he occasionally nodded his head, Arthur never took notes, wrote down assignments, or even gave a thought to homework or long-term projects that were assigned. Arthur didn't seem to notice that everyone else did these things, and he was always genuinely shocked when a test was given or an assignment came due. He often wondered how others knew ahead of time when something was going to happen, and he was awe struck when he saw that Sally had written out a point-by-point outline from one of the teacher's lectures.

What should be taught? _____

c. ___ Malinda could recite all of the guidelines for giving a good speech. She knew she should have a "set" to get attention, then tell her audience what she intended to cover, give content information in a few succinct points, and, finally, review the important points. She understood the importance of eye contact, projection, and the use of humor. But when she ran for student body president, she spoke very quietly to her shoes in a rambling style that soon bored her audience. Later, when her English teacher asked Malinda how her speech had gone, Malinda asked, "What speech?"

What should be taught? _____

9. Which of the following statements about goals and objectives is false?

a. The use of goals and objectives is one way educators maintain professional accountability.

b. IEPs, which are required for all remedial and at-risk students, must include objectives for each activity a student engages in each day.

c. Without goals and objectives, there is nothing against which progress can be judged, which results in no basis on which to evaluate instruction.

d. Goals and objectives facilitate motivation because students learn better when targets are specified and communicated to students.

10. Goals usually specify the target behavior and the direction of change that is desired. Objectives are more specific and contain a statement of content, observable behavior, conditions under which the behavior will be performed, and the criteria for success. For each of these goals, write two objectives that would be appropriate en route to the goal.

    a. Goal: Enricki will improve reading in subject matter area textbooks.
        Objective #1:

        Objective #2:

    b. Goal: Pamela Kay will increase the number of study strategies she utilizes to improve reading comprehension.
        Objective #1:

        Objective #2:

11. Quality goals and objectives must be measurable, useful, and calibrated in units that are both small enough to show variation in the behavior when change occurs and large enough to maintain an achievable pace through the breadth of the curriculum.

Only one of the following has all three qualities. Which one is it?

a. Franklin will improve his appreciation of numerical systems used around the world throughout history. He will demonstrate his appreciation orally and in writing.

b. Emilio will master the content of the audio library's series on inventors. Mastery will be judged as 85% or better on tests that are given on the material.

c. Agnes will get better at reading prose and poems in reading materials both in school and out of school.

d. Leah will improve writing skills so that all of ten randomly selected written assignments will contain complete sentences with correct punctuation.

12. Which of the following statements about criterion level standards is <u>false</u>?

a. Proficiency level standards are arbitrary, but <u>some</u> statement about them must be made so the objective can be measured.

b. Some standards are established by sampling other students who have already mastered the skill.

c. Criteria for accuracy, fluency, and automaticity for any given skill should be considered and specified.

d. Although criterion standards may be individualized for a student, teachers should be careful not to routinely ask less of students with remedial or special needs lest their performance remain substandard.

13. Here's the objective:
Sven will orally read words in context from literature based chapter books at the fourth-grade level at 125 words per minute with no more than 3 errors per minute.

a) Modify the objective for individualization purposes by changing the criteria.

b) Modify the original objective by changing the content.

c) Modify the original objective by changing the behavior.

d) Modify the original objective by changing the conditions.

e) Modify the original objective by recalibrating the objective (the size of the curricular "slice").

14. Match the term to its definition.

a. _____ Subtask   1. The process of isolating, sequencing, and defining all of the essential components of a task.

b. _____ Task

                                     2. The rules, procedures, and algorithms students

c. _____ Task analysis   follow to combine subtasks into larger tasks.

d. _____ Strategy   3. The performance of an objective.

4. Small unit of behavior necessary for completion of a step en route to an objective.

~~~~ ~~~~ ~~~~ ~~~~ ~~~~ ~~~~ ~~~~ ~~~~

CHAPTER FOUR

THINKING ABOUT INSTRUCTION

In this section you will learn:

...the characteristics of "hands on" instruction;

...the difference between giving assignments and instructing;

...teacher actions that improve student learning;

...critical attributes of strategy instruction;

...the concept of the acquisition stage of learning; and

...effective strategies for special-learner needs in the general classroom.

1. Since the primary defining characteristic of students in need of remedial or special education is their failure to keep pace with their general-education peers while moving through the curriculum, the authors of this text advocate a "hands on" approach to instruction. "Hands on" means direct, interactive instruction. Consider the following items and categorize them as either requiring teacher interaction <u>Yes</u> or student centered <u>No</u>.

Yes   a.   Ms. Perkins asks the group to speak in unison, listing in sequence the three steps necessary to solve the problem. As they respond, she listens to be sure they know the right steps in the correct sequence.

No   b.   The history teacher assigns chapter five and the first ten questions of the summary section. Students are expected to copy each question and then write its answer using information from the textbook.

Yes   c.   Mr. Murray is a good lecturer. He always starts with an entertaining story and then develops three or four major points, supporting each with related information. As he lectures, he moves around the classroom to make sure students are taking notes in an organized manner. At the end of his lecture, he always summarizes the important content and usually gives a brief preview of the content that will be covered next.

Yes   d.   As students finish writing the in-class essay assignment, Ms. Bower checks each one to be sure that each student has used paragraphs that begin with a topic sentence and include at least three supporting sentences. When she finds instances where that format was not followed, she asks the student to list the characteristics of a paragraph. She then pairs that student with a peer partner who has finished the assignment so that they can work together to reconstruct one of the troublesome paragraphs.

No   e.   Mr. Leckvold is very clear about his expectations for class assignments. They must be neat, they must be finished within the allotted class period, and they must be placed in the tray labeled "Assignments." Once the assignment has been turned in, Mr. Leckvold gives credit for its completion by placing a check mark by students' names in the grade book. If any student fails to turn in two or more assignments in the grading period, his or her grade will be decreased by one full grade.

2.   The text states, "One of the biggest threats to good instruction is the belief that the core of teaching is assignment giving." Here is your opportunity to change a threat to a promise. Change each of the following assignments into a teacher action that will have a higher probability of influencing student learning. Hint: consider using explanation, demonstration, guided practice, timely correction, task specific feedback, or other teacher action supported by the effective teaching literature. The first example is completed for you.

a. Today's lesson has been on mammals. As a group we listed the critical and noncritical attributes of a mammal.

The assignment:
>   Now use your textbook to help as you answer the first eight questions at the end of chapter five titled, Facts About Mammals.

Revised:
>   Now, work with your partner as you sort this list of 20 animals into mammal and nonmammal categories. Be prepared to explain why you categorized each as you have. (This teacher has presented an activity designed to provide practice for students as they demonstrate their level of comprehension about the defining characteristics of mammals.)

b.   Yesterday, I showed you the chemical abbreviations used for elements on the periodic table. Today, you'll have a chance to review that information.

The assignment:
>   This worksheet lists all of the elements. You are to fill in the chemical abbreviation for each and turn in the worksheet when you are finished.

Revised:

c. So that is how you should use the punctuation marks of commas, colons, and semi-colons.

The assignment:
>Write an essay at least three pages long, and pay attention to how you punctuate it.

Revised:

3.   Which of the following statements is <u>false</u>?

   a.   Academic learning time increases with teacher direction.

   b.   In general-education classrooms, 50% to 70% of time allocated to instruction is spent doing independent, non-teacher directed activities.

   c.   Academic learning time increases when instruction is designed to match the curricular objectives.

   d.   It is good practice to maintain the lesson sequence presented in published materials adopted by the school district.

4.   Effective instruction is characterized by aligning several variables. Sort the actions and strategies listed below into the appropriate category.

Teacher instructional action:

Type of thought process:

Teacher format of instruction
(matched to student learning stage):

   a.   Acquisition instruction
   b.   Factual knowledge
   c.   Responding to student efforts
   d.   Fluency instruction
   e.   Strategy knowledge
   f.   Delivery of information
   g.   Application
   h.   Asking questions
   i.   Conceptual knowledge
   j.   Presenting activities

5. Sometimes students need to learn strategies to either apply what they already know or to learn new information. When teachers want to teach <u>strategies</u>, they should use good instructional techniques to do so. Which of the following best represents the critical attributes for strategy instruction?

    a. Define the strategy. List its critical and non-critical attributes. Give examples and non-examples, then present test items to see if the student understands.

    b. The teacher orally talks through the process, demonstrating use of the strategy. The student uses the process, also orally talking through each step. Experiences are arranged to provide practice, and the student self-monitors application.

    c. The teacher describes when the strategy should be used, assigns work that might require its use, then reinforces the student when he or she does choose to use it.

    d. The strategy is broken down into its component parts, each part is written on a flashcard and the student memorizes the sequence by drill and practice.

6. Which of the following would be the most effective teacher choice if a student was accurate but not yet automatic in performing an important task that should be a routine behavior?

    a. Arrange for drill and practice of the skill to occur frequently. Use contingent reinforcement for improved rates of performance.

    b. Increase the amount of instruction. Use carefully sequenced step-by-step directions to explain how and when to use the skill.

    c. Elaborate correction procedures are called for here. Be very clear about how to check for errors and follow the same correction procedure each time an error is made.

    d. There is no formula. Each student is different and it is a mistake to believe that a set of student performance characteristics has implications for instruction that can be generalized across students.

7. Describe the teacher behaviors that should be associated with instruction of a student who is at the acquisition stage of learning.

8. Sometimes...let's be honest, MANY times a student will demonstrate mastery of a task in an instructional setting, but fail to generalize that skill to other settings where its use would be appropriate. Which of the following is not a reasonable explanation of why that occurs?

    a. The skill was not learned to a fluent level.

    b. The student is uncertain about how to do the larger task of which the previously learned skill is only part.

    c. The student, because she is learning disabled, lacks the capacity to generalize.

    d. The student fails to recognize the situational cue that should prompt use of the skill.

9. We know a teacher who got the key to her classroom stuck in the lock in the door one morning. One of her students, a thirteen-year-old with moderate disabilities, volunteered to try to get it out while the teacher took care of other morning duties. After a while, the teacher noticed that the student was gone...with her keys...**and her car.** Yes, the student from a self-contained special-education class had not only successfully removed the key that had been stuck in the lock, but she had also figured out which key went with the teacher's car **and she drove it away!** This student's parents had no idea that she had any concept of how to drive a car, let alone how to drive to a friend's house and pick him up to go for a picnic...paid for by the spare change in the car's ashtray.

    This is no fable, but try to guess the moral, anyway. What is the point of this "stranger than fiction" story?

    a. Beats me. Maybe this is like the seventh inning stretch.

    b. When a task is meaningful, a student, even one with learning problems, will make every effort to learn it.

28

c.   This is an example of acquisition through practice. The repetition of riding in her parents' car all over town allowed the student to acquire the skill of driving.

d.   Never give your keys to someone who covets your possessions.

10.   The emphasis in special and remedial education is on keeping students with special instructional needs in the general-education classroom. For those students to be accommodated in that setting, teachers need effective procedures for group instruction. One such procedure is teacher-directed lessons that include modeling, guided practice, monitoring, and feedback. Please describe two other effective group instruction procedures.

a.

b.

~~~~ ~~~~ ~~~~ ~~~~ ~~~~ ~~~~ ~~~~

CHAPTER FIVE

EVALUATION AND DECISION MAKING

In this section you will learn:

...the difference between evaluating and testing;

...how to test assumed causes;

...how to sample behavior;

...how to test student performance with "identify" or "produce" items;

...some strengths and weaknesses of portfolio assessment; and

...the difference between formative and summative evaluation.

1. Evaluation is not the same as testing. Testing is the measurement of something by sampling it. Evaluation requires the comparison of performance to a standard. The purpose of evaluation is to determine if there is a discrepancy between the way things are and the way they should be.

    Which of the following represent testing (T) and which represent evaluation (E)?

    a. __T__   Susan scored 65 on the reading section.

    b. _____   Seven-year-old Juan reads words in context at a rate of 115 per minute with 2 errors. His peers average 75 words per minute with 5 errors.

    c. _____   Hank needs to demonstrate competency in mathematics to meet high school graduation requirements by performing basic computations, conversion, and problem solving with fractions, transformation of metric to standard measures, and the completion of simple algebra problems. He must successful solve 80% of the problems in each sub-section within one hour.

    d. _____   Vickie earned 20 points on her written story in language arts. The story had a well-developed theme and contained a variety of descriptive modifiers. It contained six complete paragraphs and had no punctuation errors, although there were seven misspelled words.

2. The thoughtful process of evaluation requires which three of the following? Circle the components of evaluation.

    a. Good measures of current performance levels.

    b. Carefully constructed standardized tests that have been normed on large, representative populations.

    c. Good estimates of the standards the student should be meeting.

    d. Active decision making on the part of the evaluator.

e.   More items presented in the test sample than the student can complete during the time allotted.

3.   In order to make good decisions about student needs, teachers need a trustworthy process to gather information.

Which of the following is the sequence of steps in the decision-making process suggested by the authors of the text?

a.   Ask the student to describe her strengths and weaknesses, and then test to see if her appraisal is correct. Adjust instruction where necessary.

b.   First, survey performance to collect some information about the student. Next, develop an assumed cause that might explain the facts that are known. Directly measure performance to confirm or reject your hypothesis, and finally, make decisions based on what you have learned.

c.   Use norm-referenced tests to give guidance about what should be taught to students. These tests are generally well researched and normed with a representative cast of thousands. A teacher should test, consider the score, and then place students in appropriate groups for instruction.

d.   Test, place, test with formative measures, adjust instruction if necessary, test for summative purposes, assign grade, take a break.

4.   Here is the <u>fact</u>: Garrett does not successfully answer comprehension questions about stories he reads in his third-grade reader. He averages one correct response for every two questions he attempts.

Which of the following <u>assumed causes</u> could productively be tested? There may be more than one reasonable answer.

a.   Garrett allocates less attention to major ideas, sequence, characters, and implications of the story than he should. If he were taught to ask himself key questions before and during reading, his comprehension would increase.

b.   Garrett reads too slowly for the words in the story to appear to relate to each other. If his reading fluency increased, his understanding would also increase.

c. Garrett does not have enough prior knowledge for the content of the stories he is reading to make sense to him. He is not a middle-class kind of kid, but the stories are very traditional, "Gee whiz, the family goes on vacation in the station wagon!" kind of stories. If he were given stories he could relate to, his comprehension would increase.

d. Garrett is not an able learner. In fact, he is not an average learner, and he has poor comprehension because he does not have a lot of understanding to work with from the beginning. He would understand more if less were asked of him.

5. Educational evaluators have to be good at seeing relationships. The entire inclusive set of skills, thought processes, and attitudes that affect learning cannot be directly observed, even by a "marathon evaluator." Instead of trying to measure every aspect of a student's prior knowledge, evaluators **sample** observed behavior and then make inferences about what a student already can do and what still needs to be learned.

For each of the following, identify which sample would provide the best information from which inferences could be made:

a. An evaluator wants to know if the student is ready to join the next higher reading group where students are reading at grade level at an average of 100 words per minute with 2 to 4 errors.

   1. Give the student an informal reading inventory to see if she is reading at grade level.

   2. Ask the student to read from the current reader used by the target group and count the number of correct and error words per minute.

   3. Administer the reading section of a standardized achievement test like the WRAT or CAT to see if the student scores within grade-level range.

b. What level of arithmetic skill does Carlos, the new student, have? Initial observations of his responses to a screening test indicated that he can do some addition and some subtraction, but his responses to problems requiring regrouping seemed associated with frowning, eraser biting, and errors. The teacher will find more specific information by:

1. Asking him what he knows. Students know when something is hard or easy for them. Sample by verbal report.

2. Use Key Math or another reliable achievement test to identify skills that are troublesome for Carlos.

3. Ask Carlos to complete several examples of both addition and subtraction problems. Each probe should have problems that do and do not require regrouping.

6. Fill in the blank by each example to identify the format (*identify* or *produce*) of each question. The first one is completed for you.

a. Which of the following are reptiles?

   frog snake hawk lizard turtle

   Format: _____identify_____

b. Draw an example of a complete circuit.

   Format: _____

c. What is the fourth planet from the sun?

   a. Venus
   b. Mars
   c. Earth
   d. Saturn

   Format: _____

d.   Match each word to its Tongan equivalent.

_____ Water   a. Uha
_____ Sun   b. Langi
_____ Sky   c. La'a
_____ Rain   d. Vai

Format: _____

e.   Write a compound sentence.

Format: _____

7.   Which of the following is a <u>false</u> statement about portfolio assessment?

a.   Often the best samples of behavior are collected through the analysis of classroom work assignments.

b.   One of the strengths of portfolio assessment is that it is not necessary to compare the student's work to any defined standard. The student's work is simply compared to previous work of the same student.

c.   To gather portfolio samples, teachers routinely collect and catalog work that the student completes on routine assignments and projects.

d.   Portfolio assessment has emerged as an alternative to traditional tests because of dissatisfaction with artificial means of sampling student performance.

8.   Please fill in the blanks:

The major purpose of a norm-referenced test is to compare a student's performance with _____.

The primary use of a norm-referenced test is to _____.

The purpose of a criterion-referenced test is to compare a student's performance with _____.

The primary use of a criterion-referenced test is to _____
_____.

9.   There are two general types of evaluation, summative and formative. **Summative** information provides a sample of performance from which evaluators can infer how much (or how little) a student has learned as a result of instruction.   Grades, promotion, and placement decisions often rely on **a summary of what was learned.**

Formative evaluation results from monitoring during the process of instruction while the skill is **still being formed.** This information is used to change the nature of the treatment (instruction or task) while learning is still occurring.

Consider each of the following scenarios and identify which type of evaluation is occurring.

a.   Jamal has taken an achievement test to see if he qualifies for special services.

        Formative evaluation   Summative evaluation

b.   Wilma takes a one-minute probe each day and charts the rate of correct and error responses on a graph that both she and the teacher monitor to see if Wilma is still learning at the desired rate. If Wilma is not, the teacher adjusts instruction.

        Formative evaluation   Summative evaluation

c.   Each student in Mr. Diaz's class writes an essay each week. Once he reads the essays, Mr. Diaz uses what he finds to select the content for his "Mend It On Monday" lesson.

        Formative evaluation   Summative evaluation

d.   Greg must pass his history test with a B+ or better in order to receive a final grade of at least a B.

        Formative evaluation   Summative evaluation

10. What do the text authors suggest is the relationship between individualizing instruction and evaluation?

   a. The first step in individualizing instruction should be identification of the student's learning style through the use of tests and questionnaires.

   b. The most important information that will inform instructional decisions will result from summative tests.

   c. The best way to choose an instructional method to meet the needs of an individual student is to pick a method, place the student in it, and use formative evaluation to see how he or she does.

   d. The diversity of classrooms today makes it impossible to truly individualize instruction. Best evaluation efforts will result from achievement tests that screen and place students in homogeneous groups.

11. Grades, raw counts, and percent scores do not show the rate of growth. On the following chart, draw an example of progress that shows growth.

```
150-----------------------------------------------------------
145-----------------------------------------------------------
140-----------------------------------------------------------
135-----------------------------------------------------------
130-----------------------------------------------------------
125-----------------------------------------------------------
120-----------------------------------------------------------
115-----------------------------------------------------------
110-----------------------------------------------------------
105-----------------------------------------------------------
100-----------------------------------------------------------
```

M T W T F   M T W T F   M T W T F
Daily Samples

12.   Draw an example of data that shows the teacher is using assisted assessment:

70
65
60
55
50
45
40
35
30
25
//
5

_____

13.   One of the following statements about formative evaluation is <u>false</u>. Which one is it?

   a.   One of the strengths of formative evaluation is that it provides a means by which evaluators can measure the discrepancy between the desired standard and the student's performance.

   b.   Formative data is usually based on samples taken frequently - sometimes daily, sometimes weekly.

   c.   Research clearly demonstrates that teachers who periodically review formative data and base teaching decisions on it are more effective teachers than those who don't.

   d.   Formative data procedures are both more effective and easier to use than traditional methods of evaluating student performance.

MONITORING STUDENT PROGRESS

Is Robert's comprehension improving?

YES   NO

Is Sasha's oral reading rate changing?

YES   NO

Do Ellie's social skills differ significantly from her peers?

<u>Ellie</u>   15.5, 16.6, 16, 17, 15, 15.5, 15, 15.5, 15, 14.5, 15, 14.5, 14.5

Peers 19.5, 18.5, 20.5, 19.5, 20.5, 20, 21, 20, 21.5, 20.5, 20, 20.5, 21
<u>(ecological ceiling)</u>

YES   NO

Is Allen's arithmetic performance changing?

YES   NO

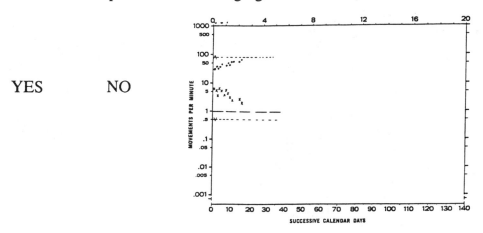

Is Desmond spelling more accurately?   YES   NO

60%, 65%, 80%, 70%, 65%, 60%, 75%, 70%, 75%, 80%

You probably found it easier to make the judgments necessary to answer these questions when a visual display was provided. Charted data efficiently communicate information just as a photograph provides details that even well-written prose cannot. The visual display should reveal current performance, direction of change, and how close the student is to meeting the goal. Depending on the type of data displayed on the chart, the reader may also gain information about accuracy and mastery levels of performance. Prose description and raw scores may provide the same information, but only after careful analysis by the reader.

It is easy to tell that Robert's comprehension is not improving because the trend of his scores is changing in the wrong direction. The seventeen days of data on the chart indicate that he is less successful in the last half of the month than he was in the first half.

Sasha, on the other hand, is demonstrating change. Her correct scores are climbing and her error scores are decreasing. Allen's chart demonstrates a similar pattern since correct response data points are approaching the goal and error data points are decreasing.

It was probably difficult to decide if Ellie's social skills differ significantly from her peers or if Desmond is becoming a more accurate speller since only raw scores were presented. Here are the same data presented in a visual display:

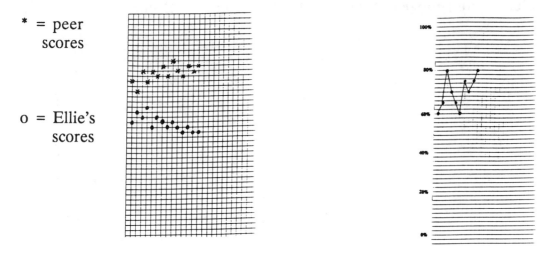

* = peer scores

o = Ellie's scores

Ellie's social skill data   Desmond's spelling scores

It should now be clear that not only does Ellie have lower rates of the desired social skills than her peers, but she is moving in the wrong direction. Her rates are decreasing rather than increasing. Desmond, on the other hand, is gradually scoring higher and higher on the measure of spelling performance.

If there is any doubt in your mind about the reason for this discussion, let us throw out all subtlety:

WHEN YOU ARE MONITORING STUDENT PERFORMANCE OVER TIME, CHART THE INFORMATION IN A VISUAL DISPLAY SO THAT YOU CAN SEE THE EFFECT OF INSTRUCTION. VISUAL DISPLAYS WILL SHOW YOU WHEN TO CHANGE TEACHING ACTIONS AND WILL HELP KEEP YOU FROM CHANGING WHEN YOU SHOULDN'T.

There are a number of methods that can be used to chart student performance scores that are derived from curriculum-based measures. The type of chart used, how frequently the student's performance is measured, and the guidelines used to inform the decision-making process may vary, but there are at least three shared attributes across all curriculum-based measurement systems.

Tucker (1987) identified three key features of curriculum-based assessment. They are: 1) test stimuli are drawn from the student's curricula; 2) CBA utilizes repeated testing across time; and 3) the assessment information is used to make instructional decisions.

The first attribute, <u>test stimuli are drawn from the student's curricula</u>, requires that evaluators know the objectives to be taught, and that they then periodically sample student performance to measure progress toward those objectives. Procedures for developing curriculum-based measures based on classroom learning objectives are described in a section in this study guide titled <u>Constructing Probes</u>. Please refer to that section for information about those procedures.

The second characteristic, <u>repeated testing across time</u>, means that student performance must be sampled often enough for learning patterns to emerge from the charted data. Some teachers sample behavior twice a week, some twice a month, and some sample student performance daily. To some extent, the frequency of sampling is influenced by the number of objectives measured. If several objectives are measured in the same probe, sampling can occur less frequently than if only one small objective is measured.

Some teacher judgment is required when deciding how frequently objectives should be measured. We believe that it is better to err on the side of sampling behavior frequently rather than infrequently. (One of us believes that daily measures are just about right.) The bottom line here is that the behavior should be monitored frequently enough that meaningful changes can be made **early** in the teaching sequence if learning does not occur at the desired rate. Curriculum-based measurement is meant to be <u>formative</u> evaluation, after all, and that means that the teacher responsible for designing and delivering instruction must be able to respond to learning patterns quickly when performance is poor. For example, if measurement occurs infrequently, important patterns may be missed. If Meredith's performance on Monday and Tuesday is always lower than her performance later in the week, measurement of her performance twice a month on Wednesdays would miss that important information.

The third attribute of curriculum-based measurement is <u>the assessment information is used to make instructional decisions</u>. What guidelines are used for decision making? The answer to this is influenced by the type of decision an evaluator wants to make. If the decision is whether or not a student is adequately progressing toward broad annual goals, bi-weekly measurement on items that sample year-long objectives will provide a long-range picture (Fuchs and Deno, 1991). If an extended trend line appears to reach the end-of-the-year target, the teacher will probably be satisfied. If it does not, changes should be made.

If the decision to be made is whether or not a short-term objective has been reached, more specific decision guidelines will be necessary. In this case, measurement should occur more frequently and actual student progress compared to a day-to-day standard of expected performance.

The <u>Constructing Probes</u> section in this study guide describes a procedure for identifying the discrepancy between expected and actual performance, and then calculating how many objectives per teaching unit must be mastered for the student to eliminate the discrepancy. If that procedure is followed, failure to maintain an adequate pace through the target objectives would be a signal that change in instruction, task, or motivation is necessary.

Another decision guideline is based on learning rate as represented by trend of learning. Trend is determined by the direction and degree of change that emerges in the charted data. Some evaluators evaluate the adequacy of learning by visually inspecting the general trend of the data. White and Haring (1980) have designed more precise decision guidelines that are used with daily measurement of student performance. They recommend that a student's learning trend be compared to a gradually increasing daily standard called a dynamic aim line. When a student fails to match the daily standard for three consecutive days, teachers are advised to intervene in the learning process.

Median scores can also be used to describe changes in performance, and then compared to the median scores of the achievement of typical students. But remember that single scores that summarize a group of scores are not as sensitive to change in the short run as are learning slopes (trends).

In summary:

* Decisions about the adequacy of student learning will be easier to make if the student's data are charted for visual display. A picture **really is** worth a thousand words.

* Repeated measures of performance should be taken often enough that learning patterns emerge early in the teaching sequence. This is necessary to provide enough information for teachers to actually <u>USE</u> the data to make instructional decisions.

* Teachers should determine what decision guidelines will provide the necessary sensitivity to change in learning (discrepancy, trend, summary scores,...) and consistently use them.

CHAPTER SIX

TOOLS FOR DECISION MAKING

In this section you will learn:

...the concept of measurement error;

...definitions of reliability and validity;

...to recognize the difference between content- and criterion-referenced items;

...performance levels: accuracy, fluency, and automaticity;

...percent, rate, and interval sampling measurement procedures;

...the difference between behaviors and states; and

...the concept of critical effect.

1. Evaluators make inferences about what a student knows when they measure samples of observable behaviors representing the broader construct we call KNOWLEDGE. Error in measurement occurs when performance is influenced by a variable other than the element the evaluator is trying to measure. In each of the following scenarios, identify at least two sources of error. An example is provided in the first scenario.

    a. Jeb's teacher wanted to know if Jeb understood that proper paragraphs should contain a topic sentence followed by supporting sentences. To test this, she presented him with three pages of sentences in paragraph form and asked him to identify those that were "proper paragraphs."

    Sources of error: 1) The match between Jeb's word knowledge skill and the vocabulary used in the sentences

    2) _____

    _____

b.　K. W. was integrated into a sixth-grade general-education class, but he had difficulty writing project reports that compared to his classmates'. His teacher wanted to know what strategy K. W. used to organize, write, and edit his reports, so she decided to analyze the errors he made in previous reports. She read three reports and wrote down every conceptual, mechanical, or factual error contained in them. From those errors, she inferred the strategic errors K. W. had made in preparing the reports.

Sources of error: _____

_____

_____

_____

_____

c.　Katie scored poorly on the Wide Range Achievement Test reading sub-test. She scored two full grade levels below her grade placement when she read words categorized by grade level and presented one-by-one in a work list.

Sources of error: _____

_____

_____

_____

_____

2.　Identify whether the following represent _Validity_ or _Reliability_.

_____ To measure Ruth Ann's driving skill, the instructor asked her to drive to the shopping center, to parallel park, and to return to school by way of the freeway.

_____ The coach was concerned about the team's consistency so she measured field point and free throw averages for each player, each game.

_____ Juan's IEP included the goal of improved cooperation with his parents as well as with his teachers. At the beginning of his social skills training program, his parents were asked to help define what they considered to be cooperative behaviors so those behaviors could be measured.

_____ Forest took alternate forms of a comprehensive arithmetic test every two weeks through the year to measure progress through the curriculum.

3. Let's say that you want to know if Lidia can read a story and then state the main idea in her own words. You have an informal reading inventory (IRI) with several short stories in it, and you are considering using those for the stimulus stories. Which of the following is the most important consideration?

    a. Are your measurement goals the same as those of the test publishers?

    b. Will you follow the exact procedures outlined in the test manual?

    c. Will use of the stimulus stories meet YOUR purpose?

    d. Were children similar to Lidia included in the group that was used to set the normative standards of the test?

4. "To relate the results of a test to the curriculum, you must have a test that allows the scores on items or subtests to be directly keyed to the curriculum." (Ken Howell, somewhere deep in the heart of Chapter six...)

    For each of the following objectives, describe test items that would measure a student's mastery of the objective.

    a. Each student will always apply the regrouping rule in subtraction when appropriate, and never when it is not.

        Appropriate test:

b. Carlos will demonstrate his comprehension of what is read by paraphrasing the story, projecting a reasonable outcome, identifying the main idea, and recalling facts. He must successfully complete 90% of the questions asked of him in grade level reading materials.

Appropriate test:

c. Given a geometric shape, sixth grade students will write the correct formula for finding either its area, perimeter, diameter, or radius. This will be done without mistake.

Appropriate test:

5. The text makes an issue of the difference between the concepts of criterion-referenced objectives and content-referenced items. Sometimes the content of published materials show up as objectives; this is a mistake for most special and remedial learners. Those students need skill and knowledge bases that will allow them to close the gap between present performance and the performance of their peers. They do not need to cover material, they need to acquire facts, concepts, and strategies.

Can you spot the difference between criterion-referenced and content-referenced items? Label them.

_____ ...read at grade level at a rate of 150 words per minute with no more than three errors.

_____ ...sort living organisms into correct kingdom, phylum, class, and family with no errors.

_____ ...complete the entire first three units in the social studies text and all of the assigned chapter questions.

_____ read the works of five different American authors who have written short stories since 1800.

6.   Processes used to measure facts, concepts, and strategies will require students to demonstrate different behaviors. List three verbs that represent appropriate student behaviors in each category. An example is provided in the first item.

Factual knowledge:

1. The student will <u>list</u>

2.

3.

Concept knowledge:

1.

2.

3.

Strategic knowledge:

1.

2.

3.

7.   Proficiency domains identify the level of performance expected of a student. <u>Accuracy</u> means the student doesn't make any (or at least, very few) mistakes; <u>mastery</u> means the student is both accurate and fluent; and <u>automaticity</u> means the student responds accurately and quickly, without having to engage short-term memory, even when there are distractors.

Circle the term that appropriately labels the proficiency domain that is described.

a.	Her teacher notes how many of the week's twenty vocabulary words Wanda defined correctly.

Accuracy		Mastery		Automaticity

b.	As Mark writes essays for literature class, he no longer even thinks about the formation of letters or how to spell each word.

Accuracy		Mastery		Automaticity

c.	In order to obtain adequate notes from lecture classes, Luis must increase the speed of his handwriting.

Accuracy		Mastery		Automaticity

8.	Okay, time for a reality check. Chapter six describes several ways to measure behavior. Now is the time to see if you can recognize when one measurement approach is preferable to another. The types of measurement are: percent, rate, and interval sampling. Percent measures what proportion of problems attempted were completed correctly (accuracy); rate measures accuracy and fluency when both correct and error responses are monitored; and interval sampling measures what proportion of "snapshot observations" recorded the target behavior.

For each of the following, indicate which measurement procedure you would employ. State the rationale for your choice.

a.	Roberto has been learning how to maintain a steady pace when he reads words in context. He used to read so slowly that he didn't understand what he had just finished reading, and he usually didn't have time to finish reading the assigned material.

Procedure:

Rationale:

b. Lindy Lou is not every teacher's idea of a model student. She chatters, daydreams, distracts others, and makes popping noises with her gum even when her mouth is shut. Her teacher wants a measure of Lindy Lou's productive work time, but doesn't have the time to constantly watch her.

Procedure:

Rationale:

c. The class has weekly untimed spelling tests. Some students have specialized spelling words that are different from the majority of the class, but everyone has 10 words and takes the test on Friday. The teacher maintains individual scores for each student, and in some cases, charts data for IEP reporting purposes.

Procedure:

Rationale:

9. To check your understanding of the difference between behaviors/states and overt/covert behaviors, place at least one example in each of the cells in the following grid:

	BEHAVIOR	STATE
OVERT		
COVERT		

10. What might be the critical effect of:

   a. proofreading and editing a paper to correct spelling, capitalization, and punctuation errors before it is submitted?

   b. reading the comprehension questions before reading the story?

   c. monitoring each student's guided practice activity?

11. Circle each of the items that describe conditions under which it would be reasonable to gather data on a teacher as well as on a target student.

   a. You're feeling vindictive toward a teacher who refers every second student to special education.

   b. You have established a collaborative relationship with the teacher.

   c. The teacher in question is interested in obtaining data that reflects teacher/student interaction patterns.

   d. You want to practice what you are learning in this great textbook.

   e. You and the teacher in question have talked about gathering interaction data **BEFORE** you begin observing.

   f. You believe that information would be enlightening.

   g. There is absolutely no other way to help the student.

CHAPTER SEVEN

FUNDAMENTALS OF EVALUATION

In this section you will learn:

...the steps characteristic of evaluation linked to teaching objectives;

...the difference between consolidated and unconsolidated curriculum;

...the process of developing assumed causes;

...how to use a status sheet; and

...to recognize sub-tasks.

1. Opening remarks in Chapter seven state, "The purpose of a teaching-oriented evaluation...is to provide the evaluator with information regarding what students should be taught, and how it can best be taught to them." The model of teaching-oriented evaluation presented in the text has four stages. Please state in your own words: a) a brief definition and b) the purpose of each stage.

Fact finding:
a)

b)

Hypothesizing:
a)

b)

Validation:
    a)

    b)

Decision making:
    a)

    b)

2.   In the following scenario, identify each part of the evaluation process by labeling it as <u>fact finding</u>, <u>hypothesizing</u>, <u>validation</u>, or <u>decision making</u>.

1)   Miriam doesn't keep up with her peers in language arts activities, and her teacher, Ms. Smith, wants to know what she should be emphasizing in Miriam's daily work. To find out, Ms. Smith selected four different reading books and listened to Miriam read in each for about five minutes. Miriam was asked to read to find answers to some questions that Ms. Smith asked before each reading sample. This process was followed for three consecutive days.

2)   Ms. Smith also asked Miriam to spell some words from three different grade level lists in the district spelling series and to write dictated sentences. In addition, Miriam was given a story starter and instructed to write a story at least three paragraphs long. These activities were also repeated for three days in a row.

3)   Ms. Smith studied Miriam's responses to these tasks and noted that given sufficient time, Miriam spelled as accurately as the typical student at her grade level, wrote stories as well as students a grade level lower, and wrote dictated sentences as well as average. But Miriam read more slowly at all grade levels than typical readers. Her accuracy at all grade levels was acceptable, but her comprehension dropped as the grade level of the reading material increased.

4)   Given this information, Ms. Smith suspected that Miriam had difficulty keeping up with her peers in reading and spelling because her rate of responding made it difficult for her to complete her work. She was probably receiving less practice than her peers since she completed less of the activities assigned in class. Ms. Smith also believed that if Miriam would read more fluently, her comprehension would improve.

5)   An analysis of written stories revealed that fluency was not the only issue, however. Miriam's sentence structure and paragraph development did not meet grade-level expectations when compared to the student learning objectives for the previous grade. Ms. Smith inferred that Miriam did not know how to write compound or complex sentences or that paragraphs should contain a topic sentence supported by additional, related sentences.

6)   Ms. Smith gathered more information by taking additional reading samples at grade level after instructing Miriam to read faster. Ms. Smith even modeled what she wanted by demonstrating reading rates of 80 words per minute and 150 words per minute, and asking Miriam to approximate the faster reading rate. She also took a "tool skill" sample of Miriam's rate of writing letters since letter writing is the basic response unit involved in spelling and writing dictated sentences.

7)   Miriam was also asked to write four additional stories, two from story starters and two from self-generated topics. Ms. Smith noted the time it took to write three paragraphs during each story. When the stories were complete, they were analyzed for sentence formula, length of words per

sentence, number of separate adjectives and adverbs per story, and the number of sentences per paragraph.

8) The results of this testing indicated that when prompted to do so, Miriam read faster with better comprehension. She wrote letters at about half the fluency rate of competent peers in her class. Her most significant deficits were in writing skills. The only sentence formula she used was subject - verb - object and the median number of modifiers per story was three. The sentences in the story paragraphs were not related by topic.

9) Ms. Smith referred to the student-learning objectives for grade level, and set the following teaching goals:
   a) Increase reading rate to 150 words per minute with no more than 3 errors. Require 90% accuracy on comprehension questions that are previewed before reading the story.
   b) Increase the rate of writing letters (tool skill) to rates comparable to competent peers at grade level.
   c) Increase the variety of sentence formulas used in written work to include complex and compound sentences.
   d) Increase the number and variety of modifiers used in written work to levels comparable to typical grade-level peers.

3. What does it mean to say that a curriculum is consolidated?

4. Give two examples of each:

consolidated curriculum:
a)

b)

unconsolidated curriculum:

a)

b)

5.   If the curriculum is not consolidated, what do you have to do in order to compare a student's performance to an evaluative standard?

6.   What is a status sheet and what purpose does it serve?

7.   For each pair listed below, indicate what type of thought process is involved and whether or not goal "a" must be mastered before skill "b" can be taught. The first item is completed for you as an example.

       <u>A before B?</u>

   1)   <u>Yes</u>   No   a. know letter/sound <u>Factual</u>
                           b. "sounds out" correspondence words <u>Factual</u>

   2)   Yes   No   a. list planets in order from sun outward
                    _____

                    b. describe concept of orbit
                    _____

   3)   Yes   No   a. complete long division problems
                    _____

                    b. list steps in division process
                    _____

4)   Yes   No   a. decode words in context

_____

b. identify sequence of events in story

_____

5)   Yes   No   a. decode words in context

_____

b. use context cues

_____

6)   Yes   No   a. decode words in context

_____

b. read answer to comprehension question

_____

8.   Exhibit 7.5 (pp. 140-141) listed a number of "do's" and "don't's" to remember while developing assumed causes. Some of each have been scrambled in random order below. Sort the good advice from common evaluation errors by indicating **Do** or **Don't** by each and then stating a rationale for your judgment.

a.   Be comprehensive. Don't assume that the first thing a student can't do is the only, or most important, thing he needs to be taught.

   DO   **DON'T**   (Circle one)

   Rationale:

b.   Assume that if a student skips an item, he doesn't know it. If he had <u>known</u> it, he wouldn't have skipped it.

   DO   **DON'T**

   Rationale:

c.   Stick to alterable variables that can be influenced by instruction. Don't focus on variables such as I.Q. score, family status, low birth weight, or other variables not likely to be changed through classroom interaction.

DO   **DON'T**

Rationale:

d.   Understand that for a student to pass content class objectives (like literature, science, social studies), she must read the textbook, and must therefore be taught to read as the first remediation step.

DO   **DON'T**

Rationale:

e.   Select instructional goals that match a teaching style that you like. Go with your personal teaching strengths.

DO   **DON'T**

Rationale:

f.   Test all the elements of a task, including content behavior, conditions, and criteria.

DO   **DON'T**

Rationale:

9.   Look at Exhibit 7.3 (p. 137) in the textbook. Note which items the student has passed, not passed, or for which the results are not clear (as indicated with a "?"). Write teaching objectives for those items that provide enough information for you to do so.

CHAPTER EIGHT

FUNDAMENTALS OF INSTRUCTION

In this section you will learn

...teacher actions associated with student learning;

...how TIES identifies potential teacher actions to enhance learning;

...thought process categories: facts, concepts, and strategies; and

...additional information about accuracy, mastery, and automaticity.

1. Let's play a game. The guide-master (that's me) will describe a series of teacher actions, and the guide-reader (guess who that is) will name the thought process. Remember the thought process categories are: Facts, Concepts, and Strategies.

    a. The teacher has reviewed relevant prior knowledge and demonstrated how an example of the core idea discussed in the lesson can be changed to a non-example. He has asked several students to explain how they know an answer given by another student is correct, and he periodically challenges correct answers by asking students to support a response. After the teacher is finished with the group lesson, students are assigned an activity that requires them to sort items into categories and to change some non-examples into examples by changing the necessary attributes.

        Thought process: _____

    b. The teacher has demonstrated a procedure for arriving at a solution to a problem. She hasn't emphasized the answer, only the way to obtain the answer. Students are asked to supply rules, steps, and procedures and during seat work, they are required to identify the missing steps when given an incomplete series of directions. They are also asked to practice identifying situations where the procedure will and will not work.

        Thought process: _____

    c. During this lesson, students are encouraged to make rapid responses to simple, direct questions. The instructor uses drill and practice that is distributed across the day in several short sessions rather than one long lesson. Students receive frequent feedback on accuracy and rate, and items that are missed are repeated several times.

Thought process: _____

d. Ms. Jackson's lesson encouraged students to focus on the process, not the completion of the task. She didn't care if students finished every problem, only if they knew how they solved the problem. Students were asked to explain what went wrong when they made a mistake, and to practice generating and evaluating alternative solutions.

Thought process: _____

2. Now let's try the same thing for behavior outcomes. Given a description of student performance, identify whether the student is operating at an accuracy, mastery, or automatic level.

a. The student requires extensive explanation and demonstration of the lesson. The teacher monitors all responses and makes sure the student does not practice errors. The student engages in guided practice, but not in independent practice.

Behavioral outcome level: _____

b. The teacher emphasizes answers, not the process, and praises fluent work. The student engages in drill and practice and completes independent practice activities with a success rate of 90% to 100%.

Behavioral outcome level: _____

c. The lesson emphasizes how existing skills can be generalized to other tasks and environments. The student is asked to modify the skill to meet new demands in "real world" examples. The student meets or exceeds the criterion expected in the basic core skill.

Behavioral outcome level: _____

3. The Instructional Environment Scale (TIES) was authored by Ysseldyke & Christenson (1987) and draws upon teacher-effectiveness studies designed to identify teacher behaviors that make a difference to student achievement. The six categories of teacher actions described in TIES are:

1. Prepare for Instruction   4. Respond to Efforts
2. Deliver Information   5. Use Activities
3. Ask Questions   6. Evaluate

Use the category numbers to sort the following TIES items into the appropriate grouping.

___   Transitions are short and brief.

___   Various cuing and prompting techniques are used to elicit accurate responses from the student.

___   The teacher circulates among students during seatwork activities to provide assistance and to check work.

___   Practice opportunities are provided until the student makes only infrequent, careless mistakes.

___   Specific suggestions to correct student errors are provided.

___   The student's attention is gained and focused during instruction.

___   The lesson explanation emphasizes a step-by-step description of the process to follow to solve the problem.

___   The student is given a warning for transitions between lessons.

4. Somewhere out there is a teacher who does not follow the guidelines suggested by TIES or this textbook. The following description might be from a lesson in that teacher's classroom. Underline the teacher behaviors that violate the guidelines described in this text, and suggest an alternate behavior.

1   Teacher X expected her students to know how to act like good

2   students since seventh graders have already had six years of practice

3 at being students, but sometimes their behavior really got out of hand.

4 Today's lesson had to begin with a stern reprimand and a reminder that

5 seventh-grade students should be more sophisticated than fourth-grade

6 students. The lesson started a little late, but once everyone settled down,

7 Ms. X presented a lesson on levers as simple machines. She hadn't had

8 time to organize the equipment for the lesson, so she assigned pairs of

9 students to select one person to go get the fulcrums and levers from two

10 locations in the back of class. When everyone returned to their desk, she

11 asked students to tell her what they already knew about levers.

12 Responses indicated that there was great diversity in what students

13 already knew, so she reassigned peer partners so that the high performers

14 were with high performers and low performers with low performers.

15 Ms. X then began the lesson. She talked about how levers could be used

16 to move heavy objects and showed pictures of workers removing stumps,

17   moving rocks, and using crowbars. Students appeared to be listening to

18   some of her lecture while they set up playful uses of the levers and

19   fulcrums at their desks. Ms. X had to interrupt her lesson once or twice

20   to intervene in an object-flipping contest that developed between Gerald

21   and Darrel who had learned that the levers could be used as a primitive

22   catapult for pieces of eraser, paper clips, and other small objects.

23   Time seemed to slip away very quickly because of all the interruptions,

24   but at the end of the period, Ms. X asked if there were any questions

25   about levers; no one seemed to have any. Ms. X inferred that the

26   students would have attended better without the levers at their desks,

27   and planned for a continuation of the lesson for the next day that would

28   be based on written essay responses rather than "hands on" lever

29   experimentation.

CHAPTER NINE

ELIGIBILITY DECISIONS

In this section you will learn:

...why some students who need special service do not receive it;

...the functions and the weaknesses associated with labeling students;

...how curriculum-based measurement seeks functional information about students;

...strengths and limitations of curriculum-based measurement; and

...how curriculum-based measurement can be used to make eligibility decisions.

1. The text states that it is possible to NEED remedial or special services without being ELIGIBLE for services. Imagine that you are talking with the parent of a student who reads three years behind grade level but is not <u>eligible</u> for extra help. Explain to the parent how that can happen.

2. What are the benefits of labeling?

    What are the harmful effects of labeling?

3.   Which of the following do you believe best describes the textbook authors'
      position on labeling?

      a.   It is important for teachers to know when a student with remedial or
            special-education characteristics has been labeled. Labels cue teachers
            to select those special teaching strategies needed to work with the
            identified student.

      b.   For students with remedial or mild disabilities, labels do not contribute
            to the selection of teaching strategies and should make little impact on
            teaching decisions. There is no such thing as a teaching prescription that
            comes with a label.

4.   The text states that curriculum-based measurement (CBM) relies on **functional**
      information for use by teacher assistance teams or during the pre-referral
      process. What does **functional** mean in this context, and how is that different
      from information derived from measures of global achievement?

5.   Identify at least two limitations of curriculum-based measurement.

      1)

      2)

6.   Explain how this observation made by John Dewey is relevant to the information
      in chapter eight:

      "This intelligence-testing business reminds me of the way they used to weigh
      hogs in Texas. They would get a long plank, put it over a cross-bar, and
      somehow tie the hog on one end of the plank. They'd search all around till they
      found a stone that would balance the weight of the hog and they'd put that on
      the other end of the plank. Then they'd guess the weight of the stone."

64

John Dewey (1859-1952). American teacher, philosopher, reformer from the Concise Columbia Dictionary of Quotations. Avon Books, 1989. Robert Andrews, Editor. P. 138.

7.   The text suggested that CBM could be used to describe performance using any of the following three procedures. Describe each with enough explanation that your instructor could be confident that you understand how it would be carried out.

   a. Achievement/expectancy comparison:

   b. Percentile scores:

   c. Aptitude/achievement discrepancy:

8.   Describe how CBM could be used to answer the following questions.

   a.   Is one school's math program more effective in computation development than another school's?

b.   Are the low achieving students in my class improving at a rate that will close their achievement gap?

c.   What eighth-grade-level science concepts does Garrett need to learn?

9.   Summarize the strengths of CBM for making eligibility decisions.

~~~~   ~~~~   ~~~~   ~~~~   ~~~~   ~~~~   ~~~~   ~~~~

CHAPTER TEN

COMPREHENSION

In this section you will learn:

...strategies to improve students' reading comprehension;

...how to administer and interpret cloze and maze comprehension tests;

...specific-level comprehension tests;

...enabling skills for comprehension; and

...how to determine the next appropriate action when given a description of student performance.

1. Listed below are five reading comprehension strategies used by readers as they try to understand written text. For each strategy, specify at least one observable behavior that indicates a reader is using that strategy.

    a.   Active reading
         Example: Takes notes and/or highlights

    Now you do the others...

    b.   Monitors meaning

    c.   Adjusts task for difficulty

    d.   Connects text to prior knowledge

    e.   Clarifies

2. Circle the correct word for this selection from Chapter 10 in the text. No peeking until you have selected a word for each blank. Come on, try it...this is what your students will experience when you begin survey-level testing. You may read ahead or return to a completed item to change it if you wish, but don't work longer than ten minutes on this task.

    Tindal and Marston (1990) have proposed one way to avoid the problems of definition that come with the term comprehension. Instead of talking about ____ (reading) (decoding) (concepts) and comprehension, they talk ____ (about) (thinking) (of) reading and reacting.

    Use ____ (about) (only) (of) the term **reacting** shifts ____ (the) (some) (critical) focus from psychological process, ____ (that) (because) (which) cannot be observed, to ____ (behaviors) (ideas) (concepts) and products that can. ____ (One) (For) (An) example, students may react ____ (since) (to) (because) what they read by ____ (answering) (asking) (understanding) questions, retelling, paraphrasing, or _____ (reading) (like) (completing) cloze passages. Each of _____ (these) (several) (scholarly) techniques can be used _____ (after) (by) (to) illustrate a student's comprehension -- _____ (but) (because) (and) few people would agree _____ (to) (that) (eagerly) any of them are _____ (real) (reliable) (pure) measures of it.

The _____ (prototypical) (easy) (concept) "diagnostic reading inventory," for _____ (use) (ever) (example), is made up of _____ (words) (then) (passages) followed by questions. The _____ (purpose) (student) (teacher) reads each passage and _____ (then) (sometimes) (someone) answers questions before reading _____ (a) (quickly) (the) next passage. In these _____ (moments) (cases) (classrooms), the interval between reading _____ (the) (certain) (a) passage and answering the _____ (error) (teacher) (questions) is a minute or _____ (sometimes) (two) (moment). What if you waited _____ (30) (mega) (few) minutes before asking the _____ (answers) (questions) (brilliance)? What if you waited _____ (some) (rapidly) (a) week? If you did _____ (glide) (wait) (hope) longer, the student's score _____ (would) (might) (is) almost certainly be different (_____) (apparently) (drop) (probably lower), because what was _____ (once) (never) (suddenly) "comprehended" may no longer _____ (still) (want) (be) recalled. Therefore, a student's _____ (ideas) (score) (approval) on post-passage questions _____ (develops) (depends) (related) not only on what _____ (they) (can) (he) understands but on what (they) (can) (he) remembers. Many educators seem to accept this confusion, though few of them would agree that memory and comprehension are synonymous.

3. What procedure was illustrated in question 2?

Score your own responses and categorize your performance.

Too hard _____ Less than 80% (28 or fewer items)

Instructional _____ 80% to 90% percent (29-31)

Too easy _____ 90% or more (32 or more correct responses)

4. The text described these seven specific-level testing procedures: assisted monitoring, retell, awareness of reading, assisted activation of prior knowledge, make predictions, assisted search, and referent knowledge. Five of them are

described here. We've supplied the descriptions, you provide the label that identifies the test procedure.

a. _____ Collect passages of about 250 words of varying difficulty from classroom texts or published tests. Tell the student that you want him to read a passage and tell you what he has read. The reaction is scored according to the thoroughness and accuracy of the student's response.

b. _____ Ask the student to begin reading from an expository passage and at the end of each paragraph, ask the student to speculate what will be in the next paragraph. Rate the student's responses by deciding if the reaction follows logically from the text.

c. _____ Have the student read a passage that contains approximately 25 pronouns such as *her, their, its,* or *those.* Return to specific examples and ask the student to tell what the word means or to whom or what it refers.

d. _____ Ask the student to read and tell him that each time he makes and error, you will tap the desk. Instruct him to fix the error each time he hears a tap. Tap only when errors violate meaning and determine if the student self-corrects when cued to do so.

e. _____ Select reading passages at the student's instructional level and ask pre-reading questions designed to focus the student's attention on topics contained in the sample. The questions should be related to the content of the passage, but not stated with the exact vocabulary or sentence structure of the material.

5.   What **ENABLING** skills are necessary before students can adequately react to reading text? Identify and give a brief description of each.

   a. P_____ K_____

   b. D_____

c. Semantics (V_____)

d. Syntax (G_____)

6.   Survey-level and specific-level tests serve different purposes. Which of the following questions best describes the goal of:

Survey-level testing

   a.   Does the student use active reading as a comprehension strategy?
   b.   Does the student adequately comprehend text?
   c.   What reading-level performance does the student demonstrate?
   d.   Does the student enjoy reading?

Specific-level testing
   a.   Does the student use comprehension strategies?
   b.   Does the student have the enabling skills necessary for comprehension to occur?
   c.   Does the student use reading in subject matter assignments?
   d.   Do the student's parents encourage reading?

7.   Because you have no information about Stoner's reading performance, the first thing you do is to listen to her read a new story from her reader and then have her retell the story while you note how many idea units she successfully included. Of twenty idea units you had counted ahead of time, Stoner recalled four. Next, you ask her to do a maze activity using a new story from the basal reader. Her word selections were 45% accurate.

From these survey activities, you are confident that Stoner does indeed have difficulties with comprehension. Which of the following activities would you choose to do next? Briefly explain why you selected the one you did and give a rationale for not selecting the others.

   a.   Select an easier reader for Stoner. Clearly she is in over her head and is being asked to read in material that is too hard for her.
   b.   Get rid of the basal reader altogether and use reading material from the library.

> c. Rule out the lack of prior knowledge as a cause of poor comprehension by testing her in stories that interest her.
>
> d. Teach her to use comprehension strategies that focus on active reading and comprehension-monitoring procedures.

Your choice for next action:

Rationale:

Rejected action #1:

Rationale:

Rejected action #2:

Rationale:

Rejected action #3:

Rationale:

8. You discover that Victor cannot define words that appear within the context of a sentence. What should you conclude?

9. Trina reads at a consistent rate without expression or intonation. She seldom corrects errors that violate the meaning of the passage. What comprehension strategy might she be missing?

10. Lupe makes reading errors that violate meaning. Fortunately, she self-corrects most of them. What variables should you consider as you try to decide if you should simply ignore this problem or use a remedial teaching recommendation?

11. When searching text, Ralph can't find the answers to comprehension questions. What are the three mnemonic devices you could use to teach him a strategy he could use?

12. Joey took a maze survey test and scored 35%. He didn't answer the questions accurately, either. What is the first thing you should check?

13. Tony retells a story and includes major ideas and supporting details. However, he doesn't generalize beyond the text and he is so concise, his story borders on being terse. What rank (1-5) would he earn for response quality? (P. 202 of the text).

14. What teaching recommendation is described in each of the following?
    a. A procedure that has students take on the role of teacher. The student participates in instruction and summarizing and includes instruction on questioning, clarification, and prediction.

    _____

    b. This procedure helps students develop skills in a) identifying the author's conclusions, b) determining what evidence is presented, c) determining if the author is qualified or biased, and d) identifying faulty arguments. What is it?

    _____

72

c. A device used to organize what is read visually so specific relationships of selected story elements are highlighted.

_____

~~~~ ~~~~ ~~~~ ~~~~ ~~~~ ~~~~ ~~~~ ~~~~

CHAPTER ELEVEN

READING AND DECODING

In this section you will learn:

...differences in how adequate readers and remedial readers are instructed;

...how to conduct decoding survey-level tests;

...characteristics of code-based instruction;

...specific-level testing procedures; and

...what to look for in an error analysis.

1. Read each of the following and designate whether the student involved is most likely to be an adequate reader (A) or a remedial/corrective reader (R/C).

<u>R/C</u> Spends less time in silent reading than peers

_____ Spends a high proportion of reading instruction time reading words from the text

_____ Spends a high proportion of reading time doing independent and noninteractive worksheets

_____ Knows both how Superman died and how he was resurrected

_____ More likely to be interrupted during reading tasks

_____ May spend as little as two minutes at active reading a day

_____ Least likely to spend time on letters, sounds, and words in isolation

2.   When conducting decoding survey-level tests, you should sample from

a.   grade-level readers
b.   readers all from the same series, but different levels of difficulty
c.   multiple texts from a variety of curricular areas in which the student is expected to perform
d.   published informal reading inventories

JUSTIFY YOUR SELECTION OR REJECTION OF EACH.

Rationale:
a.

b.

c.

d.

3.   Each of the following statements is **FALSE** (erroneous, mistaken, incorrect, wrong). Explain <u>why</u> each is false.

a.   Code curriculum means teaching students to sound out words phonetically.

b.   The key to teaching decoding lies in the selection of the right book.

c.   It is important to know if a student has good visual discrimination skills before beginning to teach him to read.

d.   Fluency is not important in decoding.

4.   If you want to test (a specific skill) what <u>stimulus unit</u> should you present?

If you want to test <u>persistence</u>, present <u>long, hard problems</u>.

If you want to test <u>sounds</u>, present _____.

If you want to test <u>words</u>, present _____.

5.   Several times in Chapters ten and eleven, the authors have stated that omissions should not be counted as errors when monitoring a student's correct and error count in a reading passage. Now why do you suppose that is? Does it mean omissions are unimportant? State a rationale here:

6.   Read the following description. Identify what procedure is being used, and then explain why you would carry it out.

Collect at least three passages from texts used in class (250 words per passage) that the student would be expected to read if she had no problems in reading. Set up a tape recorder and get a stopwatch. Ask the student to read passages at her expected level as quickly and carefully as she can. Time her for one minute, marking errors on your copy of the passage. Calculate the number of words read correctly and incorrectly.

What procedure is this?

Why would you do it?

NOTE: IT MIGHT BE HELPFUL TO USE EXHIBIT 11.4 (p. 229) IN THE TEXT AS YOU RESPOND TO ITEMS 7-12 (if you haven't cut it out already).

7. Jim is a slow but accurate reader. You give him the re-reading test and his rate increases from 80 words per minute (wpm) to 87 wpm. Now what should you do?

8. You decide to check 5th-grader Deborah for error patterns. You have her read a 250-word passage. This gives you a large error sample because she misses more than half the words. She never self-corrects, although she makes lots of hesitations. Next you categorize the errors. Unfortunately, many of the errors cannot be classified and the rest are evenly divided between categories. The whole exercise seems like a mess. Where did things go wrong?

9. Joey leaves the endings off of words during passage reading. How can you find out if he doesn't know endings or isn't attending to them?

10. T. J. is inaccurate. You tell her to very carefully read a passage and try not to make any errors. She does so, and her accuracy improves to CAP. What should be done with T. J.?

11. Allie, a 6th-grader, reads 100 wpm but is only 80% accurate at grade level. Her accuracy does not improve when she is told to read carefully and she does not self-correct. Her errors seldom violate the meaning. What now?

12. Seven-year-old Patrick cannot read words. When sitting with you and a simple children's storybook, he doesn't hold it right-side-up or turn the pages from front to back. He can't identify sentence beginnings and endings or individual letters. He does correctly provide predictable words when they are omitted from a sentence or rhyme, and he can blend words in an oral "word game." What should you do?

13. Give an example of each of the following types of errors. Write a sentence to help illustrate your example.

    a. Insertion that is contextually appropriate
       Example:

       Explanation:

    b. Omission that affects passage meaning
       Example:

       Explanation:

    c. Error is phonetically similar to the stimulus word
       Example:

       Explanation:

d.   Error involving a CVC + e

Example:

Explanation:

14.   Note the errors in the following passage and identify the error pattern.

Passage: When I was a girl, my family had a dog named Laddie. He was *[Lady]* *(substitution)* a mixed breed shepherd, and I've never seen another dog just like him. He was big and *[bred]* *[sheepherd]* *[crepitition]* shaggy with several colors in his patchy coat. He may not have looked like a particular *[shady]* kind of dog, but his instincts were all shepherd. *[instints (omission)]* *[Sheepherd]*

Our house was small, and a person of average height could reach the eaves of *[H]* the roof while standing flat footed on the ground. In one corner of the house, a family *[awhile / self correction]* *(hesitation)*

of swallows built a nest every summer. One year they had more babies than there was room for in the nest. The baby birds began to fall out of the nest before they could fly. *[started]* When a baby fell out of the nest, Laddie would spend all day standing guard *[Lady]* *[and]* *[ing]* while the baby bird chirped from where it lay on the ground. The adult birds would *[cripped]* *(insertions)* swoop down behind Laddie and feed the baby. Our cat would watch, but she knew that *[Swing]* *[Lady]* *[bird]* she could not get by Laddie. *[Lady]*

When daddy came home from work, he would pick up the baby swallow and put *[My]* *[. He]* it back in the nest and Laddie would be at ease until the next baby fell out. That *[Lady]* *[H H]* summer, Laddie guarded birds on three different days, and the cat never got close *[Lady]* *[H]* *[the]*

enough to do any harm.

78

No, Laddie didn't look like a famous breed of shepherd, but after that summer we all knew he was a genuine swallow shepherd.

Lady H bred sheepherd genine sheepherd

Categorize the errors in the passage about Laddie

Error Categories: <u>Number of errors:</u>

Mispronunciations:

Insertions:

Omissions:

Hesitations:

Repetitions:

Does not attend to punctuation:

Does not pause at punctuation:

Pauses at end of line:

Self-corrects:

<u>CONTENT CATEGORIES</u>

Words: errors involving whole words
- Polysyllabic Words
- Contractions
- Compound Words
- Sight Words
- Silent Letters

Units: errors involving combined letter units
- Endings (suffixes)
- Clusters
- R-controlled vowels

Vowel teams
Consonant Digraphs
CVC words

Conversions: errors involving sound modification
    Double consonant words
    Vowel + e Conversions

Sounds: errors involving individual letters and sounds
    Vowels
    Consonants
    Sequence
    Sounds
    Symbols

ERROR CATEGORY CHECKLIST FOR MEANING VIOLATION

	Violates meaning	Does not violate meaning	Cannot classify	Errors self-corrected
% of total				
% of total self corrected				

15. Karna is currently practicing an oral "warm-up", and reviewing words she has previously missed before she reads orally for her teacher. Look at her charted data and decide whether or not she is showing adequate progress.

Adequate progress?

YES   NO

Desired learning rate

Rationale:

Actual learning rate

80

CHAPTER TWELVE

LANGUAGE

In this chapter you will learn:

 ...the body of knowledge included in the categories of semantics, syntax, and pragmatics;

 ...common misconceptions about language-problems;

 ...similarities between LEP students and language problem students;

 ...how to obtain language samples for both survey-level and specific-level testing;

 ...how to analyze a language sample; and

 ...teaching strategies for teaching language skills in the classroom.

1. Chapter twelve focuses on three elements of language: semantics (vocabulary), syntax (structural rules), and how language is used (pragmatics). Identify examples of each by sorting the following into one of those three categories. Signify **SY** for syntax, **SM** for semantics, or **PG** for pragmatics.

_____	Names months of the year	_____	Uses past tense
_____	Considers audience	_____	Identifies colors
_____	Uses varied forms of do	_____	Uses idioms
_____	Repairs communication	_____	Uses passive voice
_____	Names animals/insects	_____	Uses persuasion

2. Use the same **SY**, **SM**, and **PG** notation to identify the type of error made in each of the following: (Assume each skill would be expected for the child's age level.)

_____ Failure to sequence events when telling a story

_____ "The toys was broke."

_____ Missing knowledge of opposites (small-large)

_____ "Mine is more bigger."

_____ Does not label emotions

_____ Does not participate in discussions

3. Below are a series of statements regarding beliefs about language development and language problems. Take a stand on each by justifying it or providing an argument against it.

a. Some children do not learn language as quickly as their peers.

b. It's the content of the message that's important, so any sentence form is okay as long as the teacher knows what the student means to say.

c. Children's language deficits are the by-product of immaturity, and children just grow out of them.

d. Language is learned through early interactions with family members, and not in school. Teachers do not have the responsibility to teach language.

4. Eight-year-old Miho is a limited English proficiency student who has been in the United States for only three months. She has no language deficiencies in Japanese. One of her classmates, Thomas, has syntax, semantic, and pragmatic language deficiencies in English, his first and only language. Both need language instruction. A. Do they need the same general language instruction? B. Are there any assumptions that you would make about one student that would not apply to the second student?

    a.

    b.

5. Describe general language sampling procedures. Include these items in your description:

    a. How many utterances should be included in the sample?
    b. How many settings should be observed?
    c. Which is preferable...a spontaneous or a prompted interaction?
    d. Under what circumstances is it appropriate to have another child present?
    e. If you use stimulus materials such as photographs or toys, how should you present them?

6.   What is the purpose of survey-level testing language skills?

7.   What is the mean length of this utterance:

"We didn't go to the...to the big store."

8.   You collected a representative language sample from Thomas but he said so little you are unsure about how to analyze it. Now what?

9.   Al was referred because his teacher says Al has a language problem. You have him and a friend come in for a language sample and he seems to do just fine. But when you see him in class, he rarely talks. What do you do next?

10.   You took a language sample from Robert and found three areas in which he made syntax errors. Are these the only areas you might test at the specific level? Yes or no, and why?

11.   Specific-level testing is used to find answers to the questions listed below. Let's assume that a particularly challenging student has demonstrated problems within every area. Please list one teaching strategy to match each category of concern.

84

1) Does the setting inhibit the student's verbal communication? If yes, ...

2) Are there patterns of pragmatic errors? If yes, ...

3) Is the student competent in communication? If no, ...

4) Are the student's utterances adequately complex? If not, try this ...

5) Are there patterns of syntactical errors and omissions? If there are, ...

6) Are there patterns of errors or omissions in the student's vocabulary usage? If yes, ...

7) Can the student use context to determine the meaning of words? If not, try ...

12. Here are data on Joel's mean length of utterance language samples. Is he progressing satisfactorily? Justify your response.

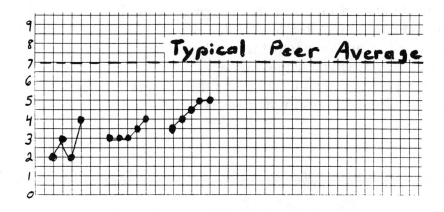

Mean length of utterance

CHAPTER THIRTEEN

WRITTEN EXPRESSION

In this section, you will learn:

...three aspects of the author role in written communication: 1) purpose, 2) process, and 3) product;

...the components of written products and the evidence that defines them;

...a procedure for identifying idea units (T units) in sentences;

...an analytic scale for rating story sophistication;

...survey-level testing procedures to evaluate written communication skills;

...specific-level testing procedures;

...how to count word sequence samples; and

...four instructional strategies for improving written communication skills.

1. In an old Woody Allen movie, a hapless bank robber slipped a note to a bank teller. The note said something like "I have a gub." The teller was confused. She made quite a fuss over the meaninglessness of the note and asked other bank employees to help interpret it.
As the tellers argued about the note's message, the would-be-robber left the bank embarrassed and without money.
Which aspect of communication was the primary problem for him? Purpose? Process? Product? Justify your selection.

2. Written products allow teachers to determine how well a student has mastered writing. Therefore, it is important for teachers to know what <u>evidence</u> would be

used to evaluate the various components of written communication products. Match each component to its supporting evidence. (Text Exhibit 13.2 on page 295 will help you.)

_____ Fluency   a.   Fewer repetitions of favored words and use of more sophisticated words.

_____ Syntactic maturity   b.   Attention to organization of thought, originality, and style.

_____ Vocabulary or semantic maturity   c.   Production of sample sentences and elaboration into compositions of gradually increasing length.

_____ Content   d.   Mechanical aspects of writing such as margins, grammar, spelling, and punctuation.

_____ Conventions   e.   Production of sentences of increasing complexity.

3. You're ready to evaluate Sam's written communication. Because you have no information on Sam, you use the following story starter: "Describe as many animals as you can that live by the ocean." The sample doesn't seem to be of any use. What could be the reason?

4. What is a T-unit?

5. How many T-units are in the following sentence?

"While I was in Bellingham, a town known for it's sprawling, downtown pulp-mill, I happened upon an old friend."

6. You have checked Ben's syntactic maturity using T-units. He passed the test, but no one seems to understand what he's trying to communicate when he

writes. How can you explain this?

7. Use Tindal and Hasbrouck's five-point analytic scale from figure 13.4 on page 298 of the text to rate the following story.

Story Idea _____   Organiz-Cohesion _____   Conven-Mechan _____

My sister leaned a majic trick from him. The trick was to go inside a closit. Say some majic words and turn out the lite. Turn the lite on again and a qarter is in your hand and it looks like the qarter come from the air. Tom wants to git mony for a bike like that.

8. When analyzing a writing sample, the product must be compared to a standard. It is possible to establish local standards based on the performance of students in your own school. Describe the process used to do that.

9. Briefly describe the procedure you would follow to complete survey-level testing of written communication skills.

10. Sally has written communication problems. These problems don't seem to be mechanical so her evaluator gives some specific-level tests, one of which reveals word sequences with punctuation problems. What should be done next? (See Figure 13.5 on page 300 of the text for assistance.)

11. Use the guidelines given in Exhibit 13.7 (p. 301) to score the following word sequence samples.

    a. I asked my grandma I could go to movie

    b. She want to do it

    c. Ralph and he runned away form the polite.

    d. My cat can't sleep on the chair any more.

    e. Another words, my mother mad when he sleeps their.

Total percent correct: _____ Total percent error: _____

12. Specific-level tests include interview/observation, word sequence tests, syntactic maturity tests, and semantic maturity tests. Identify which type of specific-level test is described in each of the following paragraphs, and then state in your own words what information you would be attempting to learn by administering each.

    a. Obtain samples of the student's writing. Score the samples by awarding one point each for words in correct sequence and for appropriate endings.

    Type of test:

    Test is given in order to learn:

b. Collect samples of the student's written communication. Determine the number of sentences that are at each of these levels: repetitive use of simple sentences; simple sentence plus various phrases; and transformation of simple sentences to include relative and subordinate clauses.

Type of test:

Test is given in order to learn:

c. During the writing process, ask the student to explain what she is doing and how she decided to take that action. Complete the status sheet for planning, reviewing, revising, and rating the adequacy of the structure and cohesion of the product.

Type of test:

Test given in order to determine:

d. Obtain samples of written work and compare the words written to a grade-level list of high-frequency words. Use a procedure described by Isaacson to judge the proportion of large words, uncommon words, and unrepeated words used in the written sample.

Type of test:

Test given in order to determine:

13. Four instructional procedures for use in teaching the writing process were recommended in Chapter 13. Briefly describe each one.

Balanced Instruction:

Teach the Writing Process:

Teach Fluency:

Sentence Combining:

14. Portfolio evaluation is used by Louise's teacher to monitor writing skills. Each student's portfolio has samples of compositions from grade-level peers rated one (poor example) through five (excellent example). The chart below shows the ratings that Louise has earned on her weekly essays. Should Louise be given more instruction in authoring skills than her peers receive?

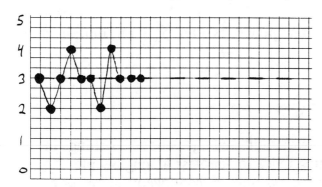

Composition ratings

CHAPTER FOURTEEN

WRITTEN MECHANICS

In this section you will learn:

...some facts about handwriting and spelling;

...the role of morphographs in spelling;

...how to score spelling samples;

...how to categorize spelling errors;

...how to summarize writing sample information; and

...what specific-level tests may reveal.

1.   The first step in assessing handwriting, spelling, and punctuation skills is to obtain samples of the student's writing and judge whether or not it is an adequate sample. What is an "adequate sample"? How do you know one when you see one?

2.   What is a morphograph and how does learning about morphographs contribute to successful spelling?

3.   True or false?
      _____ There is wide variation among people's writing in cursive, while manuscript writing tends to vary less among people.
      _____ Success in cursive writing is contingent upon prior instruction in manuscript.
      _____ There do not appear to be any significant differences in writing rates

between writing in cursive and writing in manuscript when experience and practice are comparable for those people tested.

_____ Even students who have had difficulty learning (but <u>have</u> learned) to write using manuscript should be required to switch to cursive writing.

_____ Students who have had difficulty with spelling need to learn procedures (not word lists) that they can apply to decode and spell words they have not specifically studied.

_____ Recalling the letters or clusters that make sounds is not a necessary prerequisite to good spelling.

_____ One of the most important prerequisites to good spelling is the skill to selectively attend to and perceive letters, clusters, and sounds.

4. On the next page is a story with some spelling, handwriting, and capitalization errors. Use the categories from the <u>Writing Sample Summary</u> in Exhibit 14.4 (p. 315 of the text) to describe this twelve-year-old's skills.

Total letters: _401_   **Total Errors:** ___   **Total Accuracy:** ___
Rate ___ (The assignment took 15 minutes to write)

Letter formation	Opportunities	_401_	
	Correct letter formations	___	___%
	Error letter formations	___	___%

Letters spelled	Opportunities	_401_	
	Correctly spelled letters	___	___%
	Letters spelled incorrectly	___	___%

Capitalized words	Opportunities	_12_	
	Correct capitalizations	___	___%
	Incorrect capitalizations	___	___%

Punctuated words	Opportunities	_8_	
	Correct punctuations	___	___%
	Error punctuations	___	___%

5. Use Exhibit 14.3 (p. 314) from the text to determine whether or not this student requires the use of any specific teaching strategies. What is your conclusion?

When my mom was in peace core she had a cat. Once when she went away a frend took care of the cat. It was run over by a bannanna truck and it die. The frend was worryed that my mom would think that he didn't take any noteice so he put a messege an the raydio so she could here it befor she came home. In that place, feunerals are put on the raydio. The raydio played the messege like it was a feuneral and lots of peeple herd it. One gril got in truble when she laft becaws she kuw it was a cat. Her dad didn't kow.

THE EnD

6. Use Exhibit 13.7 (that's <u>13.7</u>, in Chapter 13) and SLP 2 on page 301 in the text to score the following spelling test. Score it letter-by-letter, not word-by-word. An example is completed for you.

	Stimulus	**Response**	**Score**
a.	treasure	tresure	Tresure 3c / 4x
b.	holiday	holaday	
c.	journey	journie	
d.	tournament	turnament	
e.	champion	champeon	
f.	suitable	suitabel	
g.	challenge	chalenge	
h.	consolation	consollation	
i.	defeat	defete	
j.	sportsmanship	sportsmansip	
k.	delay	dellay	
l.	cottage	cottege	

95

m.   recreation   recreachon

7.   Exhibit 14.9 (p. 318) will help you categorize a sample of the errors made in the sample from question 6.

Stimulus	**Response**	**Error Type**
challenge	chalenge	
defeat	defete	
cottage	cottege	
suitable	suitabel	

8.   Chapter 14 described four specific-level tests for written mechanics skills. They were: 1) writing fluency, 2) letter formation, 3) spelling accuracy, and 4) capitalization and punctuation. Go beyond just the titles of the tests to describe specifically what you would learn from each test.

1)   Writing fluency

2)   Letter formation

3)   Spelling accuracy

4)   Capitalization and punctuation

9.   Danny's weekly spelling scores are shown below. What advice would you give to his teacher?

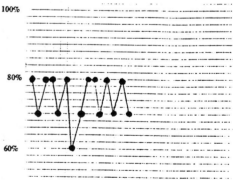

CHAPTER FIFTEEN

MATHEMATICS

In this section you will learn:

...facts about the state of the art in teaching/testing mathematics;

...three elements of the mathematics curriculum: facts, strategies, and concepts;

...what's different about survey-level testing for basic facts;

...how to calculate rate per minute from a sample test;

...use of tool skill rates to set intermediate aims;

...specific-level tests for mathematics; and

...teaching strategies for mathematics.

1.   Imagine that on your annual flight to Tonga, in the South Pacific, the person sitting next to you begins to speculate about the math skills her fourth-grade son will encounter next year in school. (You meet all kinds when you travel.) You're on the spot because she's learned that you're an educator, and are expected to know things like this. Of the following, circle the one that would be the most honest response. Justify your selection.

   a.   It depends on his ability.
   b.   It depends on how well he scores on the achievement test.
   c.   It depends on what textbook the district uses.

   Rationale:

2. Before going any further, let's be sure you understand the vocabulary used to talk about mathematics in Chapter fifteen. Please define these terms:

   a. Operations

   b. Algorithm

   c. Computation

   d. Domain

   e. CAP

   f. Intermediate aim

3. There are three computational domains in mathematics. Define and provide an example of each.

   a. F_____

   b. S_____

   c. C_____

4. Remember the cloze procedure from Chapter 10? The purpose of these study guide activities **IS** to enhance comprehension...so fill in the missing words and check your accuracy. Your goal should be approximately 13 or 14 exact word choices.

Many teachers allocate time for instruction in computation and operations but do not include adequate time for instruction in problem solving and application. To _____ extent the practice of _____ the factual and strategic _____ of computation over the _____ utilitarian content of application _____ problem solving may actually _____ the time it takes _____ to acquire computation skills _____ decrease the likelihood that _____ will maintain proficiency. When _____ and operations are taught _____, it is difficult to _____ them meaningful. Meaningless material _____ more practice if it _____ to be retained and _____ more likely to be _____ than material that is _____ in daily tasks.

Math _____ are often saturated with _____ content -- the first example _____ comes to mind is _____ topic of roman numerals. _____ sort of curricular residue _____ not be allowed to _____ with things the student _____ needs to know and _____.

Problem solving requires the _____ combination of computation knowledge _____ application knowledge. It has _____ steps: step 1 involves _____ what to do (selecting _____ operations, selecting relevant information, _____ irrelevant information, noting missing _____, and estimating correct answers); _____ 2 involves carrying it _____ (setting up equations and _____ which numbers go with _____ operation, working equations using _____ that result in correct _____, and checking results).

Problem solving is another neglected and misunderstood topic in the math curriculum.

5. One of the purposes of survey-level testing in mathematics is to find out if the student is fluent. Fluency is determined by measuring the student's rate of performance. Please describe:

    a) how to administer a rate test, and b) how you would calculate rate once the sample is completed. In your response to part "a," include information regarding directions to the student, what happens if a student omits a problem, and whether you or not you expect the student to complete all problems within the timed sample.

a)

b)

6. Your para-professional aide has been doing some survey testing for you. He has thrown away the original work and given you a list of math problems with the student's answers. Will that be sufficient for a math analysis? Please explain.

7. A student responds 7 + 6 = 1. What might be an assumed cause?

8. You are giving a computation survey test to find out if the student knows what has been taught. What can you do to limit the number of problems the student will have to work?

9. You are evaluating Andrew's operation knowledge. He misses every item on the survey test. Now what?

10. Rico is expected to do 50 written addition problems per minute. He does 15. You check his "write digit" speed and find out it is 40 digits per minute. What is your recommendation?

11. Here is Charlie's chart used to track his rate of converting improper to proper fractions. Is he progressing satisfactorily?

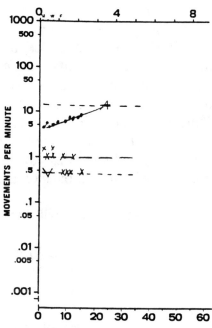

~~~~ ~~~~ ~~~~ ~~~~ ~~~~ ~~~~ ~~~~ ~~~~

CHAPTER SIXTEEN

SOCIAL SKILLS

A friend of ours spent a day at the lake with her 2 1/2 year-old son. When it was time to go, she couldn't find the car keys. She looked through her bag, pockets, folded blanket, trash, and on the ground. Her son watched her very quietly. Finally, she looked at him and asked, "Matt, where are the keys?" He said, "I throwed them in the lake." and pointed to an area of marsh grass and cattails.

The obscure moral of this story is that sometimes you just have to ask the right question in order to get an important answer.

That's what chapter 16 is all about. We have tried to provide a conceptual framework for looking at social skills so you will ask questions that will lead to useful solutions. It's not possible to provide you with everything you need to know about social behavior in a single textbook, let alone a single chapter. Even though we haven't tried to do that, the information regarding the evaluation of social skills is complex.

Before you decide not to immerse yourself in something that one of the authors has recklessly labeled complex, please remember that roughly 55% of the school day is spent managing students. Some of that management time is spent in routines such as lining up, making transitions to the next subject or class period, preparing for P.E., library, pep assemblies, etc. But as any teacher will testify, too much of it is spent with students whose behavior has interrupted the flow of instruction. Students with social skill excesses and deficits already demand a great deal of a teacher's time and energy. We hope you will view this collection of evaluation recommendations as an extra set of keys that will put you back on the road when trouble throws your first set in the lake.

In this section you will learn:

...to recognize <u>form</u> and <u>function</u> of behavior;

...overt and covert variables influencing behavior;

...how to establish standards to which student behavior can be compared;

...environmental and student-centered factors that motivate actions;

...how to conduct survey-level testing; and

...specific-level testing.

1. Believe it or not! Sort the following statements into either the believable (true) or unbelievable (false).

    _____Generally speaking, tolerance for diversity in student behavior is very similar from teacher to teacher.

    _____Low-income students are more likely to receive punishment than high income students.

_____As a group, teachers are empathetic to students who are depressed because of life stress factors.

_____Students with behavior problems often make poor choices because they choose from a very limited range of familiar options.

_____Most school actions focused on social behavior take the form of reactions to problems rather than proactive instruction.

2.   Identify the <u>form</u> and the <u>function</u> of maladaptive behavior in each of the following scenarios:

a.   When students were told to line up for lunch, Imelda elbowed Carlos so she could be first in line.

Form:

Function:

b.   During a pop quiz, Darien copied answers from P. R.'s paper to avoid flunking.

Form:

Function:

c.   Gil and Joe were best friends, but when Carol asked Gil if Joe had been invited to the tolo dance, Gil lied - hoping that Carol would forget Joe and invite him instead.

Form:

Function:

d.   Walt didn't have a student body card for Mariner High School, so he slipped into the dance through the girl's locker room.

Form:

Function:

e.   In order to appear smart, Paul raised his hand for every question, whether he knew the answer or not.

Form:

Function:

3.   Consider each of the <u>functions</u> identified in question 2 and list those that are deviant.

4.   Define and give and example of each.

Overt behavior:

Example:

Covert behavior:

Example:

5.   The text makes a case for <u>social judgment and decision making</u> being critical to successful social skills training. What are some reasons for such a strong emphasis on this point?

6. The authors suggest the use of an A-B-C (antecedent, behavior, consequence) form as a procedure to identify the antecedents and consequences of behavior. The text provided one example of use of this process in Exhibit 16.4 on page 373.

Now you try it. Your very own A-B-C starter set below has two separate scenarios. The first has suggested an antecedent (forerunner, precursor) to a behavior. Please fill in at least one probable behavior and consequence that would complete the linear sequence.

The second scenario has supplied a behavior. Please add an antecedent and consequence.

ANTECEDENT	BEHAVIOR	CONSEQUENCE
Teacher's assigned seating chart places two opposing gang members side-by-side		

ANTECEDENT	BEHAVIOR	CONSEQUENCE
	Chris nodded, smiled and said, "Thank you. I understand it much better now that you have explained it to me."	

7.   The text uses the terms ecological ceiling and ecological floor to describe the "typical" performance of students. Why is this something you should care about?

8.   Under what circumstances would it be a bad idea to use typical rates of behavior as the CAP for a target student?

9.   Remember that we select responses not just on the basis of what happens in the environment, but also on our interpretation of what is going on. What we "think" is influenced by what we attend to (attention), what we expect to occur (expectation), what we believe to be true (belief), and a pattern of associated thoughts and habits we've relied on in the past in similar situations (cognitive set).

Use those elements to analyze this real-life incident:

Larry is an executive with a zest for life. He has a Harley Davidson motor cycle and the leathers that make him look like he belongs on it. One afternoon, while he was touring, he spontaneously decided to stop at a marina and look for a yacht. He had wanted one for some time, and was now in a financial position to buy. When he walked into the showroom after parking his Harley just outside the door, a salesperson watched Larry but did not go across the room to meet him.

What do you think the salesperson would attend to so far?

What expectations do you think the salesperson might have?

Speculate about what the salesperson might believe about Larry? (What kind of self-talk can you imagine going on in the salesperson's mind as he approached Larry?)

106

What other related habits, beliefs, and patterns do you think might be included in the salesperson's cognitive set?

10. You might want to read what the key has to say about question 9 before answering this question.

What happened to Larry is repeated in thousands of interactions every day. Students with limited social skills are especially vulnerable to perplexing interactions given their limited problem-solving strategies and belief structures.

Exhibit 16.7 on page 377 of the textbook shows the operant stimulus --> response --> consequence model with perceptions and expectations added. We've provided the actual environmental events; please add reasonable cognitive variables.

ANTECEDENT	BEHAVIOR	CONSEQUENCE
Teacher announces, "It's time to line up for lunch."	Imelda elbows Carlos and crowds in front of him at the head of the line.	Imelda is sent back to her seat for one minute then is given permission to join the back of the line.

List Available responses Imelda **COULD** choose:

List the responses you think Imelda can probably think of:

List the response she chose:

List the consequence she probably expected:

List the actual consequence:

11. Some of the following descriptors are measurable/observable and some are not because they include adjectives or adverbs that are open to interpretation, or value judgments. Please identify the measurable pinpoints by circling them and change the poor pinpoints by adding or deleting words.

   a. Insults peers

   b. Sells illegal substances

   c. Inappropriately solicits answers from peers during hard assignments

   d. Causes others to stop working

   e. Signals for help from the teacher

   f. Eagerly contributes to discussions

12. The textbook offered two categories of prerequisites necessary for evaluating social skills. Type 1 prerequisites consist of overt skills and knowledge (initiates conversation, requests what is needed, can state school rules, etc.). Type 2 prerequisites are covert beliefs, expectations, and perceptions ("can do" thinking, believes teachers want to help, expects to succeed, etc.).

108

Social skill evaluation requires an assessment of both categories. Please describe the general approach we've recommended for obtaining evaluation information about each:

Identify overt target behaviors by:

Identify covert target behaviors by:

13.   Some of the following are appropriate guidelines for observing behaviors. Some are bad ideas. Please sort the good from the ugly by indicating Yes (appropriate suggestion) or No (bad idea).

_____   Observe behavior for several short periods rather than one long period.
_____   Don't prompt behaviors that don't naturally occur. That would set up an artificial response.
_____   Describe/report the circumstances under which the observation occurs.
_____   If you must collect data on interactions with another teacher, do not inform the other teacher about what you are doing lest you change the environment.
_____   Collect several days' worth of data, even if the maladaptive behavior is dangerous.
_____   Compare the median score of the last three days of data to a standard to see if there is a discrepancy between expected rates and actual rates of behavior.

14.   By using Exhibit 16.9 (p. 381), Decision Making for Social Behavior, you should identify one of four potential problems. They are: 1) missing type-1 student behaviors; 2) missing type-1 environment perquisites; 3) missing type-2 student prerequisites; and 4) missing type-2 environment prerequisites. To demonstrate your understanding of these categories, please write an example of behavior for each.

Missing type-1 student prerequisite:

Missing type-1 environment prerequisite:

Missing type-2 student prerequisite:

Missing type-2 environment prerequisite:

~~~~   ~~~~   ~~~~   ~~~~   ~~~~   ~~~~   ~~~~   ~~~~

CHAPTER SEVENTEEN

TASK-RELATED SKILLS

In this section you will learn:

...how the concepts of enabling skills and scaffolding apply to task-related behaviors;

...how to establish a standard for task-related behavior;

...to recognize study skills, problem solving skills, and basic learning strategies;

...what levels of assistance are used to teach attention, memory, and motivation skills; and

...why you should consider the role of teacher actions when students have deficits in task-related behaviors.

110

1. Explain how a student who appears very capable outside of class can literally not know how to learn in an academic setting. (Suggestion: think about scaffolding and enabling skills before you respond.)

2. Match the following:

    ___ Study skills

    ___ Test-taking skills

    ___ Task-related behaviors

    ___ Learning scaffolds

    ___ Topical knowledge

    a. Supporting knowledge that serves as a temporary conduit between prior knowledge and new information

    b. ...allow students to make use of instruction

    c. Prior knowledge required to learn new skills or concepts

    d. A wide range of skills that teachers believe enable success

    e. ...allow the student to display what she has learned.

3. 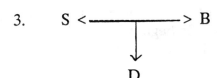   What is this and how is it used?

4. Give an example of each of the following:

    a. A study skill

    b. A problem-solving skill

    c. A basic learning strategy

5. Fill in the blanks:

    a. You can assume a student has adequate topical knowledge if _____
        _____
        _____
        _____

    b. Basic learning strategies include attention, _____, and _____.

    c. When conducting a survey-level evaluation for task-related skills, the very
        first question focuses on _____
        _____.

6. Attention, memory, and motivation can be taught with varying levels of
    assistance. What are the four levels of assistance that can be used?

    1)
    2)
    3)
    4)

7. If you had to teach a basic learning strategy such as attention using some level
    of assistance, which would be better: to start with a low level of assistance and
    increase the intrusiveness of assistance if necessary? Or begin with the highest
    level of assistance and work toward lower levels of intrusiveness?

8. Before saying, "The student has an attention problem," ask yourself if you have
    consistently employed teacher actions to promote attention. Describe two
    teacher actions that help secure or direct attention.

    a.

    b.

9.   Teachers also need to promote storage, promote recall, and teach memory skills. Describe one strategy for each:

   a.   Promote storage:

   b.   Promote recall:

   c.   Teach memory skills

10.   What would you be teaching if you supplied meaning to a task by placing a priority on it, relating it to its context, and demonstrating a personal interest in it?

ANSWER KEY

STUDY GUIDE CHAPTERS ONE - SEVENTEEN

KEY, CHAPTER ONE

TEACHER THOUGHT PROCESS

1. The authors define curriculum as a set of learning outcomes resulting from instruction. b is the correct choice. Both choices a and c are common misconceptions that result in teachers designing lessons around material that is available rather than around a student's instructional needs. The authors believe that when a teacher defines learning outcomes and teaches to them, learning has a greater probability of being more relevant and efficient.

2. The chart should look something like this:

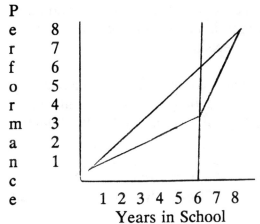

When student progress is expected to be one year's growth in one year, the characteristic that defines remedial and special-education students is failure to maintain expected movement through the curriculum. Changes in instructional programs can change the rate of movement through a set of defined learning outcomes.

3. Placement decisions are concerned with assignment to a particular category of students, assignment to use specific resources or services, or with grouping, grade retention, determination of eligibility, and duration of service.

Teaching decisions focus on what to teach and how it will be taught.

a. Teaching. The decision concerned <u>what to teach</u>.

b. Placement. This example focused on <u>assignment</u> to a specific service.

c.   Teaching.   Juan's teacher has identified a teaching strategy that will determine the <u>instructional process</u>.

d.   Teaching.   Willard is being taught <u>how to</u> solve problems.

e.   Teaching.   The cooperative learning group is being used as an <u>instructional process</u> to teach a specific skill.

f.   Placement.   Debbie is being <u>placed</u> in a group, but no indication was given of what she will be taught or how she will be taught.

4.   The best response is <u>c</u>.   Achievement test scores are norm-referenced information that are frequently used to assign, sort, retain, or promote students. Those decisions are placement decisions. Whether or not a student can add one digit to one digit at a written rate of 60 correct digits per minute is a criterion-based comparison that is useful for teaching decisions.

If you considered choice <u>a</u> for longer than two seconds, you have misread the philosophical orientation of the authors. Choice <u>b</u> ignores the usefulness of comparing student performance levels to others of the same age when making placement decisions.

5.   a)   <u>S</u>tudent variable. Since it is usually not within the role of the teacher to treat chemical dependence or change family dynamics, this is an **unalterable** variable.

b)   <u>T</u>ask variable. The student's ability to successfully complete the assigned task is limited by the reading level of the text. The nature of the task is **alterable**. The teacher could change the assignment to either reading a less difficult text with similar content or by providing audio tapes with the content.

c)   <u>I</u>nstructional variable.   Since the teacher has chosen the type of instruction used, this is an **alterable** variable. The teacher could choose to use a direct instruction approach if student success rate indicated it was necessary.

d)   <u>S</u>tudent variable. His size and other physical characteristics are just as **unalterable** as is his parent's choice of occupation. Hey, don't judge a book by its cover. This kid is known to read poetry by flashlight under his covers late at night.

116

e) Instructional variable. This is an **alterable** pattern that the teacher could change by structuring lessons that would focus students by increasing active participation.

6. There are many different correct answers you might have given, but all correct answers should have these characteristics in common:

a) Task-related suggestions should focus on what is asked of the student. The amount of work, the mode of response or the amount of time the student is expected to perform are all examples of task related variables.

b) Instructional variables focus on how the teacher presents or arranges the "input" part of the lesson. Using visuals models, requiring 90% correct responses before presenting new material or using mnemonic devices to organize a sequence of events are examples of instruction related variables.

7. 1. **d.** Using the same modifier over and over again is not an effective strategy for writing interesting essays. Teach a new strategy so the student will have multiple words from which to choose.

2. **f.** The student has demonstrated difficulty with generalization. Select an instructional technique likely to improve generalization.

3. **b.** The student lacks the prerequisite skill. This is one example of a student variable that the teacher <u>can</u> change.

4. **e.** Comparison to peer performance indicates that the student is unlikely to be able to complete the task because she is too slow. The task could be altered for this student, but unless she is permanently physically impaired, lowered standards for her performance should be a <u>temporary</u> adjustment.

8. <u>b</u> Ms. Easton made her judgment too quickly with too little information. The new student may be a shy but very able learner. He may come from a home that values respect for teachers so much that he is hesitant to be too forward. Ms. Easton lacks perspective on this student and has unwarranted confidence in her judgment.

9. <u>b</u> Although it's true that some teaching functions may resemble the orchestra leader, the pilot or the artist, the role that is the best analogy for effective <u>decision making</u> is that of the detective. Teachers gather assessment information

related to the interaction between task-student-instruction, form an idea of the nature of the problem and its potential solutions, and then test the student's response changes in the task or instruction.

10.   There are many correct responses to this question. The suggestions here are some possible responses.

   b)   1. I've mistaken a correlational relationship for cause and effect. Linda and Connie's reasons for poor learning must be different.

        2. I need more information about what Linda can and cannot do. It is not clear yet whether she lacks skills or motivation.

        3. Depending on what I learn through some direct assessment, I may need to make task and/or instructional decisions.

   c)   1. I've defined the problem too narrowly. Since Ralph doesn't have good organizational or study skills, it was not good judgment to think that teaching him one small component of organization would meet all of his needs.

        2. I need to assess to find out what other domains of study skills Ralph is missing.

        3. I need to make both task and instruction decisions.

~~~~ ~~~~ ~~~~ ~~~~ ~~~~ ~~~~ ~~~~ ~~~~

KEY, CHAPTER TWO

THINKING ABOUT LEARNING AND STUDENTS

1.   The statements made in the study guide are:

a. <u>Myth</u>. Motivation comes with the sense of control and accomplishment. Easy tasks are recognized as such by students and will not serve as a challenge met and successfully completed. In fact, tasks that are too easy may be viewed either as boring or demeaning. Have you ever tried to get an eighth-grade boy to "enjoy" a children's story about teddy bears?

b. _T_rue. How well you use what you've learned changes as a result of practice, but learning is not a gradual process.

c. _M_yth. Current theory suggests that performance is determined by attention, motivation, and memory, not by fixed capacity or strength of "modality" channels.
d. _T_rue. Early special education thought in the U.S. was that if students were distractable, it would be helpful to remove as many distractions as possible. Current evidence indicates that students will better maintain work skills if they learn to perform in the presence of distractors.

e. _T_rue. It is a rare occurrence indeed to find two children who have exactly the same learning needs. How we sort children is less important than how and what we teach them.

2.   The correct answer is **b**. Modality theory assumed that the brain contained sensory specific channels. That's where terms such as "auditory memory" and "visual learner" came from. Information processing suggests that executive function determines the selection of strategies required to respond to environmental demands.

3.   The correct response is _d_. Most students fall behind in expected progress rates because they have not focused on critical features of learning tasks or because they have not learned how to store information in long-term memory. "Special students don't always fail because they haven't got the potential to learn. They fail because they don't use their potential effectively."

4.   The third child's name is Johnnie...as in, "Johnnie's mother had three children." Since all of the problem-solving information was presented in just a few short sentences, only short-term memory played a part in finding the answer. Most adults who care enough to voluntarily work their way through a study guide have the motivation necessary to expend the 1/1000th of a calorie necessary to continue. The remaining possibility is attention, and that is, in fact, the variable involved in this cheap trick. If you did not focus on the introductory information, "Johnnie's mother had three children," it is probable that you returned to the beginning of the story to read it again to learn if you had missed critical information. The second time through, you probably had ATTENTION on your side, and solved the riddle. We sincerely hope so. Some of our friends who still haven't figured this one out are still mad at us.

5. a. Willie attributes his success to external forces and is not likely to persist at a task when he doesn't believe his efforts matter. We cannot identify him as motivated given the information we have about him.

    b. Waylen is not motivated. He is giving up the accordion forever!

    <u>c.</u> <u>Dolly is motivated</u>. She did not perform well, but she is sticking to the task and will try again. She is behaving in a way that suggests she believe what she does will make a difference.

    d. Garth has found an easy way out. He has not demonstrated that he is motivated. Students who believe that success is related to things they can control, view difficulty as a cue to work harder.

6. a. <u>Performance</u> Ms. Jensen is simply concerned with assignment completion. Accuracy or improvement of performance does not seem to be a concern, given the information provided.

    b. <u>Learning</u> Mr. Berry is engaging in a process that will identify why the error is occurring and then provide practice in the correct sequence.

    c. <u>Performance</u> Michael and his teacher both seem to be preoccupied with the accuracy score, not mastery of specific skills or knowledge base.

    d. <u>Learning</u> Ms. Hankinson has asked her students to engage in self-monitoring that measures improvement in the ability to generate facts about the science unit, and then to monitor the effect of performance in that task on another task. She has structured the activity to show change and relationships.

7. All three of your statements representing a "learning orientation" should have acknowledged improvement rather than task completion. Descriptive statements such as, "Yes, exactly! You have written a topic sentence and three supporting sentences to make that a complete paragraph!" are preferable to valuative statements like, "You are such a clever writer."

8. Most likely: <u> b</u>   Somewhat likely: <u> a</u>   Least likely: <u> c</u>

    Mr. Lovitt has the edge on promoting self-monitoring because his students must judge the difficulty of the task and check their own work. Ms. Lopez may find that some of her students choose to correct their work, but many may not. Ms. Follett is trying very hard to provide immediate feedback, but her method not only removes self-monitoring responsibility from the student, her chosen method of simply identifying correct and error responses may not be very effective (Lovitt, 1977).

9. It should be clear that only you can judge which of the items would be solved in short-term or long-term memory. The key criterion is that if the activity requires you to consciously think about it with consideration and intent, then your are using short-term memory. It is our best guess (which may be very wrong for you) that most people still have to consciously attend to programming the VCR, reciting the Gettysburg Address, and filling out that income tax long form. Only the "Happy Birthday" song is likely to be lurking at the automatic level somewhere in your long-term memory.

10. The correct response is "c." Whether or not a task should be learned to an automatic level, should be determined by how important the performance is to tasks that will be presented in the future and how frequently the student will need to use it.
    Each of the other options focuses on either a myth (capacity) or an excuse (not enough time).

11. a. Wrong. It is important to teach students to self-monitor as they work. Special educator Anita Archer has been known to say that, "Practice makes permanent. Perfect practice makes perfect."

    b. Infrequently. Since it takes time and energy to teach a task to the automatic level, the best use of instructional time is to make that kind of investment only for tasks that will continue to be important for the learner.

    c. Prior knowledge. A carpenter without an organized shop will lay tools "around here somewhere." A child without a closet will toss clothes on the floor. (Okay, okay, ...maybe even one with a closet will do that, but one without will certainly remove and drop.) A learner without a conceptual framework to which new information can be related will have difficulty understanding the relevance of new content.

    d. Executive control. This really is the key concept of this chapter. We know that special and remedial students do not differ much from general-education students in their ability to learn because we know that they can be taught attention, motivation, and memory strategies. They differ in the executive control functions of information processing.

e. Instruction. It is instruction that shall set them free and empower teachers as professionals. That's our job. It's what we do.

~~~~ ~~~~ ~~~~ ~~~~ ~~~~ ~~~~ ~~~~

KEY, CHAPTER THREE

THINKING ABOUT CURRICULUM

1. _b_, Curriculum is what is taught, often described in goals and objectives.

2. SK Writing digits is a skill.

    ST Studying for a test by paraphrasing key concepts is a strategy. It could be used for any of a number of different tests or challenges such as obtaining a driver's license, reporting brain storming ideas to an employer, and so on. This strategy is really a way to check comprehension of content.

    SK "Measure object" is a skill used in very specific situations.

    KN Knowledge of compounds is required to recognize the need for testing.

    ST The use of a calendar to track due dates is a strategy.

    KN Predicting weather relies on the application of a broad set of meteorological principles. If you don't know these principles, you can't teach them.

3. _X_ No. Curriculum for remedial and special-education students in general-education settings should not be different from their typical peers. What students need to learn remains constant. Instructional strategies, calibration of tasks, or learning pace may vary, but the goals and objectives are the same.

4. The value of an instructional method is determined by how well the curriculum is learned. When learning does not occur, it is _instruction_ that should be changed.

5.   _c_ .   When a student is having difficulty learning, it is the student's prior knowledge that is most likely to be the source of the problem.

6.   The following are potential correct answers. There may be others.

TASK ANALYSIS

1. Addition would be a necessary skill.
2. Finding a common denominator would be required.
3. Reduction of improper fractions would be necessary.

CONCEPT ANALYSIS

1. The concepts of "more" and "less"
2. The concepts of whole numbers and fractions
3. The concepts of proper/improper fractions

ERROR ANALYSIS

Student A: This student is using the wrong strategy to solve the problem. The student is simply adding numbers straight across the numerators and denominators without finding a common denominator.

Student B: This student has used the correct strategy to solve the problem, but has stopped one step too soon. The improper fraction should be reduced.

Student C: This student is adding incorrectly. That the correct strategy is being used is clear from looking at the student's written work, but the enabling skill of addition has let him down.

7.   a. No. The reader does not comprehend the writer's intent because she lacks necessary prior knowledge of the vocabulary and perhaps a few basic construction principles.

b. Yes. The student has used oral language and social behavior that are congruent with his intent.

c. No. The writer has failed to communicate the of the message because he lacked the skills (prior knowledge) necessary to make his note understandable.

d. Yes. The speaker used language that communicated the shortest route to the traveler.

8. a. <u>E</u>nabling skill. Uwanda had the concept of what was necessary, he just didn't have the enabling skill (vocabulary) that would have made it possible to ask for help.

b. <u>B</u>oth. This student seems to lack both the concepts of planning, reviewing, and organizing <u>and</u> the enabling skills of outlining and writing down assignments.

c. <u>C</u>oncept. Malinda knew the parts of a good speech, but she didn't recognize when to use the skills she had learned as a whole set of behaviors in the appropriate environment.

9. <u>b</u> It is false that goals and objectives are required for all students with remedial and "at-risk" characteristics. It is considered to be good practice to use goals and objectives, but it is not the law. It is also false that goals and objectives are necessary for every activity that <u>any</u> student engages in each day.

10. Your objectives are correct if you can underline these components:

a. content (reading in science, social studies, etc.)

b. observable behavior (read words orally, write answers to comprehension questions, see to say definition of new vocabulary word, paraphrase concept, etc.)

c. conditions (from science textbook, from word list, etc.)

d. criteria (130 words per minute, 95% correct, every time)

11. <u>d</u> is the only example that is measurable, useful, and calibrated in "reasonable" units.

12. <u>a</u> is false. Proficiency level standards are <u>not</u> arbitrary. They should be set at a level comparable to the standards used for general-education peers. Remember, it is not a student's capacity that is the major identifying feature of

students with remedial or special-education needs. It is the poor use of attention, memory, and motivation that distinguishes them from peers who succeed in the curriculum. Attention, memory, and motivation can all be taught.

13. You may have made any of hundreds of possible changes to individualize Sven's objective. We have identified <u>what part</u> of the objective should have been changed under each condition.

   a. Criteria should have changed:
       125 words per minute with no more than 3 errors

   b. Content changes should have focused on:
       words in context

   c. Behavior changes should have altered:
       orally read words

   d. Conditions should have changed:
       from literature-based chapter books

   e. Calibration of the objective:
       fourth-grade level

14. Terms and their definitions:

Subtask: **4.** Small unit of behavior necessary for completion of a step en route to an objective.

Task: **3.** What is required for the performance of an objective.

Task Analysis: **1.** The process of isolating, sequencing, and defining all of the essential components of a task.

Strategy: **2.** The rules, procedures, and algorithms students follow to combine subtasks into larger tasks.

KEY, CHAPTER FOUR

THINKING ABOUT INSTRUCTION

1. a.   <u>Yes</u> Ms. Perkins is engaging students in an overt behavior that allows her to monitor their level of mastery of a strategy. The teacher action represented in this example is <u>asking questions</u>.

   b.   <u>No</u> In this example, the history teacher has not chosen a teacher action. Students are expected to independently read the chapter and answer the questions at the end. There is no teacher interaction here.

   c.   <u>Yes</u> Mr. Murray is relying on two types of student responses to keep them engaged. He is hoping for covert attention to his lecture; the chances of that are increased by his expectation that his students will overtly take notes. This is an example of the teacher action of <u>delivery of information</u>.

   d.   <u>Yes</u> Ms. Bower is <u>responding to student efforts</u> by checking their paragraphs and asking them to self-correct after overtly reviewing the strategy used to develop a complete paragraph.

   e.   <u>No</u> This teacher has carefully defined how to complete assignments, but has not chosen any action that would require active interaction focused on learning the curriculum objectives. His students may complete assignments, but that is not the same as LEARNING.

2.   Your answers are correct if they engaged students in activities that required thoughtful responses directly related to the lesson content. Teacher-directed instruction that targets curriculum objectives and requires active participation of the students is powerful. It is more powerful than dittos, workbooks, coloring, puzzles, non-academic discussions, or feeding Squeezy - the class gerbil. Teacher-directed instruction is what enables learning to occur and what gives us the professional label: "teac<u>er</u>."

3.   We hope we aren't setting you up for lengthy arguments with your principal on this one, but the false statement is <u>d</u>. Student activities should be drawn from the next lesson in sequence in published materials **ONLY** when that activity or worksheet matches important curriculum objectives. Typically, there is poor alignment between school district objectives and textbook content; therefore, teachers should make conscious decisions about when to use the next lesson in

sequence and when to skip it.

4.   Teacher actions: c, f, h, and j. Deliver information, ask questions, present activities, and respond to student efforts.

Thought process: b, e, and i. Facts, strategies, and concepts.

Format of instruction to match student stage of learning:
a, d, and g. Acquisition, fluency, and application.

5.   _b_. The strategy is demonstrated, practiced orally, applied, and the student monitors its use.

6.   _a_. The student who is accurate but not yet automatic in an important skill that should be routine needs a teacher who can provide fluency instruction. Fluency instruction emphasizing practice rather than directions or correction procedures is needed here because the student already has demonstrated he knows _how_ to do the task. Fluency instruction will lead to mastery, which is a prerequisite for automaticity.

7.   Acquisition stage instruction should focus on how to do the task. Students at this stage still have high error rates and need to have the task demonstrated, explained, and corrected each time an error is made. Students should _not_ practice independently lest they practice up a storm ... of error responses.

8.   We hope you answered _c_. We danced that capacity myth out again just to see if you remembered that you shouldn't trust old stories. All of the other options are reasonable explanations as to why a student may fail to generalize.

9.   Although it is good advice that you should be careful about giving your keys away to someone who likes your "wheels," we meant this to be an example of the power of meaningful tasks. _b_. If you doubt that meaningfulness influences learning, ask a biology teacher which unit elicits greater attention from students, the unit on human reproduction or the unit on protozoa.
      In case you are wondering, the local police found the car sitting slightly askew in a ditch, and two happy adolescents picnicking in a city park.

10.   Other effective group instruction procedures might include peer tutoring, cooperative learning, cognitive-strategy instruction, cross-age tutoring, and other methods that combine efficient routines with teacher actions appropriate for the demands of the task to be learned. But remember - the magic isn't in the

procedure - it is in the effective use of the procedure. A poorly implemented cooperative learning lesson is no better than a poorly maintained airplane engine. You won't get far with either one.

~~~~ ~~~~ ~~~~ ~~~~ ~~~~ ~~~~ ~~~~ ~~~~

KEY, CHAPTER FIVE

EVALUATION AND DECISION MAKING

1.   a.   Testing, because performance is not compared to a standard.

     b.   Evaluation, because performance is compared to average peer performance.

     c.   Evaluation because performance is compared to a minimum acceptable score.

     d.   Testing, because we do not know what the points mean in the context of expected performance.

2.   Items a, c, and d are all necessary for evaluation to occur. There has to be a measure of the student's current level of performance (a) that is compared to an expected level of performance (c) so that the evaluator can make decisions (d) about the necessity for change.

3.   b.   This choice describes the F.A.C.T. format presented in the text.

4.   a, b, and c are all assumed causes that could productively be taken to the next step of testing or observing specific skills to see if the hypothesis generated is correct or not. Choice d is not productive because it labels Garrett as a student with limited capacity, which by now should alert the attention and memory executive functions of your mind.

5.   For the first example. 2 would be the best choice because the leap of faith that must be made from what is known to what is inferred is a shorter jump when using the text she will be asked to read in to predict if she can read with the new reading group.

In the second example, choice _3_ would provide the teacher with information that focuses most directly on a specific level skill relevant to the curriculum and instruction that could benefit Carlos.

6.   Item B is a _produce_ format because the student must create an example.

Item C is an _identify_ format because students are asked to choose from among given options. They simply have to recognize the correct response.

Item D is also an _identify_ format because the words are all provided for the student. He or she needs only to recognize the correct pairs.

Item E is a _produce_ format since the student must create a correct response from knowledge of the formula for compound sentences.

7.   The false statement is _b_. If you chose any other item, please read on. The authors of this text share an anxiety about the use of portfolio assessment becoming a popular, but inadequate way to evaluate student performance. Remember the discussion about how **evaluation** is the **comparison** of student **performance** to a **standard**? Well, if a student's behavior is compared only to her previous behavior without reference to where he or she _ought to be_, then evaluation has not taken place. Please don't go to sleep on this one. If portfolio assessment becomes more and more popular, educators must be made aware that for it to be useful, we will still have to compare samples of what is to what ought to be.

It is true that sometimes idiosyncratic standards are used to monitor if a student is learning better under one condition than another. Even then, however, it is still important to know what level of performance represents "good enough."

8.   Consider your responses correct if they contain the general idea that:

The major purpose of a norm-referenced test is to compare a student's performance with other students of the same age or class placement.

The primary use of a norm-referenced test is to determine program eligibility (make placement decisions).

The purpose of a criterion-referenced test is to compare a student's performance with skills specified in the curriculum in order to find out which are missing.

The primary use of a criterion-referenced test is to <u>determine what the student should be taught</u>.

9.   a.   Jamal's evaluation results will be used to determine how much he has learned to date. It is <u>summative</u> evaluation.

        b.   Wilma's teacher has set up a <u>formative</u> evaluation process so that either the instruction or the task could be changed while it is still possible for learning to occur.

        c.   Mr. Diaz is using <u>formative</u> evaluation, since the purpose of the weekly essay is to determine instructional goals.

        d.   Greg's grade will be used to assign a final grade. It is <u>summative.</u>

10.   <u>c</u> is the best choice. Formative evaluation provides teachers with measures of student behavior in response to tasks and instruction.

11.   To create a learning pattern, the progress line should change over several days. Change does not have to be a straight line, but the trend line should be discernable.

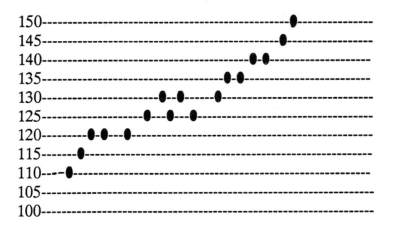

MTWTF MTWTF MTWTF MTWTF MTWTF
Daily Samples

12. Assisted assessment shows the assistance a student requires in order to learn. It is represented by an indicator (usually a vertical line) on the chart at the point where assistance was added.

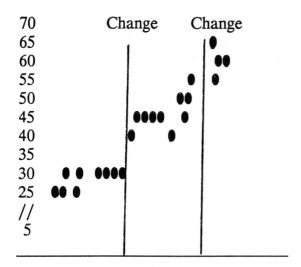

13. _d._ It is false that formative evaluation procedures are easier to use than traditional evaluation practices. Alas, formative evaluation procedures must be well organized and be administered frequently, even in the face of early release days and school assemblies. But because teachers who use formative data generally are more effective teachers, it is worth the extra effort required to use it.

~~~~   ~~~~   ~~~~   ~~~~   ~~~~   ~~~~   ~~~~   ~~~~

KEY, CHAPTER SIX

TOOLS FOR DECISION MAKING

1. a. Sources of error in the evaluation of Jeb's understanding of paragraphs might include Jeb's interpretation of what the word "proper" means in this context. He could interpret "proper" to mean polite or non-offensive. Other sources of error could be fatigue resulting from the length of the test, and Jeb's reading comprehension skills.

    b. Sources of error include mistakes in inference. None of the errors directly reflect the use of strategy. Additional error might be due to the lack of interest in the topics covered in the reports (poor task specific motivation), K. W.'s writing skills, directions given for each report, or the amount of time allocated to completing the project. This list is not inclusive.

c. As it turns out, the WRAT uses reading words in isolation to infer grade-level placement. Maybe Katie normally makes use of context cues as she reads (a very sound strategy!), but she doesn't use this strength with words in isolation. Additional sources of error might include a poor match between district-based vocabulary selection and WRAT-selected vocabulary, or Katie's anxiety/motivation to perform.

2.   <u>V</u>   Ruth Ann's driving instructor chose a direct measure of driving ability. Asking Ruth Ann to drive is a valid measure (it measures what it intends to measure) of her ability to drive.

  <u>R</u>   Reliability is a measure of consistency, and measurement of game-to-game performance will reflect dependability.

  <u>V</u>   Validity is determined by how well a test measures what it says it will measure and is often judged by experts familiar with the quality being observed. Since parents and teachers are very direct observers of "cooperation," they are the best experts available to define that quality.

<u>R/V</u>   Ah! Trick question! If alternate forms of the comprehensive test do contain the same number of items from the same domain of problems that are being taught in the classroom, this process should be both valid (it measures learning in curriculum-based objectives), and reliable (test - retest performance should not be influenced by which form of the probe is used). This is the desired state of affairs. Tests must be BOTH valid and reliable (authentic and trustworthy) to be useful for decision making.

3.   The most important consideration is whether or not use of the stimulus stories from the IRI will meet YOUR purpose. If your purpose is to measure Lidia's skill at reading and stating the main idea of a story, you should ask yourself if you have the means to validly measure those skills. In order to measure what you want to measure, you should ask yourself if you have a sufficient number of stories of reasonable length and of the correct level of reading difficulty. You should try to remove sources of error such as fatigue, and frustration level difficulty. It is possible that the stories from the IRI may serve your purpose, but *that* judgment should be made only after you have had a pithy discussion with yourself about what you want to accomplish and how that might validly be accomplished.

4. Your responses may vary from those given here and still be correct if they describe direct congruence between the objective and the measure.

    a. The appropriate test for this objective should be two-column subtraction problems, half of which require regrouping and half that do not. Problems should be presented in an order than does not allow the student to respond to the pattern of presentation rather than the problem itself. Diagonal patterning may be appropriate for ease of error analysis.

    b. The objective specifies the comprehension skills that Carlos is expected to use, and the test used to measure his comprehension must include those same parameters. The test does not have to be timed, but the reading material must be at grade level.

    c. The appropriate test should include a variety of geometrical shapes (squares, circles, rectangles, triangles) with a short goal by each one (find area, find parameter, etc.).

        Remember that the objective states that the student is to state the formula for solving the problem, not to solve the problem.

5. <u>Criterion-referenced</u> 150 words per minute with no more than 3 errors is a statement of acceptable performance.

    <u>Criterion-referenced</u> Sorting into kingdom, phylum, class, and family with no errors describes the quality of performance (criterion) necessary before the evaluator would be satisfied that the student has the necessary knowledge base.

    <u>Content-referenced</u> The "first three units" describes a section in a textbook. It does not describe the knowledge base or quality of performance expected of the student.

    <u>Content-referenced</u> "...read five different authors" does not describe the knowledge or skill base expected of the student. It does indicate "coverage" of content, but not what the student should learn through the experience.

6. Here are <u>some</u> suggestions about verbs used to describe student responses. These suggestions are neither perfect nor comprehensive. The point is, you need to think about establishing congruence between what you want to know and what you ask the student to do.

Knowledge: List, name, point to, label, match

Concepts: categorize, sort, catalog, pigeonhole, discriminate, identify attributes

Strategies: describe the process, list the steps in sequence, state the rule, tell how you solved..., explain how to do

7. a. Wanda's <u>ACCURACY</u> is the focus of the vocabulary measure.

    b. Mark is operating with <u>AUTOMATICITY</u> when he uses skills without conscious attention.

    c. Luis should be concerned about <u>FLUENCY</u> because his rate of writing has a negative impact on taking notes.

8. a. Roberto's reading behavior should be monitored with a <u>RATE</u> measure since that is the factor that prevents him from performing at expected levels.

    b. Lindy Lou's behavior could be measured with an <u>INTERVAL SAMPLING</u> procedure. With this approach, the teacher would check her behavior at assigned times and record the presence or absence of productive work behavior. The data would be summarized to indicate the percentage of intervals within which the teacher "caught" her being productive (or not).

    c. The teacher concerned about spelling test result could use <u>PERCENTAGE</u> measurement. The tests are not timed, and the major concern is <u>accuracy</u>.

9. There are many correct responses that you might have thought of as you filled the cells of the grid. Your answer should be considered correct if it meets the characteristic described in each cell. One example is supplied.

	BEHAVIOR	**STATE**
OVERT	Observable, repeatable behavior	Observable condition or location
	e.g. Orally answer question	e.g. On time for class
COVERT	Not <u>externally</u> observable	Internal condition or feeling
	e.g. Mentally rehearse social date invitation	e.g. Crave chocolate

10. The critical effect (product) of:

    a. proofreading is a paper with fewer (maybe no) errors.

    b. reading the comprehension questions before reading the story is increased correct answers to the comprehension questions.

    c. monitoring guided practice is increased teacher awareness of each student's readiness to proceed to independent practice.

11. It is reasonable to measure teacher/student interaction behaviors when:

    b. You have established a collaborative relationship with the teacher.
    c. The teacher in question is interested in obtaining data that reflects teacher/student interaction patterns.
    e. You and the teacher in question have talked about gathering interaction data BEFORE you being observing.
    g. You must do it to help the student.

    Sorry, vindictiveness is **NOT** justification for snooping.

KEY, CHAPTER SEVEN

FUNDAMENTALS OF EVALUATION

1.   Since you were asked to state a definition and purpose of each of the four stages **in your own words**, correct answers will vary in wording - but should contain the key ideas listed below.

Fact finding:
a)   The first testing or observation, usually broad-based survey tests, conducted in the initial stages of assessment.

b)   Survey level tests are given in order to identify and summarize general strengths and deficits.

Hypothesizing:
a)   The process of developing assumed causes for deficits that were identified during fact finding.

b)   This process narrows the focus of additional testing and directs the evaluator's attention by formulating assumptions that will then be tested in the next step.

Validation:
a)   Specific-level tests

b)   These tests are designed to verify (or possibly reject) the assumptions formed after fact finding and the formation of an explanation (hypothesis).

Decision making:
a)   This is the stage in which decisions are made regarding the need for additional testing or, if testing results appear to be definitive, recommendations regarding the goals are established for the learner.

b)   Ultimately, this is the last stage of the evaluation process and should result in a list of instructional objectives that teachers can then use to create an individualized teaching program.

2. Fact finding: Paragraphs one and two
Hypothesizing: Paragraphs four and five
Verification: Paragraphs six and seven
Decision making: Paragraphs eight and nine

3. "Consolidated" means objectives from the content area can share some set of common strategic steps or conceptual attributes.

4. Consolidated curriculum examples (your responses will probably be different):
a) Basic arithmetic facts
b) Writing skills (letters, words, sentences, etc.)

Unconsolidated examples:
a) Words in stories composed by students
b) Names of the presidents

5. If the curriculum is not consolidated, select exemplars, or examples of products, that illustrate acceptable levels of accuracy/mastery/automaticity. These can be used as standards to which performance can be compared. In the absence of known acceptable examples, consult with "experts" who can assist in the definition of a standard.

6. A status sheet delineates the essential subtasks required in the curriculum. It identifies the content that should be tested and can serve as a summary sheet for items that have been passed or not passed.

7.
2) <u>NO</u> a. <u>Factual</u> b. <u>Conceptual</u>

3) <u>NO</u> a. <u>Factual</u> b. <u>Strategic</u>

4) <u>NO</u> a. <u>Factual</u> b. <u>Conceptual</u>

5) <u>YES</u> a. <u>Factual</u> b. <u>Strategic</u>

6) <u>YES</u> a. <u>Factual</u> b. <u>Strategic</u>

8. a. <u>Do</u> Rationale: Students seldom have only one missing prerequisite and it isn't safe to assume the first thing they can't do is the only thing they can't do.

b.   <u>Don't</u> Rationale: The absence of behavior is not the same as observable behavior. Cue the student to complete those, or similar, items in order to obtain observable behavior.

c.   <u>Do</u>   Variables that are not easily changed through school experiences may be interesting but not cost-effective to measure for teaching purposes.

d.   <u>Don't</u> What a student needs to know is determined by the curriculum, not by the way the curriculum is taught. The <u>content</u> can be taught through means other than reading.

e.   <u>Don't</u> Personal preference for teaching actions should not determine teacher choice. Student need should determine teacher action.

f.   <u>Do</u>   Since tasks contain behavior, conditions and criteria, all elements should be tested or observed.

9.   Appropriate teaching goals might be:

a)   Teach decoding skills for silent letter patterns, cluster, and r-controlled vowels to accuracy levels.

b)   Increase fluency of reading in context materials that include suffixes, consonant digraphs, and consonant teams.

c)   Increase fluency of reading in context in all grade level materials.

~~~~   ~~~~   ~~~~   ~~~~   ~~~~   ~~~~   ~~~~   ~~~~

KEY, CHAPTER EIGHT

FUNDAMENTALS OF INSTRUCTION

1.   The thought process for each lesson is as follows:

   a. Concept lesson

b. Strategy lesson

c. Fact lesson

d. Strategy lesson

If you missed any of these items, please review the information in exhibits 8.2, 8.3, and 8.4 in Chapter eight.

2. The behavioral outcome levels were presented in hierarchical sequence:

    a. Accuracy...an emphasis on being correct

    b. Mastery...an emphasis on being correct <u>and</u> fluent

    c. Automaticity...an emphasis on being automatic

3.

1. Prepare for Instruction	4. Respond to Efforts
2. Deliver Information	5. Use Activities
3. Ask Questions	6. Evaluate

__1__   Transitions are short and brief.

__3__   Various cuing and prompting techniques are used to elicit accurate responses from the student.

__6__   The teacher circulates among students during seatwork activities to provide assistance and to check work.

__5__   Practice opportunities are provided until the student makes only infrequent, careless mistakes.

__4__   Specific suggestions to correct student errors are provided.

__2__   The student's attention is gained and focused during instruction.

__2__   The lesson explanation emphasizes a step-by-step description of the process to follow to solve the problem.

<u>1</u>   The student is given a warning for transitions between lessons.

4.   By now, you should understand that there are many choices that a teacher could make to effectively organize the teaching/learning environment. The "key" presents only some suggestions that would improve the lesson as presented by Ms. X.. Our hope is that you identified errors in teacher actions and replace them with appropriate suggestions. Here are <u>some</u> better ideas:

Line 1:   Teacher X maintained a small number of important rules and communicated them through discussion of rules and routines.

Lines 5-7:   Today's lesson began with a review of information presented in a previous related lesson and a statement of how this lesson contributes to the unit goal. The lesson started on time.

Lines 9-10:   Students knew the established routine for obtaining equipment used in science lessons and collected the materials Ms. X had organized before class and placed in the equipment pick-up area.

Lines 10-13:   The steps involved in completing the lesson were identified through a task analysis and the student's instructional skill levels were considered when Ms. X assigned tasks.

Lines 13-14:   Peer partners were assigned at the onset of the lesson based on similar instructional needs, not on labels reflecting assumed abilities.

Lines 15-18:   Ms. X required frequent guided practice responses from students and she monitored their responses so she could adjust instruction by providing more examples or alternate explanations. Students were actively engaged as they responded to teacher-directed questions throughout the lesson.

Lines 18-19:   The practice activities were directly related to the instructional goal.

Lines 19-22:   Disruptions were infrequent because Ms. X maintained lesson momentum with high rates of student engagement by asking frequent, relevant questions and providing clear, guided practice activities using the fulcrums and levers.

Lines 24-25: Students were asked to show, demonstrate, explain, and display their responses overtly.

Lines 25-29: All of the activities students were asked to complete were closely related to the objective of the lesson.

~~~ ~~~ ~~~ ~~~ ~~~ ~~~ ~~~

KEY, CHAPTER NINE

ELIGIBILITY DECISIONS

1. Your explanation to the parent should clarify that, yes, there is a discrepancy between the reading level that is expected of Junior and his actual reading level, but that his performance (or status) does not meet the legal requirements that would make him eligible for **special** services. (By the way, this does not let you, the teacher, off the hook. Junior should still receive whatever classroom resources are available to help him with his reading. He is just not eligible for <u>specially funded</u> programs. He is still entitled to school services as are other "typical" students.) By the way, we suggest that you avoid trying to reassure the parent by saying, "Don't worry, he'll be farther behind next year - then he'll qualify."

2. Applying labels to students entitles them to additional funding sources that may provide the assistance the student needs.

    The drawbacks to labeling include students feeling like damaged goods (stigmatized) when they are called "remedial" or "special." Most students know that there is a kind of "special" that is desirable (when they win the door prize or get a second dessert) and a "special" that is not so desirable (when they have to wear thick glasses with the head strap or receive remedial help during story time).

    Another disadvantage of labeling is that some teachers believe that children with labels are not likely to learn, so they expend less effort in trying to teach them. This only increases the probability that the student will not learn as efficiently or as much as his or her peers. Still another disadvantage is that some teachers, upon hearing the label, conclude that the student is now the responsibility of special education.

3.   We hope you chose b . Students with labels do not come with tags that recommend unique teaching strategies. Teachers still have to identify the individual's specific needs and strategies that will accelerate the learning process. Those learning strategies will almost always be drawn from procedures that are also effective with a wide variety of general education students. Besides, it is a violation of Federal Law to base most decisions on the fact that a student is labeled.

4.   **Functional** means that the data resulting from CBM measures provide information that can be readily applied toward the selection of teaching goals and teacher actions. A CBM measure may indicate that Sally can write complete individual sentences, but she cannot write meaningful paragraphs. That information can be used without complicated analysis to establish a goal to teach Sally proper paragraph construction.

Global measures of achievement generally result in a normative comparison to other students of the same grade level, but cannot be used to establish teaching goals.

5.   Limitations of CBM include:
   1)   Most CBM measures have focused on basic skills and there are not many examples of complex concept or strategic knowledge bases that have been measured with CBM.

   2)   Most CBM has been used at the elementary level, and although it has been used to make _teaching_ decisions at the secondary level, information about making _eligibility_ decisions is not as available.

6.   Gee, this is a lot like explaining the punch line of a joke, never an enviable task. The moral of the story is: don't take the complex route simply because that is the way it has always been done. If the reason for measuring a student's performance is to make teaching decisions, then take direct measures (CBM) of the facts/strategies/concepts that are to be taught. Estimate the weight of the pig, not the rock.

7.   a.   Achievement/expectancy comparison: This model defines a disability in terms of the discrepancy between what the student has achieved and what the system expects of the student. Expectancy levels are determined by the typical achievement of the student's peers.

     b.   Percentiles: Arrange class (school, district) scores in percentile groupings

142

and note which students fall above and below the percentile level established by you or your district as the eligibility marker. See Appendix A for information about using a percentile scale.

    c.   Aptitude/achievement approach: In this system, average scores on CBM probes in other academic areas, or scores on tests of adaptive skills, can be used to <u>infer</u> that the student will successfully learn new skills.

8.   a.   When comparing one program to another, median scores from a district-developed probe can be used if it measures the teaching goals that are common to both.

    b.   Individual progress can be compared to median scores from district, school, or class measures. Repeated measures of target students' performances on probes administered two or three times a week (some would suggest daily) can also be used to monitor individual progress toward established aims.

    c.   Survey and specific level CBM measures will identify the needs of specific students.

9.   Your answer might contain one or more of the following:

CBM is significantly cheaper than a broad battery of global measures of achievement.

CBM measures student performance in the district curriculum. Therefore, the results require less speculation about how the student compares to his/her local peers.

Even when CBM is used to make eligibility decisions, the functional information that results from testing can generally be used to make teaching decisions, as well.

CBM focuses on <u>alterable</u> variables that teachers can influence through their actions.

KEY, CHAPTER TEN

COMPREHENSION

1. Some indicators may represent more than one type of strategy, but the point here is to encourage you to connect observable indicators with the use of strategic skills. Compare your responses to Exhibit 10.5 in the text to judge the accuracy of your reponses.

2. The passage you reacted to was from the first, second, and third paragraphs on page 182 of Chapter ten. Ideally, this type of exercise would not have occurred after the reactor had already read the entire text, but since this study guide is designed to <u>augment</u>, not replace the text, we sincerely hope that you did read Chapter ten before completing question 2. Correct responses are:

    Tindal and Marston (1990) have proposed one way to avoid the problems of definition that come with the term comprehension. Instead of talking about **decoding**, and comprehension, they talk **about** reading and reacting.

    Use **of** the term **reacting** shifts **the** focus from psychological processes, **which** cannot be observed, to **behaviors** and products that can. **For** example, students may react **to** what they read by **answering** questions, retelling, paraphrasing, or **completing** cloze passages. Each of **these** techniques can be used **to** illustrate a student's comprehension -- **but** few people would agree **that** any of them are **pure** measures of it.

    The **prototypical** "diagnostic reading inventory," for **example**, is made up of **passages** followed by questions. The **student** reads each passage and **then** answers questions before reading **the** next passage. In these **cases**, the interval between reading **the** passage and answering the **questions** is a minute or **two**. What if you waited **30** minutes before asking the **questions**? What if you waited **a** week? If you did **wait** longer, the student's score **would** almost certainly be different (**probably** lower), because what was **once** "comprehended" may no longer **be** recalled. Therefore, a student's **score** on post-passage questions **depends** not only on what **he** understands but on what **he** remembers. Many educators seem to accept this confusion, though few of them would agree that memory and comprehension are synonymous.

3. The process demonstrated in question 2 was the <u>maze</u> test. Your experience with the maze test varied from prescribed process in two ways. You read the material before responding to the exercise, and the choices presented to you did

144

not always follow the guideline for controlling the difficulty of the distractors. Only sometimes was one of the distractors syntactically correct but semantically incorrect when the other distractor was both syntactically and semantically incorrect. Sometimes, both distractors were syntactically correct, and this increased the difficulty of some of the items.

How did you score? We hope you scored in the instructional range, but remember that the criteria for maze is not absolute.

4.   The specific-level testing procedures described in item four, were:
   a. Retell/Paraphrasing
   b. Prediction
   c. Referent Knowledge
   d. Assisted Monitoring
   e. Assisted Search

5.   a.   Prior Knowledge

Prior knowledge refers to the student's basic core of information about the topic covered in the passage.

b.   Decoding

Decoding skills are the basic reading skills that allow a student to break written code using the relationship between printed text and sounds. (If this definition doesn't seem familiar to you, it could be because it comes from Chapter eleven, not Chapter ten. Consider your own response correct if it generally means the same thing.)

c.   Semantics (Vocabulary)

Semantic skills include two elements: (1) vocabulary knowledge associated with words, and (2) understanding derived from the meaning of a word in context.

d.   Syntax (Grammar)

Syntax is an understanding of the rules that govern word order, sentence structure, use of verb tense, pronoun assignment, and so on. It is associated with an understanding of basic language structure.

6.   Teachers who use survey-level comprehension tests are seeking an answer to **b**, "Does the student adequately comprehend text?" If the answer is "yes," no additional tests for comprehension are necessary. If the answer is "no," then specific level tests should be given to find out **a**, "Does the student use comprehension strategies?" and **b**, "Does the student have the enabling skills necessary for comprehension to occur?"

(Yes, we know that this is the first time in ten chapters that a multiple-choice item has had two correct responses. We hope that the strategy of reading/considering every item is a tenacious characteristic in your response repertoire.)

7.   Next action:

c, Rule out the lack of prior knowledge. When problems are identified at the survey level, that is a cue to proceed to specific-level testing. Checking for prior knowledge is an important specific-level test activity.

First rejected option: Select an easier reader. This action would be premature. So far, you have identified that Stoner has a problem reacting to text, but you do not yet have enough information to justify this choice.

Second rejected option: Get rid of the basal reader. The survey-level test indicates that Stoner does not have all of the strategic skill necessary to react successfully to text. Your task is to find out which strategic skill(s) she is missing and then teach them. Changing the material that she responds to is not an intervention that has anything to do with the use of strategies. It is an action that should be based on other information unrelated to observations about Stoner's use of reaction strategies.

Third rejected option: Teach her to use comprehension strategies that focus on active reading and comprehension. This is a teaching recommendation that might emerge after specific-level tests have identified which strategies Stoner lacks, but it is too soon to prescribe it.

8.   Victor cannot define words within the context of a sentence. Your conclusion should be that you should test the enabling skill of semantic performance. Semantics (vocabulary) is an enabling skill and might require instruction along with comprehension strategies. Test for it.

9.   Trina most likely is not using active and reflective reading strategies or monitoring meaning while she reads. The fact that she seldom correct errors that violate meaning indicates that she is passively decoding without attending to the content of what she is reading.

10. Lupe, on the other hand, does self-correct words that violate the meaning of a passage. You should ask yourself if her reading rate and comprehension seem adequate, and if Lupe immediately self-corrects when she makes and an error. If the answer to both questions is "yes," then Lupe's errors are not important and you should ignore them.

11. The text refers to a procedure designed by Raphael and Pearson (1985, p. 213) that teaches students to determine sources of answers by using these three mnemonics: **1. Right There** (the words used for the question **and** the answer are "right there" in the same sentence); **2. Think and Search** (the answer is in the text, but distributed across several sentences or paragraphs); and **3. On My Own** (the answer is not in the text, it is implied).

12. Since Joey scored poorly on both a maze test and on questions about the text, you should next ask him to identify the main idea of the story or of specific passages. If he cannot identify the main idea, it's possible that Joey lacks the enabling skill of prior knowledge necessary to react to the text material. If he can identify the main idea, ask him to paraphrase the story. If he can, then begin specific-level testing to identify which strategies he is missing.

13. Tony would score a 3 on Tindal and Marston's scale. He did not include a central thesis and his retell coherence, completeness, and comprehensibility were adequate, but not strong. Three is not a strong score, and Tony will probably be a candidate for teaching tactics such as prereading questions, story maps, and semantic webbing or for monitoring meaning while reading.

14. a.   Reciprocal teaching
     b.   Critical reading
     c.   Story maps

     Descriptions were not provided for prereading questioning, monitoring meaning, or active and reflective reading. All six teaching strategies are described in more detail in the text.

KEY, CHAPTER ELEVEN

READING AND DECODING

1.   __A__   Spends a high proportion of reading instruction time reading from the text

    __R/C__   Spends a high proportion of reading time   doing independent and noninteractive worksheets

    __?__   Now, who could know that? Professional reading literature certainly doesn't help us here.

    __R/C__   More likely to be interrupted while reading than peers who are adequate readers

    __R/C__   May spend as little as two minutes at active reading per day

    __A__   Least likely to spend time receiving instruction on isolated skills (letters, sounds)

2.   a.   Grade-level readers: Reject. What is grade level? Materials with the same "grade level" designation may be very dissimilar in difficulty and/or the skills emphasized.

    b.   Readers from same series, different levels: Reject. It is not likely that all of the student's curricular goals would be taught from texts by the same publisher, and you really want a broad sample of the student's skill in decoding across the curriculum. (If your district has a cut-rate deal with a publisher who has a monopoly on text sales, ignore this answer.)

    c.   Texts in which the student is expected to perform: This is it! By sampling in a variety of texts across the curriculum, it is possible to obtain more revealing information about the student's skills.

    d.   Published informal reading inventories: Reject. Informal reading inventories do provide a sample of stories with graduated difficulty, but they may not be similar to the demands of the materials the student will be expected to use. This is even true of the one we are providing in this workbook.

3.   a.   a is false because code instruction includes many skills including concepts of print, phonemic awareness, letter recognition, letter-sound correspondence, use of contextual clues, reading fluency, and more.

b.	Teaching <u>skills</u> is not the same as <u>placing</u> a student in a text. "Finding the right book" implies that once a good fit is found, the student will concurrently be introduced to material that will mend any weak bits of his or her reading repertoire. It doesn't happen that way. It is more functional to identify what <u>skills</u> a student needs to be taught, than to select a variety of strategies and sources to help reach those objectives.

c.	It is true that students need to "discriminate" between letters, sounds, and words as they learn to read. But useful statements focus on which letters, sounds, etc. a student can or cannot identify, rather than on a generalized "ability" to distinguish one item from another.

d.	If students can't decode rapidly and accurately, they won't cover the same amount of content as their more fluent peers. This pattern will persist in assignment after assignment after assignment through their school careers. Slow and inaccurate readers are destined to experience fewer learning opportunities in virtually all subject areas which use print to communicate information.

4.	If you want to test <u>sounds</u>, present <u>words</u>.

	If you want to test <u>words</u>, present <u>phrases</u>.

5.	The primary reason for not counting omissions as errors is that we want to avoid speculation. If you had stopped the student and called attention to the omitted word, he might have read it correctly or incorrectly. Who knows? And precisely because we <u>don't</u> know, we recommend that the omitted word not be included in counts of "words read correctly" or "words read incorrectly."

6.	The procedure described is a <u>survey-level test</u> for decoding. The purpose of survey-level testing is to determine if the student's oral reading skill is good enough to promote expected levels of reaction to print. This judgment is made by comparing a student's performance to rates characteristic of successful readers.

7.	Jim is a slow, inaccurate reader who did not increase his reading rate by 40% when given the rereading test. You need to continue with specific-level testing. The next step would be to take a closer look at error responses.

8.	The passage is too hard for Deborah. For a passage to be used to fairly categorize errors, the reader should read 80% to 85% of the words correctly. In addition to that, here's the thing about flow charts... they may not be as aesthetically pleasing to look at as a Monet water lily painting, but they <u>do</u>

149

efficiently organize complex information. By starting the assessment process with a look at error patterns, you have ignored a number of other skills that would have been considered first if you had started at the beginning. You need you find out if Deborah self-monitors before you focus on error patterns.

9.   To find out if Joey leaves the endings off of words because he isn't attending to them, use an assisted-monitoring procedure. Cue him to correct his error each time an error has been made. If he can correct it, you have evidence that he isn't attending to word endings. If he doesn't correct himself when given a cue to do so, he probably doesn't know endings. A second, and perhaps easier procedure, is to compare accuracy on words with and without underlined endings.

10. T. J. improved her reading accuracy when she was told to attend to accuracy, and is now reading at expected levels. She needs to consistently self-monitor her reading performance. (Wouldn't it be nice if all reading problems were this straight-forward?)

11. Allie reads both slower and more inaccurately (100 wpm with 80% accuracy) than successful 6th-grade students (140 wpm with 95% accuracy). Since there may be deficits in both fluency and accuracy skills, it would be appropriate to carry out specific-level testing to see if she responds to assisted self-monitoring. If accuracy improves, but her rate remains low, she should also be tested to see if her rate improves when given the rereading test.

12. You have gone far enough with specific-level testing for Patrick. He has demonstrated that he lacks some beginning reading skills and you should be able to write specific teaching objectives from what you already know. Teach him letter recognition, left-to-right page orientation, front-to-back book orientation, and other missing print-awareness skills. Please note that all of these skills can be taught while having a good time reading books and telling stories together. They should not be taught as isolated skills.

13. There will be many, many, many correct answers to these questions, so please consider the examples listed here as only a sample of potential responses.

     a.   An insertion that is contextually appropriate:

          The text reads: "Sounds are not the only thing some people think of when they hear the word decoding." The reader reads: "Sounds are not the only thing _that_ some people think of when they hear the word

150

decoding."

A word was inserted, but it did not change the meaning of the sentence.

b.   Omission that affects passage meaning:

The text reads: "A man in Belfast said that anyone who isn't confused here, doesn't really understand what is going on." The reader reads: "A man in Belfast said that anyone who isn't _____ here, doesn't really understand what is going on."

The omitted word changes the tone of irony intended by the author. This omission affects the meaning of the sentence.

c.   Error is phonetically similar to the stimulus word:

The text reads: "He is a very fit athlete and he enhances the team." The reader reads: "He is a very f<u>a</u>t athlete and he enhances the team."

In this case, fit and fat are phonetically similar but the one small difference between them significantly changes meaning.

d.   Error involving a CVC + E word:

The text reads: "Where is the mate to my sock?" but the student reads, "Where is the <u>mat</u> to my sock?"

The student has not applied the CVC + E rule and has therefore not used the long vowel/silent e pattern.

14.   Error Categories: <u>Number of errors:</u>

Error Category	Number of errors
Mispronunciations: bred/breed sheepherd/shepherd instints/instincts cripped/chirped genine/genuine	9
Insertions: Lady/Laddie shady/shaggy started/began and guarding/guard swing/swoop bird/baby my/when	14
Omissions: patchy particular for different	4
Hesitations: height at ease guarded famous	5

Repetitions: just like him, average (3), eaves, while standing flat footed, swallows (2), swallows (3)	11
Does not attend to punctuation: "...home from work. He would..." for "...home from work, he would..."	1
Does not pause at punctuation:	0
Pauses at end of line:	0
Self-corrects: "...while standing flat footed on the ground."	1

CONTENT CATEGORIES

Words: errors involving whole words
    Polysyllabic Words   genine/genuine
    Contractions
    Compound Words
    Sight Words shady/shaggy   swing/swoop   bird/baby   my/when
    Silent Letters

Units: errors involving combined letter units
    Endings (suffixes)
    Clusters
    R-controlled vowels
    Vowel teams
    Consonant Digraphs   instints/instincts   cripped/chirped
    CVC words

Conversions: errors involving sound modification
    Double consonant words
    Vowel + e Conversions

Sounds: errors involving individual letters and sounds
    Vowels   Lady/Laddie   bred/breed   sheepherd/shepherd
    Consonants
    Sequence
    Sounds
    Symbols

ERROR CATEGORY CHECKLIST FOR MEANING VIOLATION

	Violates meaning	Does not violate meaning	Cannot classify	Errors self-corrected
% of total	shady/shaggy my/when 2 of 45 errors 4%	sheepherd, bred, started, swing, bird 9 of 45 errors 20%	instints/instincts genine/genuine cripped/chirped 3 of 45 errors = 6%	swallows, average while standing flat footed swallow 4 of 45 errors = 8%
% of total self corrected	0%	100%		

15.   Karna's learning trend is <u>not</u> satisfactory. Notice that the line signifying the desired learning path is directed upward, toward the objective of 150 words per minute, but her actual learning trend is headed downward. Decisions guidelines provided by White and Haring (1980) for use with rate data would indicate that a decision to change the program is warranted.

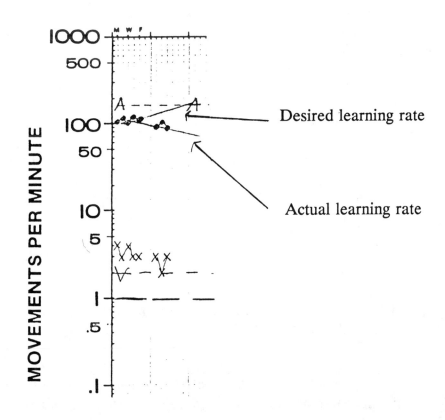

153

KEY, CHAPTER TWELVE

LANGUAGE

1. Your responses should look like this:

__SM__	Names months	__SY__	Uses past tense
__PG__	Considers audience	__SM__	Identifies colors
__SY__	Uses forms of "do"	__SM__	Uses idioms
__PG__	Repairs communication	__SY__	Uses passive voice
__SM__	Names animals/insects	__PG__	Uses persuasion

2. __PG__   Failure to sequence is a problem with pragmatics. The process of communication is interrupted when the listener has to organize information in order to understand it.

    __SY__   "The toys is broke" violates rules governing noun-verb agreement as well as use of forms of the verb "to be." Rules governing grammar are syntax rules.

    __SM__   Knowledge of opposites is semantic/vocabulary knowledge.

    __SY__   "Mine is more bigger" violates rules governing comparative forms. It is a syntax error.

    __SM__   Having the appropriate vocabulary to label emotions is a semantic skill.

    __PG__   Failure to participate in discussions indicates a deficit in the delivery of information. It is a pragmatics issue.

3. a.   <u>Some children do not learn language as quickly as their peers</u>. Now what's to disagree with here? Yes, children learn language at different rates and language norms are fairly broad as a result. This is a correct statement, but don't forget that language deficits interfere with learning.

Teachers should be aware of age-related language expectations so they can recognize the difference between routine differences and genuine problems.

b. <u>Any sentence form is okay as long as the teacher knows what the student means to say.</u> We hope you rejected this position. Simply because a specific teacher has interpreted a student's obscured message doesn't mean the rest of the world will also be able to do that. Language deficits disrupt learning and they negatively influence judgments made about individuals. Therefore, they should be targets for intervention just as poor reading, arithmetic, spelling, or writing skills should be.

c. <u>Will children just grow out of it?</u> We reject this statement, too. There are individual differences in language development rates, but simply growing older is not the answer for children with language deficits. They need instruction, not more birthdays.

d. <u>Teachers do not have the responsibility to teach language in school.</u> If a student of common school age demonstrates language deficits, it means that he or she didn't learn language "spontaneously" and needs instruction. Who is responsible for that instruction? Since learning language structure, vocabulary and process is an all-day-everyday activity, the best instructor would be the person with continuous contact with the student. The speech/language clinician should be a valuable team member who can help identify goals and teaching strategies, but it is the teacher working most directly with the student who will have the greatest opportunity to instruct.

There is an old restaurant proverb somewhere that says, "You may not have ordered the milk. You may not have spilled the milk. But if you are the one with the cloth and you find the milk, you are the one who must wipe it up." (One of us used to be a waitress.)

4. a. Do Miho and Thomas need the same general <u>language</u> instruction? Probably, yes. Miho is functionally disabled in English just as Thomas is, and the techniques used to help them with language may not differ a great deal.

b. Miho has obtained academic literacy in one language and knows what that is like. Thomas has not. Therefore, there are some differences in the assumptions that can be made about Miho. She may also experience some interference points between the Japanese language and English. For example, in Japanese the verb is usually placed at the end of the sentence, whereas in English it usually comes earlier in the sequence. She will also need to learn the cultural expectations of the classroom in order to understand pragmatic interactions. Don't forget, Miho has a well-developed language and that language should be honored even as she learns English!

Both students require direct, "hands on" instruction that should occur in many settings, with many people, throughout the school day.

5.   The following information should be included in your description of language sampling procedures.

   a.   A minimum of 50 utterances is recommended, 50% of which should be complete sentences.
   b.   Three different settings should be sampled, at least one of which should be a social setting.
   c.   Spontaneous interactions are preferred to prompted conversations.
   d.   Other children might be present during spontaneous language interactions or during prompted discussion, especially when the child is unresponsive with an adult.
   e.   Items should be presented one at a time without specific questions that can be answered with "yes/no," short phrase statements, or lists.

6.   Survey-level testing is done in order to find out if the child has a language problem and to focus attention on what additional testing may be necessary.

7.   "We didn't go to the ...to the big store" is eight words long. Contractions are counted as two words and repeated words are counted only once.

8.   If the language sample was genuinely representative of Thomas's language output, you will need to go directly to specific-level testing in all areas. He has significant deficits somewhere, and it is your assignment, Inspector X, to identify them.

9.   Now let's think this through. Al produces/uses language in one setting - but not another. It might be that the environment influences his use of language. Exhibit 12.8 (p. 277) provides a series of 15 questions that can be used as an evaluation form to determine if the classroom provides the opportunity for the student to learn and use language.

10. Robert made syntax errors in three areas. First, you should determine whether that performance meets expected standards for his age level. If it does, relax. If not, continue with specific-level testing to determine whether or not there are consistent error patterns. Remember that any testing procedure only **samples** behavior, and the presence of excessive errors in a sampling situation may represent best or worst performance. Closer evaluation may be necessary to determine "typical" performance.

11. Your answers may vary, but here are some appropriate suggestions:

    1) If the setting inhibits verbal communication, modify the setting to increase opportunities for communication. Increase the opportunities for the student to respond by using open-ended responses. Provide multiple language models and be sure that classroom presentations are meaningful. Refer to items on Exhibit 12.8 (p. 277) for additional ideas.

    2) If there are patterns of pragmatic errors, you must integrate skills in syntax and semantics as you link interactions to codes the student already knows. Role playing is often used to teach information about the communication process. Lessons should include information about a) the purpose of the skill, b) a variety of examples of situations in which the student needs the skill, and c) critical components of the skill. The student will also need generalization practice after the skill has been demonstrated in the context of a lesson.

    3) If the student is not competent in communication, he or she will not be adequately demonstrating the skills listed in Exhibit 12.10 (p. 279) in the text. Students with this type of deficit may respond to a direct teaching approach where the teacher tells the student exactly what he needs to do, how to do it, and then provides opportunities for him to do it. He might also benefit from immediate and frequent feedback when an "error" occurs.

    4) If the mean length of verbal utterances is below expectations, the student may benefit from strategies to expand both the number and richness of ideas and structure of language. Focus on the purpose, intent, and audience of communication. Take the student's simple statement and model it back, with expanded description and complexity, demonstrating language models closer to the goal for that student.

5)   If the student makes syntactical errors and omissions, teach sentence structure. Introduce unfamiliar word or sentence formation rules with at least ten illustrative examples. Introduce the rules first through recognition and then through production tasks. Test application of the rules with examples that include vocabulary not previously used.

6)   If the student has patterns of errors or omissions in vocabulary usage, use teaching recommendations 1 (p. 284), 4 (p. 286), and 7 (p. 289). Use a direct approach to instruction; teach new vocabulary, synonyms, and morphemes; and use strategies to expand the attributes and variety of the student's verbal interactions.

7)   If the student doesn't use context to determine the meaning of words, she may respond to a direct teaching approach that explicitly cues the student to monitor context, and lessons focused on teaching word meaning (semantics).

12. Joel's trend is moving in the desired direction, and that would indicate that learning is taking place. This chart does display the expected standard as well as Joel's pace of growth. However, the chart does not specify the desired rate of growth, and that information would make the charted data even more useful.

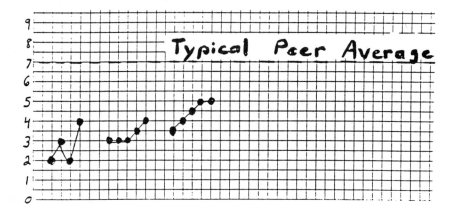

Mean length of utterance

KEY, CHAPTER THIRTEEN

WRITTEN EXPRESSION

1. The bank robber failed to communicate the <u>purpose</u> of his note. If the tellers had understood that the man meant to commit a crime, his poor handwriting/spelling would probably not have interfered with the interaction. The tellers were not afraid because they didn't know the intent of the would-be robber.

2. Fluency: <u>c</u> Production of sample sentences and elaboration into compositions of gradually increasing length.

   Syntactic maturity: <u>e</u> Production of sentences of increasing complexity.

   Vocabulary/semantic maturity: <u>a</u> Fewer repetitions of favored words and use of more sophisticated words.

   Content: <u>b</u> Attention to organization of thought, originality, and style.

   Conventions: <u>d</u> Mechanical aspects of writing such as margins, grammar, spelling, and punctuation.

3. Sam may not respond to the story starter asking him to describe animals that live by the ocean because he lacks prior knowledge of coastline life. He could be a farm boy from Nebraska or a Hopi Indian boy from Nevada. Story starters should be as culture free as possible.

4. A T-unit is a group of words that will stand alone with all subordinate clauses. (Exhibit 13.8, p. 303.)

5. "While I was in Bellingham, ..." contains one T-unit. The core idea is the meeting of an old friend. This core idea is supported by two subordinate clauses.

6. If you have followed the sequence recommended in Exhibit 13.5 on page 300 of the text, you should note that Ben has checked out on every element except semantics. The next step should be to check the adequacy of his vocabulary. If his work isn't "understandable," he probably has difficulty with word meaning and usage.

7.   Story Idea _3_   Organiz-Cohesion _3_   Conven-Mech _3_

Some judgment is needed in scoring using the analytic scale. These factors were considered in the rankings given above:

Story Idea: Lacks detail, plot somewhat haphazard, word choice predicable with only some adjectives/adverbs.

Organization-Cohesion: Events somewhat random, sometimes lacks referents, often lacks transition.

Convention-Mechanics: Spelling somewhat a problem, sentence structure somewhat a problem.

8.   To establish local standards...

At each grade level:
a) give students a story starter with two minutes to plan and three minutes to write;

b) summarize grade-level performance by counting and averaging total words, total words spelled correctly, total words spelled incorrectly, and total words in correct sequence;

c) summarize those scores and record them for future comparisons;

d) have at least three teachers sort grade-level samples (based on their judgment of quality) into five ranked piles of equal number; and then

e) for each grade level, select samples at each rank and put them into a notebook so future student products can be compared to them.

Note that these procedures will provide both grade-level "scores" (step b) and products (steps d and e) to which a specific student's written product can be compared.

9.   Survey-level testing is completed by:

a)   collecting at least two samples. One sample has a time provision so that the student may review and revise. Both samples have a two minute

160

planning provision and a three minute time limit for writing. The revision is untimed.

b)   scoring the samples, using an analytic scale (Exhibit 13.4, p. 298) or established local standards.

10.   Sally appears to have either syntax or semantic problems. Your next step would be to sort out which it is by testing her syntactic maturity with the procedures described in specific-level procedure three. You'll need to analyze her sentence complexity.

11.   Words are judged on the basis of the word appearing in sequence, correctly spelled, and with correct semantic and syntactic form.

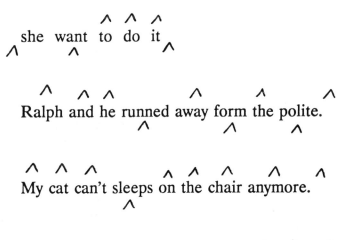

A caret is placed over each correct word. A caret indicating an incorrect response is placed before the word "I" because the word "if" has been omitted and "I" is not the appropriate word to appear in that sequence. A caret is placed before "movie" because an article (a or the) has been omitted. The final error caret signifies that the sentence has no punctuation and therefore does not end appropriately.

Total correct: 34 (70%)   Total incorrect: 14 (30%)

12. a. Word sequence test
Given to learn whether or not the student can produce a correct sequence of words/phrases reflecting both fluency and syntactical maturity.

b. Syntactic maturity
Given to learn if the student can expand and increase sentence complexity at appropriate curriculum level.

c. Interview/observation
Completed to learn if the student uses the <u>process</u> of writing effectively and if the student can produce an adequate <u>product</u>.

d. Semantic maturity test
Given to learn if the student chooses vocabulary generally expected at her curriculum level. How does she compare to local standards and her own speaking vocabulary?

13. Four instructional strategies for teaching writing skills are:

<u>Balanced Instruction</u>: Provide explicit instruction in both the writing process and in the mechanics of writing (authoring and secretarial skills). Teach planning skills and give instruction in a variety of writing forms.

<u>Teach the Writing Process</u>: Focus on the process of planning, reviewing, revising, and transcribing. Students who would benefit from this procedure should have few problems with writing mechanics. Use explicit models to demonstrate each step of the process. Students should also be encouraged to set their own goals, self-monitor, and use collaborative interaction to gain feedback.

<u>Teach Fluency</u>: Increase student quantity of reading and writing, reading and writing in a variety of genre, writing for and interacting with an audience, and rewriting in response to the audience. Students should also monitor the fluency of their writing performance.

<u>Sentence Combining</u>: Use explicit instruction in taking short sentences and making them more complex. Model how to combine ideas by using conjunctions and adding clauses.

14. The rating scale used for the portfolio evaluation in Louise's class places her comfortably in the average range of performance. Her composition scores average out at three, indicating authoring skills typical of those at her grade level.

~~~ ~~~ ~~~ ~~~ ~~~ ~~~ ~~~ ~~~

KEY, CHAPTER FOURTEEN

WRITTEN MECHANICS

1. How long is an adequate sample? A spelling sample should be at least 100 letters long, a capitalization/punctuation sample should be at least 100 words long.

2. A morphograph is a unit of meaning and includes affixes, root words, and non-word bases. They are the building blocks of all words and knowing common morphographs allows a student to apply phonics rules to combine them to spell words.

3.   __T__ There is wide variation among individual's writing in cursive, and less variation in manuscript.

      __F__ Success in cursive writing is contingent upon prior instruction in manuscript. (No, it's not.)

      __T__ There do not appear to be any significant differences in writing rates between writing in cursive and writing in manuscript when experience and practice are comparable for those people tested.

      __F__ Even students who have had difficulty learning (but _have_ learned) to write using manuscript should be required to switch to cursive writing. (Given that manuscript is an acceptable format in most written interactions in society, students should not be required to switch.)

      __T__ Students who have had difficulty with spelling need to learn procedures (not word lists) which they can apply to decode and spell words they have not specifically studied.

      __F__ Recalling the letters or clusters that make sounds is not a necessary prerequisite to good spelling. (Yes, it is. It is the most important prerequisite.)

      __T__ One of the most important prerequisites to good spelling is the skill to selectively attend to and perceive letters, clusters, and sounds.

4.   We anticipate that letter formation counts may provide the most variation in scoring. The letter formation counts listed below were obtained by categorizing letters as error responses if they were printed rather than written in cursive, if the form of the letter made it difficult to read, or if the letter was placed either above the line or below the line.

Spelling responses were scored following the letter sequence format described in Exhibit 13.7 for use when scoring running text.

Total letters: __401__   **Total Errors: 43%**   **Total Accuracy: 57%**
Rate   __27 lpm__   (Total opportunities divided by total correct/total error.)

Letter formation	Opportunities	401	
	Correct letter formations	122	30 %
	Error letter formations	279	70 %

Letters spelled	Opportunities	401	
	Correctly spelled letters	330	82 %
	Letters spelled incorrectly	71	18 %

Capitalized words	Opportunities	14	
	Correct capitalizations	8	57 %
	Incorrect capitalizations	6	43 %

Punctuated words	Opportunities	8	
	Correct punctuation	8	100 %
	Error punctuation	0	0 %

5.   The writing sample contains several mechanics problems. With an **error** score of 70% in letter formation, 43% in capitalization, and 18% in spelling, this student will require specific level testing in all three areas. Even this survey-level sample indicates that the student sometimes uses cursive letters and sometime manuscript letters. Additionally, letter formation and placement errors increase in the last part of the story, indicating that fatigue may be a problem for the student. Spelling errors are primarily phonetic errors (raydio for radio and becaws for because) but there are some non-phonetic errors (kuw for knew, kow for know). Capitalization problems appear to be related to letter

formation errors since most of them occur when capital letters were inserted in the middle of words (THe for The, EnD for end).

6.

Stimulus	Response	Score
holiday	^^ ^^^ holaday ^	6c/1x
journey	^ ^^^^ journie ^^	5c/2x
tournament	^ turnament ^^^^^ ^^^	1c/8x
champion	^^^^ ^^ champeon ^	7c/1x
suitable	^ ^^^^^ suitabel ^^	6c/2x
challenge	^^^^ chalenge ^^^ ^	4c/4x
consolation	^^^^^ consollation ^^^^^^	6c/6x
defeat	^ ^^^ defete ^ ^	4c/2x
sportsmanship	^ ^ ^^ ^^^ ^^^ sportsmansip ^^	10c/2x

165

delay   ∧∧∧   3c/3x

dellay

∧∧∧

cottage   ∧∧∧∧ ∧∧   6c/1x

cottege

∧

recreation   ∧ ∧ ∧∧∧∧ ∧∧   8c/2x

recreachon

∧∧

Total: 66 correct letters, 34 error letters. Since the total number of letters adds up to 100, this student would score 66% correct with 34% error.

7.   The errors should be categorized as:

Stimulus	Response	Error Type
challenge	chalenge	3, Omission of a doubled letter
defeat	defete	9, Phonetic substitution for a syllable
cottage	cottege	7, Phonetic substitution for a vowel
suitable	suitabel	6, Transposition of letters

8.   What should you expect to learn from specific-level tests for written mechanics?

     1)   Writing fluency: Since the writing samples for this test are generally taken from three of four conditions (assignments, story starters, dictation, or copying), it is generally used to obtain information about several skills. Handwriting, spelling, capitalization, and punctuation are all observed. It is on the basis of this test that the evaluator should decide which

166

additional tests will be necessary.

2)   Letter formation: This test should help you detect whether or not the student makes important errors in letter formation and the type of error most frequently made. It should also help identify problems of fatigue or lack of automaticity.

3)   Spelling accuracy: By completing an error analysis from the spelling accuracy test, you should be able to identify error patterns characteristic of the student and whether or not fatigue is an issue.

4)   Capitalization and punctuation: This specific-level test should allow you to identify error patterns and whether or not you will need to emphasize fluency practice.

9.   Danny is consistently missing at least 20% of the words on the weekly test. We all know that we don't want dentists, physicians, or pilots who learn only 80% of the information presented to them. Imagine what might happen if Danny were tested on his words daily, rather than weekly? Or here's a radical idea, what if he had to keep practicing the error words until he could spell them correctly?! The point is, data that are charted but not used for decision making is just another kind of data storage system. You might as well just write a series of grades in a grade book.

~~~~   ~~~~   ~~~~   ~~~~   ~~~~   ~~~~   ~~~~   ~~~~

KEY, CHAPTER FIFTEEN

MATHEMATICS

1.   The most truthful answer is probably c. Many school districts allow textbooks to determine the focus of math lessons, and after first grade, there is little agreement among publishers about the sequence of math objectives. Since you are on your way to the South Pacific, you might want to change the subject to he taimi leilei te ke ilo i he otu motu anga ofa. (The good time you will have there.)

2.   a.   Operations: The application of problem solving strategies.

b.   <u>Algorithm:</u>   The formula necessary to solve a problem. An algorithm may contain several steps.

c.   <u>Computation:</u> Working problems to arrive at a solution.

d.   <u>Domain:</u> A set of problems that are grouped by one or more defined characteristics.

e.   <u>CAP:</u> Criteria for acceptable performance. CAP is the specification of the quality of performance expected for a skill to be considered "mastered."

f.   <u>Intermediate aim:</u> An achievable standard established en route to a higher level of performance. Intermediate aims are established when a student's tool skill deficits prevent typical CAP from being reached. Intermediate aims should always be viewed as a step along the way, and not a satisfactory end.

3.   **a.**   **FACTS:**   Facts are simple numerical statements that must be used correctly in order for calculations to occur properly. Examples: $7 \times 3 = 21$, $6 + 4 = 10$, $9 - 6 = 3$

    b.   **STRATEGIES:** Tactics that make it possible for students to apply knowledge of basic skills.
Examples: "Count by"s, step-by-step self talk

    c.   **CONCEPTS:**   Principles that reveal quantitative or qualitative relationships.
Examples: Decimals and fractions express the same relationship through different notations. The sum of two positive numbers cannot be smaller than either number.

4.   The criteria for successful (instructional) performance on a cloze task is 30% - 35%. That means that you should consider your comprehension to be at a reasonable level if you chose the correct word for 13 or 14 of the 39 blanks in this question.

Many teachers allocate time <u>for</u> instruction in computation and <u>operations</u> but do not include <u>adequate</u> time for instruction in <u>problem</u> solving and application. To <u>some</u> extent the practice of <u>emphasizing</u> the factual and strategic <u>content</u> of computation over the <u>more</u> utilitarian content of application and problem solving may actually <u>increase</u> the time it takes <u>students</u> to acquire computation skills <u>and</u> decrease the likelihood that <u>they</u> will maintain proficiency. When <u>computation</u> and operations are taught <u>separately</u>, it is difficult to <u>make</u> them meaningful. Meaningless material <u>requires</u> more practice if it <u>is</u> to be retained and <u>is</u> more likely to be <u>forgotten</u> than material that is <u>useful</u> in daily tasks.

Math <u>curricula</u> are often saturated with <u>marginal</u> content -- the first example <u>that</u> comes to mind is <u>the</u> topic of roman numerals. <u>This</u> sort of curricular residue <u>should</u> not be allowed to <u>compete</u> with things the student <u>genuinely</u> needs to know and <u>use</u>.

Problem solving requires the <u>functional</u> combination of computation knowledge <u>and</u> application knowledge. It has <u>two</u> steps: step 1 involves <u>deciding</u> what to do (selecting <u>correct</u> operations, selecting relevant information, <u>ignoring</u> irrelevant information, noting missing <u>information</u>, and estimating correct answers); <u>step</u> 2 involves carrying it <u>out</u> (setting up equations and <u>judging</u> which numbers go with <u>which</u> operation, working equations using <u>procedures</u> that result in correct <u>answers</u>, and checking results).

5.   a)   Rate tests require more problems than the student can complete in the allotted time. If the student finishes the problems before the time is up, you have not measured her true rate of performance because the number of problems limited her score. It's important, then, that when you are measuring fluency, you should be sure that the worksheet placed in front of the student will last longer than the time sample.

               Directions given to the student should be something like this: "I want you to work these items as quickly and as carefully as you can. Don't skip any problems unless you don't know how to do them. When you come the end of a row, start at the next row. Keep working until I tell you to stop. Please begin." At the end of one minute, tell the student to stop. This process should be followed for each domain of problems where fluency information is desired.

               Omissions are not counted as either correct or error responses.

    b)   Rate is calculated by dividing the number of responses by the amount of time in the sample. Correct and error responses should be calculated independently. Most math skills can be measured in one minute samples, making the calculation of rate per minute verrrry easy.

6. Do you need to see a student's work in order to analyze his mathematics performance? Yes, you do. Many tasks in mathematics have multiple steps that must be completed in order to arrive at the final answer. It is important to see the student's work and even to talk with the student about what steps he followed to get the answer in order to understand what he knows or doesn't know. It's time to explain that to your staff.

7. A student who finds that 7 + 6 = 1 is probably making "attention to sign errors." Provide additional problems of this type to the student to see if 5 + 3 = 2 and 8 + 2 = 6. If that's the case, your instructional task should be easy to identify.

8. To limit the number of problems you'll have to check during survey-level testing, select stimulus materials that sample a broad range of computation, applications, and problem-solving objectives, focusing only on objectives typically taught at or near the student's expected grade level. It really is okay to simply cross out items on a test that a student isn't expected to know yet.

9. Andrew missed every operations item on the survey test. What should you do now? Exhibit 15.9 on page 340 of the text advises that it's time to test for content knowledge (SPL 6). The purpose of this specific-level test is to see if the student has the content, tool, and vocabulary knowledge to complete problems. If he does, then he needs to learn how to apply what he knows. If he doesn't have this knowledge, then he needs to learn this content.

10. Rico's tool skill (writing digits) is preventing him from reaching the expected acceptable performance level. He can't write fast enough to complete as many problems as expected. There are two actions you should take: 1) instruct him in **BOTH** the appropriate math skill and the tool skill, and 2) set an intermediate aim for him. An intermediate aim would allow him to continue to progress through the math curriculum while catching up on his tool skill, and it will have to be continually raised as he learns to write digits more fluently. Eventually, his tool skill rate should be 100 digits per minute.

To set an intermediate aim:

$$\frac{\text{Task mastery rate X Current BMC rate}}{\text{Basic movement cycle rate}} = \text{Intermediate aim}$$

$$\frac{50 \times 40}{100100} = \frac{2,000}{---------} = 20$$

11. Is Charlie progressing satisfactorily? Yes. His learning trend is equal to the desired growth rate.

~~~~ ~~~~ ~~~~ ~~~~ ~~~~ ~~~~ ~~~~ ~~~~

KEY, CHAPTER SIXTEEN

SOCIAL SKILLS

1.   __F__   All teachers do not have the same personal standards for behavior, therefore, their expectations and tolerance vary greatly.

      __T__   Yes, low-income students are more likely to receive punishment from their teachers and more likely to be labeled as a bearer of "cooties" by their higher-income peers.

      __F__   Teachers in one study responded to depression with rejection and were even less accepting when it was explained that the depression might be due to life stresses. (Peterson, Wonderlich, Ravens and Mullins, 1987.)

      __T__   It's true that many students with behavior problems simply are not aware of a broad range of choices.

      __T__   Most school programs do not teach social skills as a subject matter area and focus on behavior when a problem has arisen.

2. a. Form: An elbow chop to a peer
     Function: To be first in line to lunch

   b. Form: Copying answers (okay...cheating on a test)
     Function: To avoid flunking the test

   c. Form: Lying
     Function: To get a date

d. Form: Illegal entry
Function: To attend a dance

e. Form: Bogus hand raising
Function: To appear knowledgeable

3. Trick question! (Hiss - boo.) We hope you didn't list any functions as deviant, and that's the point. Each of those students _wanted_ very normal, acceptable outcomes. Their choice of methods to achieve their goals was not appropriate, but there was nothing wrong with their motivation.

4. Overt behavior: External, observable behavior that can pass "the stranger test" of a neutral observer's agreement about the presence or absence of the behavior.

Examples: Raising hand, throwing objects, smiling, swearing

Covert behavior: Private, internally "observable" behaviors that involve thinking and feeling.

Examples: Urges to kick, voiceless humming, silently rehearsing the grocery list.

5. Judgment and decision making is emphasized because:

* Students with problems in social skill typically don't solve problems well and are usually not skilled in analyzing the connection between the selection of behavior and the consequences of that choice.

* Experience - by itself - does not necessarily teach good judgment. Bad judgment can be learned and strengthened through practice. Experience accompanied by instruction in adaptive social skills increases the probability that a student will develop a social skills repertoire that is broader and more appropriate.

6. You may have completed the sequence differently from the examples listed here, but consider your response correct if you can follow a logical linear description of behavior starting with the first column reading left to right.

172

ANTECEDENT	BEHAVIOR	CONSEQUENCE
The teacher's seating chart places two opposing gang members side-by-side	Mike spits at Ralph's feet. Ralph pulls out his "blade" and lunges at Mike.	Teachers calls the office for help. Security officers remove both students from class. Both students indefinitely expelled.

ANTECEDENT	BEHAVIOR	CONSEQUENCE
Teacher stops by student's desk and instructs on item #3.	Chris smiles and says, "Thank you. I understand it much better now that you have explained it to me."	Teacher smiles back at Chris (Increased probability that the teacher will provide help for Chris in the future)

7. Unlike academic skills, there are often no CAP established for social skills. It's sometimes difficult to even get agreement on the same social skill pinpoints. Once the pinpoints are established, it's necessary to establish acceptable performance standards, and that's where ecological ceilings and floors become important. If the goal is to increase the rate of occurrence of a specific skill, it is still necessary to define how high is high enough.

8. It would be a mistake to use typical rates of behavior (ecological floor or ceiling) as a CAP if the group average represented unacceptable rates of behaviors. In this situation, expected performance for the student who is the focus of concern should first match the group average, and then the whole class should be moved to more acceptable levels of performance. (This is the social skills version of intermediate aims, or the student should be moved to a different group.)

9. What happened with Larry and the salesperson? We will report what we believe may have happened, but we understand that your answers may be very different from ours and still be correct as long as you identified specific and connected descriptors in the appropriate categories.

Attention: The salesperson attended to the mode of transportation (motor cycle) and dress (leather pants - with fringe - and jacket).

Expectation: The salesperson appeared to expect either trouble or a waste of time because he did not welcome Larry into the showroom or offer to show him any of the boats on display.

Beliefs: We can only speculate about the salesperson's self-talk, but it might have gone something like this: "Oh here comes a poor risk. This guy might be up to no good, and I'll bet every penny he has is tied up in that bike...or at best, he's just a Sunday shopper with no intention of actually buying a yacht."

Cognitive set: If this salesperson was experienced, he had certainly spent time with financially limited "window shoppers" who enjoyed playing out the fantasy of buying the yacht of their dreams. He may have dealt with those others by being unresponsive to questions and by not volunteering any information. He carried those practiced behaviors into his interaction with Larry.

Bottom line: Because of the attention, expectations, beliefs, and cognitive set that characterized this interaction, Larry bought his yacht somewhere else. The salesman's selection of behavior was not made solely on the basis of what happened in the environment (a customer walked into the showroom) but what the salesperson <u>believed</u> was happening (here comes a rough customer who is going to waste my time). Another salesperson might have thought, "Great - an eccentric rich executive!"

10. Probable perceptions and expectations are listed below. Please note that Imelda's <u>beliefs</u> are not listed. We do not know what she believes about the importance of always being first or about her place in the pecking order, or her attitude about anyone who doesn't take what they want, and on and on. Her beliefs and cognitive set are also important factors in this interaction.

174

ANTECEDENT	Behavior	Consequence
Teacher says, line up for lunch	Imelda elbows Carlos and crowds	Imelda sent back to seat then takes place at the end of line

Available responses:
Run to the door
Quietly take a place in line
Go to the head of the line
    and crowd in
Send someone else to "save a place"

Stay in seat until personally
    invited to line up
Stay in seat and ignore the
    teacher's direction

Perceived responses:
Run to the door

Go to the head of the line and crowd in

Selected response:
Go to the front and crowd in

Expected consequence:
First in line (first to eat)

Actual consequence:
Sent to seat for one minute   Placed at end of line

11.   a.   Insults peers. "Insults" is open to interpretation and that mysterious stranger that roams from classroom to classroom participating in the "stranger test" would probably have difficulty with this one. Is pointing a finger or snapping fingers at someone an insult? It is to some. Is swearing at someone an insult? It's not to everyone. This pinpoint would be more clearly described with a verb or two such as: calls peers names, or gags/makes bowel noises in proximity to peers.

      b.   Sells illegal substances. "Sells" is observable and what is illegal is defined by law. This pinpoint is measurable.

      c.   Inappropriately solicits answers from peers during hard assignments. The terms "inappropriate" and "hard" are both open to interpretation. Copies answers from peers is a better pinpoint.

d. Causes others to stop working. Can you be sure that when a peer stops working it is because someone else "made" them? Sometimes we stop working even when nobody else is around, and sometimes we keep working in the middle of chaos. This pinpoint can be improved by describing the behavior the student does that causes the result. "Calls out," "sings," "throws objects" are all observable.

e. Signals for help from teacher. This pinpoint is probably okay as written. "Signals" is often a hand raise, and if that is the only signal a teacher wants, it would be best to make "raise hand" the pinpoint. But if there are many ways to indicate that help is needed, the broader descriptor will work.

f. Eagerly contributes to discussions. "Eagerly" is a value judgment word and should be omitted.

12. <u>Identify overt target behaviors by:</u> making sure that the first choice for measuring overt behaviors is to observe the student in the environment where the behavior would be expected to occur and determine the discrepancy between actual and expected rates of behavior. (Remember that <u>rate of behavior</u> is the preferred way of measuring behavior.) You might also need to met with those who believe there are significant social skill problems and work with them to obtain target pinpoints that will pass both the "stranger test" and the "so what test."

<u>Identify covert target behaviors by:</u> asking the student questions that will impart information about thoughts and feelings. The text lists several methods for asking questions designed to help in this process (pages 384-386). Suggestions include open questions, multiple choice, role playing, and structured interviews. Remember that the purpose of this process is to learn if the student maintains beliefs and expectations that serve as a maladaptive influence on his or her selection of a response to environmental conditions.

13. <u>Y</u> Observe behavior for several short periods rather than one long period.
    <u>N</u> Don't prompt behaviors that don't naturally occur. That would set up an artificial response.
    <u>Y</u> Describe/report the circumstances under which the observation occurs.

176

  N   If you must collect data on interactions with another teacher, do not inform the other teacher about what you are doing lest you change the environment.

  N   Collect several days' worth of data, even if the maladaptive behavior is dangerous.

  Y   Compare the median score of the last three days of data to a standard to see if there is a discrepancy between expected rates and actual rates of behavior.

14.   <u>Missing type-1 student prerequisite:</u>
A student missing type-1 prerequisites would be lacking overt skills and knowledge such as asking for help when it's needed, complimenting a peer, or smiling when complimented.

<u>Missing type-1 environment prerequisite:</u>
A missing environmental prerequisite would mean that the environmental cues that usually cue specific social skills to occur are lacking. Examples are the student is never told what the classroom rules are or what "good student behavior" means.

<u>Missing type-2 student prerequisite:</u>
The student may value the maladaptive behavior more than the target behavior. (John would rather that peers fear him than like him.)

<u>Missing type-2 environment prerequisite:</u>
The disadvantages of the maladaptive behavior have never been taught to the student. (John doesn't understand and has never been taught that fear and respect are not the same thing and that fear will cause peers to avoid him.)

~~~~ ~~~~ ~~~~ ~~~~ ~~~~ ~~~~ ~~~~ ~~~~

KEY, CHAPTER SEVENTEEN

TASK-RELATED SKILLS

1.   A student may appear to be capable outside of class but unable to learn in an academic setting because she does not have the enabling skills that allow most students to benefit from instruction. Curricular expectations increase as students

progress through school, and if significant study/memory/test taking/attention /organization (and on and on) skills are missing, the student may not have the prior knowledge that would link new information to an existing foundation. No foundation may exist, and the skills to build one are missing.

2. Study skills   <u>b</u>   ...allow student to make use of instruction.

    Test-taking skills   <u>e</u>   ...allow the student to display what she has learned.

    Task-related skills   <u>d</u>   a wide range of skills that teachers believe enable success

    Learning scaffolds   <u>a</u>   Supporting knowledge that serves as a temporary conduit between prior knowledge and new information

    Topical knowledge   <u>c</u>   Prior knowledge required to learn new skills or concepts

3. S <------------------> B   S stands for <u>standard</u>

                 | B stands for <u>behavior</u> and
                 |
                 | D stands for <u>discrepancy</u>.
                 ↓
                 D
                                     The comparison represented in the graphic is used when judging whether a specific student's performance is sufficiently different from the standard to warrant additional evaluation and goal setting.

4. An example of a study skill: Organization of material by using labeled notebooks or folders to store materials; or taking materials home, completing homework, and bringing homework back to school.

Examples of problem solving:	The student recognizes the problem and can identify goals and obstacles. The student thinks before acting and can explain what the consequences will be if specific choices are made.
Examples of basic learning	The student uses selective attention and focuses on relevant cues while ignoring irrelevant cues. The student perseveres in the face of difficulty and can state the value of a task.

5. Fill in the blanks:

    a. You can assume a student has adequate topical knowledge if <u>he has taken prerequisite classes and received acceptable grades in them and if he understands the text and topical vocabulary.</u>

    b. Basic learning strategies include attention, <u>memory</u>, and <u>motivation</u>.

    c. When conducting a survey-level evaluation for task-related skills, the very first focus is on <u>if the student is failing to learn form classroom instruction (making expected progress in a particular class).</u>

6. Levels of assistance for basic learning strategies are listed here in order from least intrusive to most intrusive:

    1) Prompts, 2) Directions, 3) practice, 4) Lessons

7. Levels of assistance should be introduced from least intrusive to most intrusive with the more intrusive levels introduced only if it is necessary to do so. If a student can successfully begin to use a strategy after receiving a prompt to do so, it is neither desirable nor necessary to introduce other levels of assistance. To do so may encourage dependency on artificial cues and prolong the time that will have to be invested in that particular skill.

8.   Teacher actions that promote attention include:

   a.   Making lessons meaningful
   b.   Providing labels for the things you want the student to attend to and using them consistently
   c.   Emphasizing the relevant attributes of a task

   See Exhibit 17.7 on pages 418-420 for additional examples.

9.   Examples of storage, recall, and memory strategies are:

   a.   To promote storage: Link current lessons to previous lessons. Summarize and review the main lesson points after the lesson.

   b.   To promote recall: Teach skills to high proficiency levels. Provide practice on the responses targeted for recall.

   c.   To promote memory: Teach the student to use a) elaboration, b) organization, and c) mnemonic strategies. Teach the student to review previous lessons.

   Exhibit 17.8 on pages 421-422 provides other examples.

10. You would be teaching <u>motivation</u> if you supplied meaning to a task by placing a priority on it, related it to its context, and demonstrated a personal interest in it.

REFERENCES

Fuchs, L. S., and Deno, S. L. Paradigmatic Distinctions Between Instructionally Relevant Measurement Models. <u>Exceptional Children</u>. May, 1991, pp. 488-500.

Lovitt, T. C. <u>In Spite of My Resistance, I've Learned From Children</u>. Charles Merrill, 1977.

Peterson, L., Wonderlich, S.A., Reaven, N.M., & Mullins, L.L. (1987). Adult educators' response to depression and stress in children. *Journal of Social and Clinical Psychology,* 5(1), 51-58.

Tucker, J. Curriculum Based Assessment Is No Fad. <u>The Collaborative Educator</u>. <u>1</u> (4). 1987.

White, O. R. and Haring, N. G. <u>Exceptional Teaching</u>, Second Edition. Charles Merrill Publishing Company. 1980.

Ysseldyke, J.E., & Christenson, S.L. (1987). *TIES: The Instructional Environment Scale.* Austin, TX: Pro-Ed.

Constructing Probes

You are about to find out why it is easier (but not necessarily better) to select a CRT rather than to make one.

Over the next several pages we will focus on: calibrating curriculum, planning a test, selecting and writing items, assuring an adequate sample, testing strategies, testing rate, and standardizing criteria. These activities are all necessary in developing curriculum-based measures (many of them are also discussed on pages 126-136 of the text).

Calibrating Curriculum

Calibrating a test means adjusting its curriculum coverage to complement an interval of instructional time. This is a time-consuming task best accomplished during curriculum development. A CRT must measure the same slice (portion) of curriculum being taught by the teacher. This is important for two reasons: (1) It assures adequate sampling and (2) it allows repeated measurement and monitoring. Because special/remedial teachers teach in relation to short-term objectives, which by convention take approximately 4 to 6 weeks to teach, specific-level tests/observations should be calibrated at 4 to 6 weeks. (If your idea of short term is 10-15 weeks, the principles and procedures we are about to explain will also apply, but the time intervals will be longer.)

Step 1. _Summarize long-term discrepancy_. Find the long-term objectives the student has not met. These are specified in some form (usually global) in the school district's curriculum guide. Locate where the student (let's call this kid Vicki) is currently working and where she should be working. Subtract this actual performance from the expected performance. For example, suppose the curriculum indicates that Vicki should have mastered 78 separate long-term math objectives. If she has only mastered 50, the summary would look like this:

Expected Performance:	78
Actual Performance:	- 50
Discrepancy:	28

Step 2. _Establish aim date_. Deciding how long it will take to catch a student up is difficult. Usually the duration of service is decided in a child study team meeting with the input of the group. For this example, let's say that the group projects the need

for one year of special math instruction.

Step 3. <u>Find the total</u>. Add to the discrepancy the number of objectives students in regular programs will be expected to learn during the catch-up period. Remember that to catch up, a remedial student must actually cover more objectives per time unit than a regular student. Vicki has been given one year to catch up. In that year let's assume 20 new long-term objectives will be presented to all students. We now have:

       28 old objectives
    + <u>20</u> new objectives
       48

Vicki's Progress Goal is 48 objectives in one year.

Step 4. <u>Set a Weekly Goal</u>. This is done by dividing the number of objectives by the number of weeks available for instruction. Throwing out the first and last weeks plus a couple more for state-mandated achievement testing and parent conferences, let's say that we are going to get 30 weeks of actual instruction during the year. That's 48 objectives divided by 30 weeks or 1.6 long-term objectives per week (48 / 30 = 1.6).

Step 5. <u>Calibrate the objectives</u>. We think a short-term objective takes from 4 to 6 weeks to teach so our calibration interval is 4 to 6 weeks. To allow time for problems to occur and be corrected we'll take the outside time 6 weeks and multiply it by the weekly factor obtained in step 4 (6 x 1.6 = 9.6) to get a progress expectation of 9.6 math objectives for each 6-week period. The 48 original objectives can now be clumped into five groups of about 10 objectives each. Each group of 10 objectives will be taught together.

Step 6. <u>Consolidate the objectives if possible</u>. This means taking each of the objective chunks produced in step 5 and trying to treat them as one task. It may be that this is not possible and Vicki will end up working on 9 or 10 separate tasks, but if the 10 objectives can be merged into two or three related domains it will limit the number of tests Vicki will have to take and the number her teacher will have to write. Consolidation is carried out by examining the content domains in each objective as well as the strategic steps required to carry the objective out. For example, if several objectives cover percents and decimals they can be merged because percents and decimals share the concept of proportion and the application of division.

In the six steps above we used objectives as the basis of calibration. It is also possible to use materials. For example, let's say that Vicki's performance lag has put her one and a half math books behind the other students. If the regular students will cover one additional book this year she has a total of 2.5 math books to cover in 30 weeks. If each book has 100 pages, that's a weekly expectation of 8.3 pages (100 pages by 2.5 books / 30 weeks = 8.3 pages a week). 8.3 pages a week is about 50 pages every 6 weeks. To calibrate a probe in this case you go to the text pages and see what they are teaching. This means looking at the 50 pages to be covered and devising one or more tests to measure their content. As with the objective method, the aim is to recognize skills that span the entire time period. If four skills are identified you want to produce four 6-week probes, not a series of four covering 1.25 weeks each. (The danger of this system is that it assumes the materials are appropriate and that each page is worth doing.)

Planning a Test

This discussion will describe how to plan a CRT inventory for a 4- to 6-week unit of instruction. A unit of instruction may contain several objectives and each one may require its own probe. Each separate probe in the inventory will measure only one objective. The next few pages will elaborate on the following steps.

1.   Recognize content
2.   Sequence content
3.   Recognize and sequence behavior
4.   Recognize and sequence conditions
5.   Assemble a table of specifications
6.   Discard nonapplicable objectives
7.   Write items for each square

Step 1. <u>Recognize content</u>. Once the curriculum has been calibrated, take each short-term objective and identify its content element. Content may be factual, strategic, or conceptual (see Exhibit 6.10, page 107).

Recognizing the content elements of tasks is a straightforward, logical, and convergent activity. It begins with a general statement of content from which subtropics are recognized. It is best if several people generate these lists using reference materials, in order to benefit from the thinking of those who know the content area well. Once identified, each item of content should be judged according to the following criteria:

1.   Is it relevant? Is the main task of value to the student?
2.   Is it complete? Has any essential content been omitted?
3.   Is it trivial? Is content included which is too easy for the target student?

184

4.	It is necessary? Is all content necessary to master the main task?
5.	Is it redundant? Do any of the content statements overlap with other content statements? (Thiagarajan, Semmel, & Semmel, 1974).

Step 2. <u>Sequence Content</u>. Even though it seems as if critics of education want teachers to teach everything at the same time, they can't. Therefore, content must be put into a sequence. Sequencing content allows us to recognize a coordinated series of lessons.

If all content topics are of equal difficulty, then the most convenient system for sequencing should be identified and used. Those systems that do not require ordering content according to difficulty are:

Logically--Using this system, content is grouped into units defined by some similarity. Animals, for example, can be grouped according to what they eat. But the study of animals that eat grass isn't necessarily easier than the study of animals who eat cows.

Chronologically--Time may be used to present tasks as the content itself evolved or as the content was discovered. Even though it may seem obvious to start at the first, that doesn't make the first step easy. In fact, sometimes it's easier to show people where they are going before you get them started.

Student interest or teacher priority--This includes such age-old techniques as teaching what you know while you study up on something to teach next. It also includes asking the kids what they would like to know about.

Utility--This means arranging the content according to how the student will use it. This involves a little research. One technique is to ask parents if there is a skill they'd like their kids to start using. Utility is one way of ordering content that will vary a lot from location to location.

If content elements differ in difficulty, they can be ordered by the way they function in the "real" world. For example, a swimming teacher might have objectives specifying "getting into water" and "kicking in water." Obviously "getting into water" has to come first because it is included in "kicking in water." Similarly teaching a student to "identify faculty arguments" must be preceded by "identify author conclusion" because arguments can only be judged in reference to conclusions (Carnine, Silbert, & Kameenui, 1990).

If content can be sequenced according to difficulty or complexity it should be.

The obvious thing to do is to put the easiest material in the first lessons. Prerequisite content relationships (task ladders) are occasionally quite clear and easy to find in the literature. If these relationships are not clear, then the sequence should be viewed as a hypothesis to be validated through instruction and evaluation. By convention, lists of content start with the easiest (or first taught) at the bottom and the hardest (last taught) at the top, as shown in Exhibit 3.9.

Step 3. <u>Recognize and sequence behavior</u>. Every objective, must describe what a student will do to show that he or she "knows" the content. Here are some examples:

"On the midterm exam the student will write three definitions of learning with 100% accuracy." What is the "know" word in this objective? Write.

"Given a list of 60 CVC words, the student will pronounce the words within 1 minute with no more than two errors." What will the student do to demonstrate knowledge in this objective? Pronounce the words.

The same behavior occurring under different conditions (e.g., spelling while writing a letter vs. spelling on a spelling test) or at different proficiency levels (spelling quickly vs. spelling slowly) may indicate different degrees of knowledge. We can sequence categories of behavior that indicate different degrees of learning. These behavior categories include **response type** (identify/produce) and **proficiency level** (accuracy, mastery, automaticity).

Step 4. <u>Recognize and sequence conditions</u>. The conditions under which a behavior is carried out also indicate different degrees of knowledge. For example, the automatic level involves accurate and quick response under real-world conditions. Conditions can also be arranged into sequences that make the behavior harder to carry out and indicate that a higher level of learning has taken place. This is particularly important for special/remedial students, who, as a group, seem to have trouble generalizing what they have learned.

Step 5. <u>Assemble a table of specifications</u>. Assemble the content, behavior, and conditions from steps 1-4 into a table of specifications as shown in Exhibit 6.5.

Step 6. <u>Discard nonapplicable objectives</u>. Look at the table and mark out any squares (objectives) that do not make sense or do not seem to be worth instructional time.

Step 7. <u>Write items for each square</u>. The issue of how many items are needed for an adequate sample is a fairly hot one in test development circles. For the kind of testing we're talking about here (specific-level probes for short term objectives), 10 items per objective or strategy step is conventional and probably sufficient. For mastery (rate) objectives, the number of items needs to be increased (or the duration of the test modified, as described below) until the student has the opportunity to do 50% more items than called for in the objective's CAP. (If the CAP is 60, the total number of items should be 90.)

Selecting and Writing Items

The type of item used depends on several factors. Obviously the aim is to select items that are as useful as possible which means they must be both reliable and valid. Items can be categorized into select and supply headings. Supply items are those that require the student to produce an answer and include computation, reading, fill-in-the-blank, cloze, short answer, essay, and project completion. Select items include multiple choice, matching, maze (modified cloze), and true/false.

We would expect to find supply items used for most basic skills (select items are regularly reserved for higher level content or extremely low levels of basic skill knowledge). The best way to choose an item type is to look at the item and ask "Does this item have lifelike stimuli and require lifelike responses, under lifelike conditions?"

Rate Tests. If a test is designed to collect rate data the items should be randomly distributed in terms of difficulty, meaning the sheet will not begin with easy problems and then move to harder ones. The easy and hard problems should be scattered on the page.

When a written test is used, the problems on the sheet should be legible and spaced to facilitate the student's work. To make scoring easier, the number of responses possible in each row can be written down the margin, as shown in Exhibit 5.10. Note that even though the probe in Exhibit 5.10 is designed to test regrouping some items in 5.10 do not require regrouping; these non-instances are included to test the strategy for deciding when to regroup.

A student's rate of response depends on skill, the number of opportunities, and the time allowed. If the objective stipulates that 50 digits need to be written in 1 minute, a sufficient number of opportunities must be on the page. Ideally there should be 50% more opportunities than the objective calls for. To get the best idea of student rate, students taking rate tests should be encouraged to skip items they do not know.

Including 50% more problems means that few students will ever finish a probe.

Some kids may become upset when they see all of that work and can't ever seem to get it done. Therefore, you will want to put them at ease by saying, "Work as fast but as carefully as you can. If you come to one you do not know, skip it. Don't worry about finishing the page. There are more problems here than anyone needs to do."

The prominent consideration when developing rate tests is to avoid anything that artificially reduces or puts a ceiling on response fluency. It is important to allow many opportunities for the behavior to occur. (We are trying to interpret behavior, so the more we have, the happier we are.) If you find yourself with low frequencies of behavior, you may solve your problem four ways: (a) extend the time interval for the test, (b) provide more opportunities (items), (c) slice the behavior, (d) move to a response class. We will briefly elaborate on each of these.

Time. Time extension is an obvious way to increase the total number of behaviors counted (though not necessarily their rate). Suppose it takes 10 seconds to do a three-place multiplication problem with regrouping. If you allow the students 1 minute, the most problems she can do is six. You can raise this ceiling on her behavior by timing for 2 minutes. In 2 minutes she will have the opportunity to do 12 problems (too much time can cause fatigue. Although successful students can write 100 or more digits per minute, they can't keep up this rate for more than a couple of minutes).

Opportunities. Providing more opportunities is also an obvious way to obtain an increase in frequency. If there are only five problems, the ceiling count must be five. Change the number to 20 and you provide the opportunity for more behavior.

Slice (re-calibrate). Sometimes you can "slice" a behavior to raise the frequency. When you slice, you segment the behavior and count components. For example, if you want to "stop smoking," you can count (a) packs a day, (b) cigarettes a day, or (c) puffs a day. As a rule, higher frequency behaviors are easier to change than low frequency ones. Therefore, puffs are easier to change than packs, and since decreasing both leads to "stop smoking" it is better to count puffs. Examples of academic slicing include counting digits instead of problems or syllables spelled instead of words.

Classes. The last way to increase frequency is to count an entire class of behavior instead of one member of the class. This is done by first defining a response class. A response class is composed of behaviors that are so closely related that changing one raises the probability of changing them all. To illustrate, imagine that you work in a correctional institution, and Jennifer is sent there for stealing cars. "Steals cars" might be your pinpoint and decreasing "steals cars" your main objective. Unfortunately, there are no cars parked along the hallways of your reformatory, so during Jennifer's whole stay she never does the pinpoint and is never punished for it.

188

Similarly you may reward her day and night at 10-minute intervals for "not stealing cars" but the treatment may seem somehow peculiar to her. So what do you do? You make up a response class called "respects property of others" and intervene on and count all instances of "property crimes" including stealing extra desserts and entering rooms without permission. You hope that you will ultimately decrease the stealing of cars. By redefining the pinpoint to include all samples of the class "property crimes," you have raised the possible frequency.

Standardizing the Test

CAP is the standard of performance specified in the objective. Usually it is assumed that the performance level specified in the CAP represents minimal competency at the skill. Our actual ability to establish these minimal competency levels (or maximum incompetency levels, if you're a cynic) can be questioned.

Ideally, CAP will have already been established as part of the school program's curriculum development. If not, the burden may fall on the individual evaluator. In this case, you will probably want to follow one of the following procedures. These procedures are not particularly simple, but curriculum-based evaluation is impossible without curriculum expectations.

Academic CAP. In educational literature, criteria will be found which have been established: (a) by guessing (the worst way), (b) by asking experts, (c) by employing standardization techniques, and (d) by using research validating the effect of meeting different criteria or subsequent learning. Each technique has advantages and disadvantages. For the teacher, the best ways to get criteria are to consult experts or to standardize the objective.

Expert Judgment. One way to determine how well students should do something is to ask someone who already knows. In many cases, particularly in the basic skills, CAPs have already been established. To find them, you should consult educators, texts, or journals that deal with the content in question. Because opinions will almost certainly vary, some test developers use the levels specified by experts as an initial estimate and then administer the test to see if the standard seems to separate instructed and uninstructed students.

Standardization. When a CRT is standardized, people who are successful at the task are selected. This group is not randomly assembled. Only people who are judged to be experts at the task and who are in the same grade as the target student are selected for the standardization population. Then they all take the test and their median (middle - not average) score is found. This middle score can then be used as the CAP.

The hardest part of this system is deciding which students to use for the standardization procedure. We recommend grade-level peers rather than age-level peers. This means that if a student has been retained, you should compare him to students at his current grade level. We have found that few academic skills vary simply as a function of age; they are more apt to vary as a function of instruction and practice. A student who should be in the eighth grade but who was retained in the seventh grade has only been taught seventh grade material. Therefore, even though he is older than most seventh graders, he should still be used to establish CAP for him.

As a rule you can accept students selected by the teacher as the ones who have mastered the target skill. Teacher judgment is the ultimate standard to which tests are compared in validity studies (though it is safer to use a few students from several teachers than a lot from one). The teacher's judgment can be improved by making the selection question very specific. For example, "Name the 10 best students at addition and the 10 worst students at addition."

If the scores of the successful students are extremely variable, you may wish to collect a larger sample. For example, if the scores you got from an addition probe were 94, 92, 73, 70, 60, 55, 40, 35, 22, you wouldn't think that the median (60) was particularly descriptive of the group because the extreme scores, 94 and 22, vary from the median by as much as 273%. The easiest way to tell if a score is descriptive is to rank the scores in a frequency distribution (see Appendix A) and then to look at it.

The procedure for determining CAP for academic skills is as follows:

1. Devise a test.
2. Select a standardization population of successful grade level peers.
3. If the sample is less than 10, locate additional successful students in another class.
4. Administer the test exactly as it will be given to the special/remedial students.
5. Find the median score.
6. Rank order or graph the scores to see if the median score describes the successful group.
7. If most of the scores fall close to the median, accept the median score as CAP.
8. If scores don't fall close to the median, double the sample size and repeat the process or review the procedure used to select the sample.

Interestingly, CAPs determined by using this procedure do not vary from class to class as much as class averages do.

190

<u>Social Behavior CAP</u>.   The norm (average) is not particularly relevant to academic skills, but it is to social skills. The average has greater relevance to social behavior because in most situations the behavior of others is a primary cue individuals use to decide how to behave. In our culture, while we don't want to be called average, we don't like being considered abnormal either. The use of using average behavior as the target for special students is discussed in some detail in Chapter 16. The best approach for establishing CAP for social behavior is the ecological approach as explained on pages 387-388.

INTRODUCTION TO PART B
TESTING MATERIALS

This part of the workbook contains a brief description of the process one follows to summarize evaluation results, reproductions of critical (*) exhibits from the text, and testing materials in certain key areas. We are granting those of you who purchase this study guide the right to reproduce these materials for your own professional use (either as a student or a teacher). You do not have permission to sell, or to give away, copies of these materials (and if you do we can bet that Brooks/Cole and H & Z publications will take a very dim view of it). If you are interested in more information about the development and/or technical adequacy of these materials contact H & Z Publications at 6544 E. Meadowlark, Paradise Valley, AZ 85253.

Part B begins with a section containing advice and worksheets for summarizing evaluations. It then supplies selected * exhibits from the content chapters. The exhibits are larger than in the text so they will be easier to use. Following these exhibits are testing materials for Comprehension, Decoding, Mathematics, and Content Vocabulary. You should make copies of these exhibits and tests now so they don't get messed up. If they are too small, enlarge them when you make copies.

This study guide is not intended to be a test manual. You will need to read the directions given in the text for using and interpreting these measures.

To avoid having extraneous numbers on the tests students use, you should delete or cover the study guide page numbers in the bottom corners of the tests in Part B when copying them for students.

192

Summarizing Results

Evaluation results are summarized by utilizing the basic standard/behavior/ discrepancy model as illustrated throughout the text (particularly on pages 438-439).

Here are the steps you follow:

-write down the standard
-write down the behavior
-determine the discrepancy
-specify the goal
-specify a series of objectives that map
 intermediate steps between the current level
 of performance (the behavior) and the goal

Here are a couple of examples:

Using materials at expected level
(student in 8th grade)

	Oral Reading		Computation
Material:	8th-grade history text		End-of-text review exercises
Standard:	140 correct	<7 errors p/min	
Behavior:	60	15	65 percent
Discrepancy:			
Absolute:	+80	-8	+35 percent
Ratio:	x2.3	÷ 2.1	x1.9

Oral reading goal: Student will read 8th-grade history book with expected rate and accuracy.

3. Will read history book aloud at a rate of 140 mph with 95% accuracy (<7 errors).
2. Will read history book aloud at a rate of 100 mph with 95% accuracy (<5 errors).
1. Will read history book aloud at a rate of 60 mph with 95% accuracy (<3 errors).

Computation goal: Student will accurately work items on end-of-text review tests.

Objective: 3. Student will write answers to items with 100% accuracy.

2. Student will explain the process of working [specify content] items with 100% accuracy.

3. Student will identify items requiring knowledge of [specify content] with 100% accuracy.

Using Materials Below Expected Level

When the student lacks the skills to work productively in materials at her expected level you will need to test down and specify a sequence of materials in the objectives. For example:

	Oral Reading at Expected Level		Oral Reading at Intructional Level	
Material:	**8th**-grade history text		**4th**-grade history text	
Standard:	140 correct	<7 errors plain	140 correct	<7 errors plain
Behavior:	15 correct	22 errors	63 correct	8 errors
Discrepancy:				
Absolute:	+ 125	-15	+77	-1
Ratio:	x9.3	÷ 3.1	x2.2	÷ 1.1

Oral reading Goal*: Student will read **6th**-grade history book with expected rate and accuracy.

Objectives:

3. Will read **6th**-grade history text at a rate of 140 mph with 95% accuracy (<7 errors).

2. Will read **5th**-grade history text at a rate of 140 mph with 95% accuracy (<7 errors).

3. Will read **4th**-grade history text at a rate of 140 mph with 95% accuracy (<7 errors).

*In this case the annual goal specifies 6th-grade level because the team has decided that the discrepancy found on the initial test can't be made up in one year. The goal is acceptable because it is reasonable and specifies a decrease in the student's discrepancy.

Remember that, in all of these examples, we are only presenting one area of content. There may be other areas related to oral reading (e.g. blending or morphographs) that would also need to be taught.

CRITERIA FOR JUDGING THE PRODUCT OF AN EVALUATION

- IS THE STUDENT BRIEFLY DESCRIBED?

- IS THE TEST BRIEFLY DESCRIBED?

- IS THE TEST RELIABLE AND VALID?

- ARE DATES AND SCORES REPORTED ACCURATELY?

- IS THE STANDARD (EXPECTED SCORE) DETERMINED CORRECTLY?

- IS THE BEHAVIOR RECORDED CORRECTLY?

- IS THE DISCREPANCY CALCULATED CORRECTLY?

- IS THE GOAL REASONABLE FOR ONE YEAR, AND WILL MEETING IT DECREASE THE DISCREPANCY?

- ARE THE OBJECTIVES COMPLETE IN CONTENT, BEHAVIOR, CONDITIONS, AND CAP?

- DO THE OBJECTIVES LAY OUT A PATH FROM THE CURRENT LEVEL OF PERFORMANCE TO THE GOAL?

TESTING SUMMARY

STUDENT NAME:

GRADE LEVEL:

DATE OF TEST:

SKILL TESTED:

TEST MATERIALS:

STANDARD:

BEHAVIOR:

DISCREPANCY:

    ABSOLUTE:

    RATIO:

    ANNUAL GOAL:

    SHORT-TERM OBJECTIVES:

Exhibit 10.1 Comprehension Status Sheet

Purpose: To limit the scope of the comprehension evaluation.
Directions: Consider the indicators for each of the strategy and enabling skill categories.
Consult with anyone who may have comprehension-specific knowledge of the student.
Mark the status of each category:
"Yes" means the skill is adequate.
"No" means it should be taught.
"Unsure" means additional testing is required.

Category	Indicators	Status			Specific-level procedure (SLP)

Comprehension strategies

Category	Indicators				Specific-level procedure (SLP)
1. Active reading	1.1 Monitors meaning	Yes	No	Unsure	Select from 1–7 using this Status Sheet—or administer all 7 procedures
	1.2 Adjusts for text difficulty				
	1.3 Connects text with prior knowledge				
	1.4 Clarifies				
	1.5 Previews text				
	1.6 Develops and answers questions				
	1.7 Takes notes and/or highlights				
	1.8 Reviews				
2. Monitors meaning	2.1 Self-corrects reading errors which violate the meaning of the passage (such as non-meaningful insertions)	Yes	No	Unsure	1—Assisted monitoring 2—Retell
	2.2 Rereads confusing portions of material, or adjusts reading rate on difficult sections				
	2.3 Can predict upcoming events in the passage				
	2.4 Identifies when additional information is needed, or specifically what kind of information is needed to answer questions				
	2.5 Reads with expression and/or automation				
3. Adjusts for task difficulty	3.1 Utilizes study skills appropriately	Yes	No	Unsure	3—Awareness of reading
	3.2 Allocates study time according to passage difficulty				
	3.3 States purpose for reading				
	3.4 Accurately estimates success on passage				
	3.5 Adjusts reading rate appropriately				
4 Connects text to prior knowledge	4.1 Answers "best title" and main idea questions accurately	Yes	No	Unsure	4—Assisted Activation of Prior Knowledge 5—Prediction 6—Assisted Search
	4.2 Retells story with emphasis on major points				
	4.3 Describes author's purpose for writing				
	4.4 Can locate information in the passage which answers assigned questions				
	4.5 Can accurately apply stated criteria to the story to judge its value as entertainment or as an information source				
	4.6 Uses information gained from reading the passage to focus on subsequent topics/information in the passage				
5. Clarifies	5.1 Adjusts reading rate for material which is not understood	Yes	No	Unsure	3—Awareness of Reading 7—Referent Knowledge
	5.2 Is more likely to recall important passage details, not trivial ones				
	5.3 Answers comprehension questions in terms of stated information in passage, not necessarily prior knowledge				
	5.4 Uses multiple strategies to determine passage meaning				
	5.5 Uses multiple strategies to decode words				
	5.6 Self-corrects errors which violate meaning				
	5.7 Asks for assistance				

Enabling skills

Category	Indicators				Specific-level procedure (SLP)
6. Decoding	6.1 Reads passages with 90% accuracy	Yes	No	Unsure	1—Assisted Monitoring and/or go to Chapter 11
	6.2 Reads passages at 75% of expected rate				
	6.3 Makes few errors that violate meaning				

(continued)

Exhibit 10.1   Comprehension Status Sheet (continued)

Category	Indicators	Status			Specific-level procedure
Enabling skills *cont'd*					
7. Vocabulary	7.1 Can define words in passage	Yes	No	Unsure	Go to Chapter 12
	7.2 Can modify the definition of words in passage according to context (does not miss context-dependent vocabulary questions)				
	7.3 Balance of errors on maze exercise does not show excessive semantic errors				
	7.4 Comprehension does not increase dramatically and/or decoding errors do not decrease when key words are introduced prior to reading				
	7.5 Makes few nonmeaningful substitutions				
	7.6 Uses pronouns and tenses correctly				
8. Syntax	8.1 Balance of errors on maze exercise does not show excessive syntax errors	Yes	No	Unsure	Go to Chapter 12
	8.2 Primary language is same as texts				
	8.3 Oral language adequate (does not contain excessive syntax errors which violate the standard of adult speech) particularly in the use of subject-verb agreement, tense, and pronouns				
9. Prior knowledge	9.1 Comprehension does not vary dramatically according to familiarity with the passage topic	Yes	No	Unsure	Go to Chapter 17
	9.2 Can correctly define words in passage				
	9.3 Can relate information in passage to personal experience or to other sources of information (other passages, books, authors, classes, etc.)				
	9.4 Comprehension does not improve dramatically when a passage is previewed and unstated ideas are explained prior to reading				
	9.5 Can discuss unstated ideas accurately				

198

Exhibit 10.8   Status Sheet for Awareness of the Reading Process*

	Adequate	Not Adequate	Unsure
Before reading			
Considers purpose for reading (5, 7)	_____	_____	_____
Considers title (3)			
Scans illustrations/Figures (2, 8)			
Asks questions (6, 9, 10)			
Makes predictions (1, 4, 9, 10)			
While reading			
Remembers predictions and questions (14, 15, 17, 18)	_____	_____	_____
Decides if passage makes sense (11)			
Summarizes while reading (12, 19)			
Keeps questioning and predicting (13, 16)			
Seeks clarification (20)			
After reading			
Summarizes (22, 25)	_____	_____	_____
Reviews questions/predictions (21)			
Fits the story to what is already known (23, 24)			

Items from Paris and Jacobs (1984)

Reading awareness
1. What is hard?
2. What would help?
3. First sentences?
4. Last sentences?
5. What is important?

Planning
6. Which would you read?
7. What would you tell?
8. Asking before reading?
9. Planning before reading?
10. Which would you read?

Regulation
11. Do you reread?
12. Words you don't understand?
13. Sentences you don't understand?
14. What do you skip?
15. What do you read fast?

*Item numbers from Schmitt (1990) are in parentheses. They are found in Exhibit 10.7.

199

Exhibit 11.3* Passage Summary Sheet with Criteria for Acceptable Performance

Directions: For each passage used, record the number of corrects and errors per minute. Also record the accuracy. For each passage, check the rate and accuracy status (pass, marginal no-pass, or no-pass) for each curriculum level.

Curr. Level	Form	Expected Rate Correct	Expected Rate Error	Obtained Rate Correct	Obtained Rate Error	Status Pass	Status M. No Pass	Status No Pass	Accuracy Exp. Acc.	Accuracy Obt. Acc.	Status Pass	Status M. No Pass	Status No Pass
8		140	0-7						100-95%				
7		140	0-7						100-95%				
6		140	0-7						100-95%				
5		140	0-7						100-95%				
4		140	0-7						100-95%				
3		140	0-7						100-95%				
2		Late 120 Early 80	0-5						100-95%				
1		Late 50 Early 30	0-3						100-95%				

Expected Level (Current Grade Placement)   _____

Curriculum Level (Highest level at which mastery criterion is met)   _____

Levels above (+) or below (−) Expectation   _____

Rate Discrepancy at Instructional Level

Obtained Rate _____ ÷ Expected Rate _____ = Rate Discrepancy _____

Accuracy Discrepancy at Instructional Level

Obtained Accuracy _____ % ÷ Expected Accuracy _____ = Accuracy Discrepancy _____

Source: From K. W. Howell, S. H. Zucker & M. K. Morehead (1982) *Multilevel Academic Skills Inventory.* H & Z Publications, 6544 E. Meadowlark, Paradise Valley, AZ 85253. Reprinted with permission.

Exhibit 11.5* Awareness of Print and Sound

Directions:

1. Test the student.
2. Whenever an error occurs, write down the exact content and conditions of the test.
3. Start with production. If the student does not produce answers, move to identification.
4. Record accuracy.

	Record Accuracy		Note Conditions/
Print knowledge	Identification	Production	Content of Test
Page conventions	_____	_____	
left to right	_____	_____	
top to bottom	_____	_____	
Book conventions	_____	_____	
page by page	_____	_____	
front to back	_____	_____	
right side up	_____	_____	
Book length	_____	_____	
Word length	_____	_____	
Word boundaries	_____	_____	
Sentence boundaries	_____	_____	
Lower-case letter names	_____	_____	
Upper-case letter names	_____	_____	
Environmental print and logos	_____	_____	
Phonology with spoken language			
Distinguish word in speech streams	_____	_____	
Delete words	_____	_____	
Blend words	_____	_____	
Segment words	_____	_____	
Rhyme	_____	_____	
Blend syllables	_____	_____	
Segment syllables	_____	_____	
Delete onset/rime or phoneme	_____	_____	
Discriminate same/different phonemes	_____	_____	
Segment and blend phonemes	_____	_____	

Exhibit 11.6*   Error Pattern Checklist: Specific-Level Procedure 5b

Compare each error in the passage to the checklist (ignore errors on proper names). Make a mark next to the category in which the error seems to fit. Identify the strategic categories in which most errors occur and begin additional testing in those areas. Continue to monitor changes in error patterns.

Error Categories	No. Errors

Mispronunciations

Errors are substitutions of real words

Errors are not real words

Errors are phonetically similar to stimulus word

Insertions

Insertions are contextually appropriate

Insertions are contextually inappropriate

Omissions

Omission affects passage meaning

Omission does not affect meaning

Hesitation
Repetition

Repeats a portion of target word

Repeats preceding word

Repeats preceding words or phrases

Does not attend to punctuation

Does not pause at punctuation

Pauses at end of line

Self-corrects

Directions for Using the Error Pattern Checklist: Use the Error Pattern Checklist to categorize all decoding errors made on the passage. Ask yourself what the most probable reading strategy explanation is for each error. Check it off by marking the appropriate category. If more than two errors were made on a word, categorize only the first two.

Question	Recommendation
1. Are there clear patterns of errors?	If yes, correct the erroneous pattern by targeting it as an instructional objective.

Source: From K. W. Howell, S. H. Zucker & M. K. Morehead (1982) *Multilevel Academic Skills Inventory.* H & Z Publications, 6544 E. Meadowlark, Paradise Valley, AZ 85253. Reprinted with permission.

Exhibit 11.7* Decoding Content Checklist: Specific-Level Procedure 5c

Compare the words in the passage to the student's errors and categorize errors by content area and content subskill. Make a mark next to the subskill indicated by each error. Do not record more than two errors per word. Identify the content areas in which the most errors occurred and begin additional testing in those areas. Continue to monitor changes in error patterns.

Content Categories	No. Errors

Words: errors involving whole words

Polysyllabic Words

Contractions

Compound Words

Sight Words

Silent Letters

Units: errors involving combined letter units

Endings (Suffixes)

Clusters

R-controlled Vowels

Vowel Teams

Consonant Digraphs

Consonant Teams

CVC Words

Conversions: errors involving sound modification

Double Consonant Words

Vowel + e Conversions

Sounds: errors involving individual letters and sounds

Vowels

Consonants

Sequence

Sounds

Symbols

Directions for Using the Decoding Content Checklist: Use the Content Checklist to categorize all errors made on the passage. Ask yourself what the most probable content explanation is for each error. Decide what content category the error is from and check it off by marking the appropriate category. If more than two errors were made on a word, categorize only the first two.

Question	Recommendation
1. Are there identifiable problems of content?	If yes, conduct specific-level testing of decoding skills reflected in the errors.

Source: From K. W. Howell, S. H. Zucker & M. K. Morehead (1982) *Multilevel Academic Skills Inventory.* H & Z Publications, 6544 E. Meadowlark, Paradise Valley, AZ 85253. Reprinted with permission.

Exhibit 11.8* Error Category Checklist for Meaning Violations: SLP 5a

Directions: Tally *each* error under the appropriate category. An error violates meaning if it has the *potential* to impair the student's understanding of the author's message. Do *not* tally mispronunciations of proper nouns as meaning violations.

	Category 1 Violates Meaning	Category 2 Does Not Violate Meaning	Category 3 Cannot Classify	Errors Self-Corrected
% of total errors this category	_____	_____	_____	
% or errors this category self-corrected	_____	_____	_____	

Exhibit 12.4*   A Table of Specifications for Language Syntactic Structures

Student's Name _____

Evaluator's Name _____

Date _____

	By Imitation	Produces With Prompts or in Controlled Situations	Spontaneous
1. Noun phrase/verb phrase			
2. Regular plurals			
3. Subject pronouns			
4. Prepositional phrases			
5. Adjectives			
6. Interrogative reversals			
7. Object pronouns			
8. Negatives			
9. Verb *be* auxiliary			
10. Verb *be* copula			
11. Infinitives			
12. Determiners			
13. Conjunction *and*			
14. Possessives			
15. Noun/verb agreement			
16. Comparatives			
17. *Wh-* questions			
18. Past tense			
19. Future aspect			
20. Irregular plurals			
21. Forms of *do*			
22. Auxiliaries			
23. Derivational endings			
24. Reflexive pronouns			
25. Qualifiers			
26. Conjunctions *and, but, or*			
27. Conjunctions			
28. Indirect and direct objects			
29. Adverbs			
30. Infinitives with subject			
31. Participles			
32. Gerunds			
33. Passive voice			
34. Complex verb forms			
35. Relative adverb clauses			
36. Relative pronoun clauses			
37. Complex conjunctions			

Exhibit 12.8* Setting Observation

Opportunity to Learn Language	Yes	No
1. Is the presentation understandable—semantics and syntactic structure at correct level?	___	___
2. Is the presentation meaningful—linked to prior knowledge or interest of student?	___	___
3. Is there visual support for verbal input—pictures, graphs, role playing, objects, gestures, etc.?	___	___
4. Is the student given frequent opportunities to respond?	___	___
5. Is there monitoring for understanding?	___	___
6. Are corrections linked to critical attributes of skill and to meaningfulness?	___	___
7. Are there multiple models (peers and teachers) available?	___	___
8. Is the classroom structured to increase frequency of communications?	___	___
9. Do peers and teacher have strategies for engaging a shy student who would remain silent if given a choice?	___	___
10. Are peers and teacher comfortable communicating with all students or do they look away or move away when some students initiate contact?	___	___
11. If student is acquiring English as a second language, is the primary language and culture of the student valued?	___	___
12. Is there collaboration with other classes, activities, and the home to insure focus, quality, and frequency of opportunity?	___	___
13. Is the teacher responsive to student contributions?	___	___
14. Do class discussions typically revolve around a theme?	___	___
15. Do TIES descriptors relate to this class's:		
Clarity of directions?	___	___
Checking understanding?	___	___
Class climate?	___	___
Teacher expectation?	___	___
Motivational strategies?	___	___
Student understanding?	___	___

Exhibit 12.9* Table of Specifications for the Executive Function of Pragmatics

Directions: Beginning with the column on the right, judge the quality of usage for each example of content. If use is inadequate, move to the condition(s) found to the left. Criteria will need to be established according to context. Items marked "no pass" become objectives.

Content and Behavior	Conditions			
	Identify Correct Example	Produce After Model	Produce After Prompt	Produce Spontaneously
Plan ways to accomplish intent?				
Monitor to see if intent is being met?				
Recognize when a problem occurs?				
Analyze problem for solution?				
Recognize when assistance is needed?				
Recognize resources for solution?				
Seek appropriate help?				
Adjust responses as result of analysis?				
Recognize when intent is met?				
Verify intent is met through alternative message?				
Actively plan to incorporate new language skills into old?				

207

Exhibit 12.10* *Table of Specifications for Communication Skills*

Directions: Beginning with the column on the right, judge the quality of usage for each example of content. If use is inadequate, move to the condition(s) found to the left. Criteria will need to be established according to context. Mark items YES, NO, or UNSURE.

Content and Behavior	Identify Correct Example	Conditions			
		Produce After Model	Produce After Prompt	Produce in Familiar Content	Produce with Strangers
A. One-way communication					
1. Expresses wants					
2. Expresses opinions					
3. Expresses feelings					
4. Expresses values					
5. Follows directions					
6. Asks questions					
7. Narrates event					
8. States main idea					
9. Sequences events					
10. Subordinates details					
11. Summarizes					
12. Describes					
13. Compares and contrasts					
14. Gives instructions					
15. Explains					
B. Two-way communication					
1. Considers the listener					
2. Formulates messages					
3. Participates in discussions					
4. Uses persuasion					
5. Resolves differences					
6. Identifies speaker's biases					
7. Identifies speaker's assumptions					
8. Formulates conclusions					
C. Nonverbal communication					
1. Uses gestures					
2. Uses proximity					
3. Uses position					
4. Uses expression					
5. Uses eye contact					

Exhibit 13.4* Analytic Scales for Dimensions of Writing Using a Five-Point Anchors of Quality

Story-Idea	Organiz.-Cohesion	Conven. Mechanics
5 —includes characters —delineates a plot —contains original ideas —contains some detail —word choice —contains descriptors (adverbs and adjectives) and colorful, infrequently used, and/or some long words	**5** —overall story is organized into a beginning, a middle, and an end —events are linked and cohesive —sentences are linked, often containing some transitions to help with organization (finally, then, next, etc.)	**5** —sentence structure generally is accurate —spelling does not hinder readability —sometimes contain dialogue —handwriting is legible —punctuation does not effect readability too much —word usage generally is correct (s.v.o./homophone/s-v agreement)
4 —includes characters, but they are not original, often coming from movies —delineates a plot, although it is not as clear as 5 —contains some original ideas but is fairly predictable —contains some detail —includes descriptors (adverbs and adjectives) —word choice: contains some descriptors (adverbs and adjectives) and some colorful, infrequently used, and/or long words	**4** —story has somewhat of a beginning, middle, and an end —events appear somewhat random, but some organization exists —sample may contain some transitions to help with organization: finally, then, next etc.) —story often contains too many events, disrupting cohesion	**4** —sentence structure generally is accurate but not as good as 5 —spelling does not hinder readability too much —sometimes contains dialogue —handwriting is legible —punctuation does not affect readability too much —word usage generally is correct (s.v.o./homophone/s-v agreement)
3 —characters are predictable and undeveloped —plot is somewhat haphazard —may or may not contain original ideas —lacks detail —word choice is somewhat predictable only sometimes contains descriptors (adverbs and adjectives)	**3** —somewhat of a plot exists but story may still lack a beginning, middle or an end —events are somewhat random —often lacks transitions —sometimes lack referents	**3** —sentence structure has a few problems —spelling is somewhat of a problem —may use dialogue but does not punctuate it correctly —handwriting is legible —punctuation is fair —problems sometimes occur with word usage (s.v.o/homophone/s-v agreement)
2 —includes few if any characters —plot is not developed or apparent —contains virtually no original ideas —detail is significantly absent —events are very predictable —word choice is predictable, lacking descriptors (adverbs and adjectives)	**2** —plot lacks organization into a beginning, middle and an end —events are random, lacking in cohesion —lacks transitions —often lacks referents	**2** —sentence structure makes story difficult to read —spelling makes it difficult to read —may use dialogue but does not punctuate it correctly —handwriting is not very legible —punctuation is inconsistent and problematic —word usage is problematic (s.v.o/homophone/s-v agreement)
1 —includes few if any characters —plot is non-existent —contains no original ideas —detail is significantly absent —events are few and predictable —lacks descriptors (adverbs and adjectives)	**1** —plot is virtually nonexistent —events are few and random —lacks transitions —lacks referents	**1** —sentence structure is problematic —spelling makes it extremely difficult to read —handwriting is illegible, making it extremely difficult to decode —punctuation is virtually nonexistent —word usage is problematic (s.v.o/homophone/s-v agreement)

From "Analyzing Student Writing to Develop Instructional Strategies," by G. Tindal and J. Hasbrouck, 1991, *Learning Disabilities Research & Practice*, 6, (4), p. 239. Reprinted by permission.

Exhibit 13.6* Status Sheet for SLP 1: Interview/ Observation of Writing Process and Product

The Writing Process

Planning

	yes	no	unsure
Did the writer define a purpose or establish an intent before beginning to write?			
Did the writer develop a list of content items appropriate to purpose or intent?			
Did the writer formulate a model, map or outline (plan) to structure content appropriate to purpose or intent?			
Did the writer use the plan as a basis for writing the first draft?			

Reviewing

	yes	no	unsure
During the writing of the draft(s) does the writer go back and read what was written to check on development and structure?			

Revision

	yes	no	unsure
Is there evidence in the drafts to indicate that the writer made changes to accomplish purpose/obtain intent?			

Product

Structure

	yes	no	unsure
Does the thesis sentence focus the reader on the writer's intent or purpose?			
Does the final sentence provide an appropriate ending/conclusion?			
Are the subtopics and/or events arranged in a recognizable order?			

Cohesion

	yes	no	unsure
Do all the sentences relate to the writer's intent or purpose?			
Is there an apparent order in the presentation of the sentences?			
Does the writer make use of transitional words and devices?			

Exhibit 13.9* *A Modification of Isaacson's Syntax Scale*

Syntax

Count the number of sentences in the writing that are representative of each syntactic level. Record the number of sentences for each level in the rectangle provided. Divide the number in each rectangle by the total number of sentences and record the percentage on the line provided.

Level 1
Repetitive use of simple (kernel) sentences. For example:

I like hamburgers.
I saw a dog.
The dog ate a burger.
He was sick.

Level 1 [ ] _____ %

Level 2
First expansions-kernel sentences + various phrases. For example:

The dog ran away *from McDonald's*. (prepositional phrase)
Putting its tail between its legs, the dog ran around the corner. (participial phrase)
The dogs wants *to hide under the porch*. (infinitive phrase)
Lying in the cool darkness is the cure for the dog's illness. (gerund phrase)

The writer may also use simple compound sentences. For example:

The hamburger was bad, but the dog liked the fish.
The dog felt better, and he chased the squirrel.

Level 2 [ ] _____ %

Level 3
Transformations that combine kernel sentences with relative and subordinate clauses. For example:

The fish *which was freshly caught* smelled like the sea. (relative clause)
While the dog slept under the porch, the moon rose. (subordinate clause)

Level 3 [ ] _____ %

Exhibit 14.4* Writing Sample Summary

Error Category	Type of Condition			
	Copy Total Letters ___ Rate ___	Dictation Total Letters ___ Rate ___	Story Starter Total Letters ___ Rate ___	Assignment Total Letters ___ Rate ___
Letters **formed** incorrectly Number %				
Letters **spelled** incorrectly Number %				
Words **capitalized** incorrectly Number %				
Words **punctuated** incorrectly Number %				
Total errors **Total accuracy**				

Student _____ Grade _____ Date _____

Task _____ Evaluator _____

TIMED/UNTIMED COPY(NEAR/FAR)/MEMORY TOTAL NO. OF LETTERS _____

1. ALIGNMENT	2. RELATIVE SIZE	3. RELATIVE SPACING	4. PROPORTION OF PARTS	5. INCONSISTENT STYLE	6. INCONSISTENT MODE	7. INCONSISTENT SLANT	8. CLOSED LOOPS	9. STRAIGHT & CURVED LINES
Y a K ↓ K	c a t ↑ ca	ca t ↓ ↔	bird ↑↑ r d	bird cursive	birD ↑ cap	cat //	cut ↑ a	cat ↗ ↑

Exhibit 14.6 Handwriting errors.

213

Exhibit 14.11* Mechanics Error Summary

	Error Tally	% Errors per 100 Words
Capitalization		
First name in sentence		
Name of person		
Title		
Days of week		
Month		
Street names		
Towns, cities, states, countries		
Personal pronoun "I"		
Buildings, companies, products		
Geographical names		
Family relationships used for name		
First word of quotation		
Other		
Punctuation		
Period		
End of sentence		
Initials and abbreviations		
Question mark		
End of sentence		
Exclamation point		
Exclamatory sentence		
Emphasis		
Comma		
Items in a series		
Month, year		
City, state		
Day, month		
Direct address		
After year in sentence		
After state or country in sentence		
After introductory word in sentence		
Before conjunction joining independent clause		
Surround appositive		
Set off dependent clause		
Set off adverbial clause		
After greeting and closing in letters		

	Error Tally	% Errors per 100 Words
Apostrophe		
Contractions		
Possessions		
Semicolon		
Separation of series		
Other		
Colon		
Salutation of letter		
Expression of time		
Appositives		
Other		
Hyphen		
Compound word or phrase		
Prefix when base is capitalized		
Other		
Quotation marks		
Direct quotations		
Single within direct		
Block quotations (no marks)		
Dialogue		
Titles		
Words used as words		
Foreign words		
Special use words		
Parentheses		
Interruptions		
Technical information within text		
Underline		
Titles		
Stress		
Ellipses		
Omissions		
Dash		
Interruptions		

Exhibit 15.6* *Asking Questions*

Asking the right question is an art to be cultivated by all educators. Low-level quizzes that ask for recall or simple computation are a dime a dozen, but a good high-level open-ended question that gives students a chance to think is a treasure!

These questions might be used as teaching or "leading" questions as well as for assessment purposes. Both questions and responses may be oral, written, or demonstrated by actions taken. The questions and their responses will contribute to a climate of thoughtful reflectiveness.

Some suggestions about assessment questioning:

- Prepare a list of possible questions ahead of time, but, unless the assessment is very formal, be flexible. You may learn more by asking additional or different questions.

- Use plenty of wait time; allow students to give thoughtful answers.

- For formal assessment, leading questions and feedback are not generally used, although some assessment techniques include teaching during the examination.

- Make a written record of your observations. A checklist may or may not be appropriate.

This is a starter list. You will want to build a collection of your own good questions.

Problem Comprehension
Can students understand, define, formulate, or explain the problem or task? Can they cope with poorly defined problems?

- What is this problem about? What can you tell me about it?
- How would you interpret that?
- Would you please explain that in your own words?
- What do you know about this part?
- Do you need to define or set limits for the problem?
- Is there something that can be eliminated or that is missing?
- What assumptions do you have to make?

Approaches and Strategies
Do students have an organized approach to the problem or task? How do they record? Do they use tools (manipulatives, diagrams, graphs, calculators, computers, etc.) appropriately?

- Where could you find the needed information?
- What have you tried? What steps did you take?
- What did not work?
- How did you organize the information? Do you have a record?
- Did you have a system? a strategy? a design?
- Have you tried (tables, trees, lists, diagrams . . .)?
- Would it help to draw a diagram or make a sketch?
- How would it look if you used these materials?
- How would you research that?

Relationships
Do students see relationships and recognize the central idea? Do they relate the problem to similar problems previously done?

- What is the relationship of this to that?
- What is the same? What is different?
- Is there a pattern?
- Let's see if we can break it down. What would the parts be?
- What if you moved this part?
- Can you write another problem related to this one?

Flexibility
Can students vary the approach if one is not working? Do they persist? Do they try something else?

- Have you tried making a guess?
- Would another recording method work as well or better?
- What else have you tried?
- Give me another related problem. Is there an easier problem?
- Is there another way to (draw, explain, say, . . .) that?

Communication
Can students describe or depict the strategies they are using? Do they articulate their thought processes? Can they display or demonstrate the problem situation?

- Would you please reword that in simpler terms?
- Could you explain what you think you know right now?
- How would you explain this process to a younger child?
- Could you write an explanation for next year's students (or some other audience) of how to do this?
- Which words were most important? Why?

Curiosity and Hypotheses
Is there evidence of conjecturing, thinking ahead, checking back?

- Can you predict what will happen?
- What was your estimate or prediction?
- How do you feel about your answer?
- What do you think comes next?
- What else would you like to know?

Equality and Equity
Do all students participate to the same degree? Is the quality of participation opportunities the same?

- Did you work together? In what way?
- Have you discussed this with your group? with others?
- Where would you go for help?
- How could you help another student without telling the answer?
- Did everybody get a fair chance to talk?

Solutions
Do students reach a result? Do they consider other possibilities?

- Is that the only possible answer?
- How would you check the steps you have taken, or your answer?
- Other than retracing your steps, how can you determine if your answers are appropriate?
- Is there anything you have overlooked?
- Is the solution reasonable, considering the context?
- How did you know you were done?

(*continued*)

Exhibit 15.6* ***Asking Questions (continued)***

Examining Results
Can students generalize, prove their answers? Do they connect the ideas to other similar problems or to the real world?

- What made you think that was what you should do?
- Is there a real-life situation where this could be used?
- Where else would this strategy be useful?
- What other problem does this seem to lead to?
- Is there a general rule?
- How were you sure your answer was right?
- How would your method work with other problems?
- What questions does this raise for you?

Mathematical Learning
Did students use or learn some mathematics from the activity? Are there indications of a comprehensive curriculum?

- What were the mathematical ideas in this problem?
- What was one thing you learned (or 2 or more)?
- What are the variables in this problem? What stays constant?
- How many kinds of mathematics were used in this investigation?
- What is different about the mathematics in these two situations?
- Where would this problem fit on our mathematics chart?

Self-Assessment
Do students evaluate their own processing, actions, and progress?

- What do you need to do next?
- What are your strengths and weaknesses?
- What have you accomplished?
- Was your own group participation appropriate and helpful?
- What kind of problems are still difficult for you?

Exhibit 15.10*   Math Summary Checklist

Solve All Problems, Integrating Necessary Computation, Applications, and Problem-Solving Skills					Appropriate Curriculum Level	
					No Pass	Pass
Response	Identify	Produce				
Standard	Accuracy	Accuracy	Mastery	Automatic		
Problem Solving—Integrate Subskills						
Check work						
Estimate answer						
Work equation						
Set up equation						
Determine relevant information						
Determine correct operation/s						

Solve All Problems, Integrating Necessary Computation, Applications, and Problem-Solving Skills					Appropriate Curriculum Level	
					No Pass	Pass
Response	Identify	Produce				
Standard	Accuracy	Accuracy	Mastery	Automatic		
Applications—Integrate Subskills						
Measurement—Scaling						
Weight — Vocabulary						
Weight — Tools						
Weight — Content						
Volume — Vocabulary						
Volume — Tools						
Volume — Content						
Surface — Vocabulary						
Surface — Tools						
Surface — Content						
Linear — Vocabulary						
Linear — Tools						
Linear — Content						
Money — Vocabulary						
Money — Tools						
Money — Content						
Temperature — Vocabulary						
Temperature — Tools						
Temperature — Content						
Time — Vocabulary						
Time — Tools						
Time — Content						

(continued)

Exhibit 15.10* **Math Summary Checklist (continued)**

					Identify	Produce			Appropriate Curriculum Level	
				Solve All Problems, Integrating Necessary Computation, Applications, and Problem-Solving Skills					No Pass	Pass
Response Type					Identify	Produce				
Standard					Accuracy	Accuracy	Mastery	Automatic		
Computation—Integrate Subskills										
+	−	×	÷	Operations—Rational Numbers						
				Ratios						
				Percents						
				Decimals						
				Fractions						
				Operations—Whole Numbers						
				÷						
				×						
				−						
				+						
				Basic Facts—Integrate Subskills						
				÷						
				×						
				−						
				+						

Exhibit 15.14* **Application Survey Answer Sheet**

Content	"Select" Items				"Apply" Items			
	Easy		Hard		Easy		Hard	
	Item	Answer	Item	Answer	Item	Answer	Item	Answer
Problem solving	1	b	6	d	11	c	16	a
	2	d	7	a	12	d	17	c
	3	c	8	b	13	a	18	a
	4	a	9	d	14	c	19	b
	5	d	10	a	15	d	20	d
Money	21	d	22	b	23	a	24	c
Time & temp	25/26	b	27	b	28	b	29	c
Metric measure	30	a	31	a	32	c	33	c
Customary meas.	34	a	35	a	36	c	37	c
Geometry I	38	b	39	d	40	b	41	d
Geometry II	42	d	43	b	44	c	45	c

Source: From K. W. Howell, S. H. Zucker & M. K. Morehead (1982) *Multilevel Academic Skills Inventory.* H & Z Publications, 6544 E. Meadowlark, Paradise Valley, Az 85253. Reprinted with permission.

Exhibit 15.15*   Applications Content Test

Time

Grade	Questions	Answers	Score
3	1. One minute has how many seconds?	60	1 0
3	2. One hour has how many minutes?	60	1 0
2	3. One day has how many hours?	24	1 0
1	4. One week has how many days?	7	1 0
4	5. One month has how many weeks?	4	1 0
1	6. One year has how many months?	12	1 0
4	7. One decade has how many years?	10	1 0
4	8. One century has how many decades?	10	1 0
4	9. One year has how many days?	365	1 0
4	10. One year has how many weeks?	52	1 0
		Total	

Money

Grade	Questions	Answers	Score
1	1. How many pennies make a nickel?	5	1 0
1	2. How many pennies make a dime?	10	1 0
2	3. How many dimes are in a quarter?	2	1 0
3	4. How many dimes are in $1?	10	1 0
3	5. How many quarters are in $1?	4	1 0
2	6. A quarter plus a dime are equal to how many pennies (cents)?	35	1 0
3	7. A half-dollar is worth how many dimes?	5	1 0
3	8. Which is worth more? Three $1 bills or one $5 bill?	one $5 bill	1 0
		Total	

Geometry

Grade	Target Words	Acceptable Responses	Score
3	1. perimeter	the distance around the outside edge	1 0
3	2. area	surface measurement	1 0
3	3. square units	what you get when you multiply the length times the width	1 0
3	4. cubic units	what you get when you multiply the length times the width times the height (depth)	1 0
3	5. volume	capacity; how much something holds; space inside	1 0
5	6. circumference	the distance around a circle	1 0
		Total	

Measurement–Customary Units

Grade	Target Questions	Answers	Score
4	1. How many ounces are in a pound?	16	1 0
4	2. How many pounds make a ton?	2,000	1 0
4	3. How many cups are in 1 pint?	2	1 0
4	4. How many pints are in 1 quart?	2	1 0
4	5. How many quarts are in 1 gallon?	4	1 0
4	6. How many inches are in 1 foot?	12	1 0
4	7. How many inches are in 1 yard?	36	1 0
4	8. How many feet are in 1 yard?	3	1 0
4	9. How many feet are in 1 mile?	5,280	1 0
		Total	

Measurement–Metric Units

Grade	Target Questions	Answers	Score
4	1. What does *milli* mean?	thousandths	1 0
4	2. What does *deci* mean?	tenths	1 0
4	3. What does *centi* mean?	hundredths	1 0
4	4. What does *deca* mean?	ten	1 0
4	5. What does *hecto* mean?	hundred	1 0
4	6. What does *kilo* mean?	thousand	1 0
		Total	

Measurement–Vocabulary

Grade	Target Words	Acceptable Responses	Score
1	1. heavy	having weight	1 0
1	2. heavier	having more weight	1 0
1	3. heaviest	having the most weight	1 0
1	4. light	having little weight	1 0
1	5. lighter	having less weight	1 0
1	6. lightest	having the least weight	1 0
1	7. weight	how heavy	1 0
1	8. full	contains the maximum	1 0
1	9. fuller	contains more	1 0
1	10. fullest	contains the most	1 0
1	11. empty	contains nothing	1 0
1	12. emptier	contains less	1 0
1	13. emptiest	contains the least	1 0
1	14. more	a greater amount	1 0
1	15. less	not as much	1 0
1	16. height	tallness; how tall something is; how far up	1 0
2	17. width	how far across; how broad something is	1 0
2	18. depth	how far down; distance from front to back	1 0
1	19. length	how long something is	1 0
1	20. distance	amount of space between two things	1 0
		Total	

Scoring Summary

Subtest	Total Correct		Total Possible	Percent Correct
Time	_____	÷	_____	= _____
Money	_____	÷	_____	= _____
Geometry	_____	÷	_____	= _____
Measurement–Vocabulary	_____	÷	_____	= _____
Measurement–Customary Units	_____	÷	_____	= _____
Measurement–Metric Units	_____	÷	_____	= _____

From K. W. Howell, S. H. Zucker, and M. K. Morehead (1982), *Multilevel Academic Skills Inventory*. H. & Z Publications, 6544 E. Meadowlark, Paradise Valley, AZ 85253. Reprinted with permission.

220

Exhibit 16.18*   Social Skills Status Sheet

Directions:

1. Only use this status sheet after:
   - the maladaptive behavior(s) has been specified
   - the function of behavior has been specified
   - the target behavior(s) has been specified
2. The sheet should be filled out through collaboration with people who know the student.
3. Each question should be answered.

If a student does not engage in the target behavior, ask yourself if . . .

	Status (Yes—No—Unsure)	
Type 1 (Do Behaviors)	Odd Items	Even Items
1. . . . the student can discriminate the target and maladaptive behaviors from each other and from other behaviors.	_____	
2. . . . target and maladaptive behaviors are clearly and consistently labeled and reviewed.		_____
3. . . . the student can monitor his own behavior well enough to know when he is engaging in the target or maladaptive behavior.	_____	
4. . . . the student is encouraged to reflect on his behavior and is praised for self-corrections and/or early recognition of problems.		_____
5. . . . the student can monitor the environment well enough to recognize events that should prompt the target behavior or inhibit the maladaptive behavior.	_____	
6. . . . cause and effect relationships between events in the environment and the student's behavior are clearly explained and reviewed.		_____
7. . . . the student knows what behavior is expected of him.	_____	
8. . . . expectations are clearly explained and/or demonstrated to the student (they are also frequently reviewed).		_____
9. . . . the student has the skills/knowledge to engage in the target behavior successfully.	_____	
10. . . . the student is taught how to engage in the target behavior.		_____
11. . . . the student knows the consequences of engaging in the target behavior.	_____	
12. . . . the student is taught the consequences of engaging in the target behavior.		_____
13. . . . the student knows the consequences of engaging in the maladaptive behavior.	_____	
14. . . . the student is taught the consequences of engaging in the maladaptive behavior.		_____
15. . . . the student understands that his behaviors cause certain consequences.	_____	
16. . . . the reasons for the reactions of others to the student's behavior are explained.		_____
17. . . . there are no corporal factors which militate against the target behavior and/or promote the maladaptive behavior (e.g., allergies or seizures).	_____	
18. . . . there are environmental factors which promote the target behavior and/or militate against the maladaptive behavior.		_____
18.1 . . . examples of the target behaviors are commonly found in the student's environment.		
18.2 . . . appropriate instruction occurs in the student's classroom.		
18.3 . . . appropriate management techniques are used in the classroom.		
19. . . . the student generates solutions to problems that include the target behavior.	_____	
20. . . . the student is taught to solve problems.		_____
21. . . . the student knows that a target behavior may become maladaptive, and that maladaptive behaviors may become targets, depending on the situation/context in which the student is functioning.	_____	
22. . . . the situational cues promoting various behaviors are identified and adequately taught to the student, along with skills for analyzing new situations.		_____

If a student does not engage in the target behavior ask yourself if . . .

	Status (Yes—No—Unsure)	
Type 2 (Select Behaviors)	Odd Items	Even Items
23. . . . the student considers the consequences of engaging in the target behavior to be rewarding.	_____	
24. . . . the advantages of the target behavior are taught for the student.		_____
25. . . . the student considers the consequences of engaging in the maladaptive behavior to be aversive.	_____	
26. . . . the disadvantages of the maladaptive behavior are taught to the student.		_____
27. . . . the student values the target behavior more than the maladaptive behavior.	_____	

221

Exhibit 16.18* *Social Skills Status Sheet (continued)*

Type 2 (Select Behaviors)	Status (Yes—No—Unsure)	
	Odd Items	Even Items
28. . . . the student is taught to consider how the target and maladaptive behaviors fit within the student's belief system.		_____
29. . . . the student holds beliefs which are compatible with the target behavior and incompatible with the maladaptive behavior.	_____	
30. . . . the student is taught to develop beliefs through the active application of hypothesis formation, hypothesis testing, and reflection. This instruction must include public thinking by an exemplar and stress the need for beliefs to be ''valid.''		_____
31. . . . the student maintains an adaptive explanatory style when attributing the causes of events.	_____	
32. . . . the student is taught to avoid permanent and persuasive attributions to external causes and/or internal abilities.		_____
33. . . . the student avoids errors in thinking when developing and employing belief systems.	_____	
34. . . . the student is taught to avoid errors in cognition, irrational thoughts and a helpless cognitive set.		_____

222

Exhibit 16.20* Thinking Error Summary

Directions:

1. During interviews or specific level testing for Type 2 prerequisites make a list of statements which seem to reflect errors in thinking.
2. Rate the errors under both the Explanatory Style and Cognitive Error categories.
3. Under the Explanatory style heading review the list of statements and select those which seem to relate to a positive or negative experience. Also list "absolute" statements.
4. You may categorize the same error under more than one heading.

Explanatory Style

List statements and mark the appropriate descriptors.

	Negative	Performance Oriented	Permanent	Pervasive	Personal
a.	☐	☐	☐	☐	☐
b.	☐	☐	☐	☐	☐
c.	☐	☐	☐	☐	☐
d.		☐	☐	☐	☐

Cognitive Errors

List statements and mark the appropriate descriptors.

a.

b.

c.

d.

Errors in Problem Solving

- ☐ Lack of knowledge
- ☐ Stereotyping
- ☐ Failure to define problem
- ☐ Defining problem too narrowly
- ☐ Lack of perspective
- ☐ Fear
- ☐ Premature resolution
- ☐ Insensitivity to probabilities
- ☐ Sample size
- ☐ Misconceptions of chance
- ☐ Unwarranted confidence
- ☐ Selective or incomplete search
- ☐ Mistaking correlation for cause
- ☐ Lack of supportive environment

Irrational Thoughts

- ☐ I must be good at everything I do and it's terrible if I'm not.
- ☐ Everybody I meet must like me and it's awful if they don't.
- ☐ If people do things to me that I don't like, they must be rotten.
- ☐ You can't trust (anyone over thirty).
- ☐ When things don't go my way, it's awful.
- ☐ Everyone should treat me fairly and it's awful if they don't.
- ☐ I have no control over what happens to me in my life.
- ☐ I shouldn't have to wait for anything I want.
- ☐ When something bad happens to me, I should [think about it all the time].
- ☐ Anyone who walks away from a fight is a punk.
- ☐ I must be stupid if I make mistakes.
- ☐ I always have to win and it's terrible if I don't.
- ☐ People should not have to do anything they don't want to do.
- ☐ School is dumb. You don't need to go to school.

Helpless Cognitive Set

- ☐ Something must be completed correctly in order for me to be a success.
- ☐ I should only pick easy things to do.
- ☐ If I fail it is because I am dumb.
- ☐ If I fail it is because the task is too hard.
- ☐ If I fail I should stop working because it means I have encountered a task that is too hard for me.

Exhibit 17.1* Status Sheet for Task Related Knowledge

Directions:
1. Use this status sheet with a group of people who work with the student.
2. Carefully describe the settings and tasks on which the status designations are based.
3. Give an overall designation for each of the principle skill areas by marking the appropriate box.
4. Check or circle all those descriptors which seem to apply to the student or setting.
5. Employ the indicated SLPs.

Part A: Topical Knowledge

	Y N ?	Additional Testing
The Student Has Required Prior Knowledge:	☐ ☐ ☐	SLP 1&2

Descriptors:
Has taken prerequisite classes
Received acceptable grades in prerequisite classes
Understands text and presentations
Knows topical vocabulary
Is familiar with related topics

Part B: Support Knowledge

B.1 Instructional Environment

	Y N ?	Additional Testing
The Student Has the Skill and Knowledge Needed to Learn in this Setting:	☐ ☐ ☐	SLP 3

Descriptors:
Instructional presentation OK
Classroom environment OK
Teaching expectations OK
Cognitive emphasis OK
Motivational strategies OK
Relevant practice OK
Academic engaged time OK
Informal feedback OK
Adaptive instruction OK
Progress evaluation OK
Instructional planning OK
Checks for student understanding OK

B.2 Study and Test-Taking Skills

	Y N ?	Additional Testing
Study and test-taking skills are adequate:		SLP 4
Before class:	☐ ☐ ☐	

Descriptors:
arrives on time
enters in a pleasant manner
brings materials to class
gets ready for learning

	Y N ?	
During class:	☐ ☐ ☐	

Descriptors:
follows classroom rules
listens carefully
works during class
asks for assistance
moves quickly to new activity

	Y N ?	
After class:	☐ ☐ ☐	

Descriptors:
takes materials home
completes homework
brings homework back

	Y N ?	
Organization:	☐ ☐ ☐	

Descriptors:
organization of materials (e.g., use of notebook or folders) OK
organization of time (e.g., use of calendar, scheduling work) OK
organization of content on paper (e.g., heading, margins) OK

	Y N ?	Additional Testing
Gaining information:	☐ ☐ ☐	SLP 4

Descriptors:
reading expository material OK
reading narrative material OK
gaining information from verbal presentations (lectures, demonstrations) OK

	Y N ?	
Demonstrating knowledge or skills:	☐ ☐ ☐	

Descriptors:
completing daily assignments OK
answering written questions OK
writing narrative and expository products OK
preparing for and taking tests OK

B.3 Problem Solving and Self-Monitoring

	Y N ?	Additional Testing
The Student's Problem Solving/Self-Monitoring Is Adequate:		SLP 5
The student recognizes problems:	☐ ☐ ☐	

Descriptors:
identifies goals
identifies obstacles
recognizes types of problems
anticipates problems

	Y N ?	
The student recognizes types of problems:	☐ ☐ ☐	

Descriptors:
identifies open system
identifies closed system

	Y N ?	
The student recognizes solution:	☐ ☐ ☐	

Descriptors:
generates options
considers resources
anticipates outcomes
selects solutions

	Y N ?	
The student plans:	☐ ☐ ☐	

Descriptors:
thinks before acting
explains what will happen
has intermediate goals
allocates time

	Y N ?	
The student works:	☐ ☐ ☐	

Descriptors:
follows plan
follows schedule

	Y N ?	
The student monitors and adjusts work:	☐ ☐ ☐	

Descriptors:
self-monitors
recognizes errors
uses "means-end" analysis
changes with feedback

B.4 Basic Strategies

	Y N ?	Additional Testing
The student uses selective attention:	☐ ☐ ☐	SLP 6

Descriptors:
focuses on relevant cues
ignores irrelevant cues
uses effective techniques to focus and maintain attention

	Y N ?	Additional Testing
The student uses recall/memory:	☐ ☐ ☐	SLP 6

Descriptors:
recalls information
uses effective techniques to store and recall material

	Y N ?	Additional Testing
The student uses motivation:	☐ ☐ ☐	SLP 6

Descriptors:
perseveres in the face of difficulty
perceives value of task
maintains an adaptive explanatory style (i.e. is not "learned helplessness")
indicates feelings of control
uses effective techniques to maintain motivation

Exhibit 17.4* Checklist for Study/Test Taking and Problem Solving/Self-Monitoring

		Know		Apply	
		Recognize	Explain	With prompts	Spontan-eously

Directions:
1. Designate skills passed in each column.
2. Start on the left and move right if skill is not passed.

B.2 Study and Test Taking/SLP 4

Before Class:
  arrive on time
  enter in a pleasant
    manner
  bring materials to class
  get ready for learning

During Class:
  follow classroom rules
  listen carefully
  work during class
  ask for assistance
  move quickly to new
    activity

After Class:
  take materials home
  complete homework
  bring homework back

Organization:
  organization of materials
    (e.g., use of notebook
    or folders)
  organization of time
    (e.g., use of calendar,
    scheduling work)
  organization of content
    on paper (e.g.,
    heading, margins)

Gaining information:
  reading expository
    material
  reading narrative
    material
  gaining information from
    verbal presentations
    (lectures,
    demonstrations)

**Demonstrating
Knowledge or Skills:**
  completing daily
    assignments
  answering written
    questions
  writing narrative and
    expository products
  preparing for and taking
    tests

B.3 Problem Solving/SLP 5

Recognize Problem

Identify Problem Type:
  open system
  closed system
  identify or develop
    solutions

Select Solutions:
  consider resources
  anticipate outcomes
  plan
  carry out plan
  monitor and adjust work

Exhibit 17.5* Basic Learning Strategies and a Sequence of Assistance

Directions:
1. Take sensitive measure(s) of skill.
2. Provide first level of assistance.
3. Retest and note improvement.
4. Repeat until sufficient improvement is achieved.

	1 Prompts	2 Directions	3 Practice	4 Lessons
Attention				
Memory				
Motivation				

Comprehension Maze Tests

This section contains eight maze tests and the answers to the tests. The test passages were written using words identified at each grade level in five best-selling basal-reading series. However, because the concept of "grade level" is so impractical you may want to carefully compare the passages to the text material your student needs to read.

These maze tests were constructed to provide opportunities for either semantic or syntactic errors. On the answer sheets the correct response is given in "**Bold**" print, the semantic foil is given in "CAPITAL" letters, and the syntactic foil is given in "lower case" letters. The authors gave these tests to 237 students from grades 1-8 and obtained the following error proportions. The students were predominantly Anglo and middle class. There were very few (if any) non-English speakers in the sample:

Comprehension Error Types

	Semantic	**Syntactic**
Total Sample	67%	33%
Grade 1	51%	49%
Grade 2	60%	40%
Grade 3	55%	45%
Grade 4	53%	47%
Grade 5	63%	37%
Grade 6	64%	36%
Grade 7	72%	28%
Grade 8	88%	12%

Exhibits 10.1* and 10.8* are useful when using these tests.

My New Animal

I'll tell you about my new animal. This animal is
blue and black and white. It does not have

_____. It does not have _____. It likes
tells, spots, doors   bad, fur, tail

to be _____ and free.
      outdoors, this, park

Sometimes this _____ wakes me up.
             likes, house, animal

It _____ be very loud. I _____ outside and
  is, can, to   look, like, along

see it. _____ is outside in the _____. It is
       Let, It, I   a, sun, food

outside in _____ snow.
      the, over, happy

This animal likes _____ talk to other animals.
          go, to, on

_____ likes trees. It likes _____ and
It, They, With   a, doors, food

bugs and bread.

_____ you know what it _____ yet? It
Do, Has, Mother   car, do, is

is a bird. The bird is called a blue-jay.

The Country and the City

People who live in the country are lucky. The
countryside is full of open fields and trees. Lots of
animals run _____ there. There are
          wild, left, window

rabbits _____ raccoons and even snakes.
         but, pink, and

_____ animals live on farms.
Nobody, Oh, Many

_____ can see cows and _____,
You, The, Always   horses, hurt, balloons

sheep and chickens there.

_____ spring comes, there
Across, When, Land

are _____ everywhere. The earth
    flowers, numbers, there

is _____ with wonderful things. Baby
   above, band, filled

_____ are born. The farms _____
animals, necks, lots   do, are, both

really busy. There are _____ jobs to do.
                       many, after, table

People _____ live in the city _____
       they, see, who   can, pets, are

lucky too. The city _____ filled with people.
                    is, knew, not

There _____ open places and parks
      are, almost, wake

_____ pretty gardens. It's fun _____
angry, with, on   to, with, lots

explore! The wild animals _____ kept in
                          line, are, things

the zoo. _____ can see elephants and
         You, Color, Act

_____ and snakes there.
monkeys, bedrooms, sleeps

(Continued)

229

People _____ animals at home too.
do, cake, have

_____ cats, birds, and fish _____
Dogs, Bags, Grows   all, two, breath

make good pets. People _____ some pets
blow, keep, apple

outdoors. Some _____ live indoors with
pets, bands, tonight

people.

_____ spring comes to
Anything, Loud, When

the _____, trees get their leaves.
pretty, city, floor

_____ and flowers in windows
Gardens, Buildings, Stay

_____ to grow. Children go _____
start, run, baby   asleep, but, outdoors

to play.

There are _____ things in the country
bus, wonderful, cut

_____ in the city. Country _____
and, with, zoo   trees, some, people

visit the city and _____ fun. City people
does, have, herself

visit the country and have fun. They all feel lucky

to live where they live!

230

News

Who writes what you read in the newspaper?

Reporters write stories about things that are happening in your city.

There are other reporters _____ live in other cities.
<u>among, newspapers, who</u>

_____ write about what is _____ in
<u>They, Extra, Squirrels</u>   <u>happening, message, pointing</u>

their cities.

A _____ who is far away _____ write a news
<u>city, reporter, that</u>   <u>did, can, business</u>

story _____ send it "over the _____". When you make a
<u>and, but, reporter</u>   <u>far, books, wire</u>

_____ call, your voice goes "_____ the wire."
<u>write, telephone, cooking</u>   <u>over, until, other</u>

The reporter's _____ is sent about the _____ way. The
<u>news, city, some</u>   <u>new, same, get</u>

telephone line _____ the signals.
<u>special, happens, carries</u>

Large machines _____ the signals. They type _____ the
<u>comic, receive, go</u>   <u>out, but, call</u>

story the reporter _____. You do not have _____ wait very
<u>everyone, lived, wrote</u>   <u>to, in, other</u>

long to _____ out what's happening anywhere _____ your world.
<u>find, write, in</u>   <u>wire, for, in</u>

Of course, _____ newspaper pays to get _____ "over
<u>your, dark, with</u>   <u>machine, news, around</u>

the wire."

Reporters _____ not the only people _____ write what you
<u>are, can, story</u>   <u>can, they, who</u>

read _____ the paper. Your friends _____ neighbors write
<u>in, before, news</u>   <u>some, for, and</u>

letters to _____ newspaper. These letters tell _____ those
<u>the, and, line</u>   <u>cities, what, every</u>

people think about _____ in the news. Some _____
<u>events, wires, pays</u>   <u>also, voices, letters</u>

are printed in the _____ so everyone can read
<u>newspaper, telephone, and</u>

_____. They are usually printed _____ a special page
<u>signals, them, pays</u>   <u>early, about, on</u>

called _____ editorial page.
<u>same, in, the</u>

(Continued)

LEVEL 3

What about _____ "funny papers"? Special writers _____

the, and, call   line, write, paper

and draw the comic _____. Newspapers buy their work

strips, telephones, answer

_____ that people will buy _____ newspaper.

in, wait, so   also, button, the

There are many _____ writers who work for _____

other, long, carries   the, on, everyone

newspaper. Some write about _____ or books or shows.

in, afternoons, movies

_____ write about cooking or _____. Some write

Some, Voices, Special   begin, bowls, gardening

about sports. Some even make up the crossword puzzles! Would you like

to write for a newspaper?

The Kids in Our Neighborhood...

The kids in our neighborhood had never organized a club before. That summer, we decided to have one.

Tom's parents said we _____ use their backyard for _____ meetings.
(could, took, never) / (being, animal, our)

As soon as _____ started warming up, we _____ a clubhouse there. We
(it, he, also) / (said, built, with)

_____ some old boards from _____ house that was being_____
(found, could, junk) / (could, into, a) / (walked, torn, ahead)

down. We discovered lots _____ other good junk there.
(of, if, aroma)

_____ we were finished. We _____ every afternoon, but
(Finally, Always, Atlas) / (answers, were, met)

we _____ figure out what to_____ next. Then someone said
(couldn't, there, organized) / (with, do, go)

_____ it would be nice _____ take a vacation together. _____
(that, clubhouse, every) / (to, for, parents) / (With, An, Found)

idea was born! Where _____ we go and how_____ we earn the money?
(are, would, club) / (by, were, could)

_____ answers weren't easy. First _____ had to decide where
(To, Near, The) / (we, meetings, roamed)

_____ vacation and how much _____ would cost. We talked_____ over and
(in, were, to) / (it, she, decided) / (it, her, easy)

finally decided _____ beach was the answer. _____ parents
(on, neighborhood, the) / (Someone's, Vacation, Lots)

would have to _____ us and we would _____ money for gas.
(summer, take, figure) / (need, finish, warm)

We _____ need money to stay _____. We asked Pat and
(said, with, might) / (apologized, overnight, apparent)

_____ to figure out how _____ money we needed. They're
(Mary, clubhouse, raining) / (much, easy, over)

_____ good in math.
(but, everyone, both)

With _____ regular summer jobs already _____, the rest of us
(in, the, horn) / (taken, warmed, under)

_____ to figure out how _____ raise that money. Finally, _____
(easy, might, had) / (to, on, beach) / (clubhouse, someone, figure)

had an idea. What _____ a neighborhood newsletter? We _____ charge for
(about, with, take) / (also, did, could)

ads. If _____ charged more to buy _____ newsletter than it cost_____
(we, idea, stay) / (onto, the, afternoon) / (to, in, will)

make, we'd make money! _____ could write interesting stuff._____
(Money, Everybody, Decide) / (And, The, Our)

everyone could sell the _____ and deliver them.
(together, junk, newsletters)

Was it a success? We all had a great time at the beach.

LEVEL 4

233

Sheepdog

Thousands of sheep are lost to predators every year. Sheep are grazing animals. They often must be _____ to roam quite some _____
                                                          (sheep, left, poisoned)   (long, are, distance)
from shelter.

Farmers have _____ to help their sheep _____ several ways.
              (predators, tried, heard)   (in, because, new)
Some hunt _____ and other predators. Some _____ used to
           (shelter, coyotes, well)   (sheep, go, farmers)
use poisoned _____ to kill predators. Most _____ bait has
              (hunt, farmers, bait)   (poisoned, grazing, around)
now been _____. Some farmers put up _____ fences to keep
          (to, outlawed, walked)   (electric, roaming, train)
predators _____, but this is very _____.
           (but, often, out)   (gone, also, expensive)

Scientists are trying to _____ of new methods that _____
                          (think, bait, year)   (coyotes, help, farmers)
might use. One of _____ new methods is really _____ very old one.
                   (their, because, used)   (a, to, new)
Guard _____ are now being trained _____ used to help protect
       (shelters, dogs, expensive)   (and, but, farm)
_____.
(move, sheep, ways)

Guard dogs usually have _____ be imported from other _____.
                         (not, over, to)   (countries, dogs, tries)
Guard dogs are not _____ same as herding dogs. _____ dogs,
                    (but, now, the)   (Herding, Predator, About)
such as border _____, move sheep from place _____ place. They
                (outlawed, sheep, collies)   (guard, to, but)
also keep _____ from straying away from _____ flock. Herding
           (now, sheep, farmers)   (the, away, and)
dogs are _____ with the flock only _____ the farmer wants
          (expensive, lost, usually)   (when, but, near)
to _____ the sheep.
   (put, dog, move)

(Continued)

Guard dogs, _____ the other hand, are _____ the sheep
           but, on, new   method, because, with

all the _____. They do not control _____ flock, but they do
     time, about, control   dog, the, around

_____ intruders. Most guard dogs _____ European breeds. The
control, keep, bait   are, flock, do

Komondor _____ from Hungary and the _____ Pyrenees Dog from
       farmer, uses, Dog   Great, control, often

the _____ between France and Spain _____ two examples.
    also, mountains, electricity   are, can, sheep

Most guard _____ are long-tailed and _____. Each
      mountains, over, dogs   sheltered, scientists, floppy-eared

will grow to _____ weight of about one _____ pounds.
      around, very, a   hundred, expensive, but

Usually, all a _____ dog has to do _____ to scare predators away
      guard, lost, grow   will, is, never

_____ its barking. If they have to, guard dogs will fight to protect their
around, place, with

sheep. They are strong and sure fighters who do not often lose.

235

Soapmaking

Soap was first made from animal fats, oils, and the lye from burnt wood ashes.

The ancient Romans may have been the first people to use what we call soap. There

was a place _____ outside the city of _____. There animals were
near, just, growing   France, old, Rome

killed _____ burned as sacrifices to _____ gods. When it rained, _____ fat
but, and, almost   the, a, tell   in, snow, the

from the animals _____ the burnt wood ashes _____ carried downhill
but, wolves, and   were, had, never

to a _____. Many people washed their _____ at that
riverbank, mountain, talk   automobiles, astounded, clothes

riverbank. They _____ it was easier to _____ their clothes
claimed, soapmaking, imported   transfer, get, usually

clean there.

_____ centuries passed before crude _____ cakes were made
Several, Business, About   were, downhill, soap

and _____. By that time, someone _____ thought of adding perfume
sold, planted, easier   could, with, had

_____ soap. Usually, only the _____ could afford to buy _____ soap
under, to, bought   animals, rich, very   the, killed, in

cakes.

Soap was _____ in America too. Settlers _____ fat and grease
used, eaten, clothes   became, and, used

from _____ and boiled them with _____ ashes. Bacon grease,
passing, only, cooking   wood, river, bake

tallow _____ sheep, and lard all _____ their way into
because, Roman, from   washed, found, with

that _____ bar of soap.
will, homemade, outside

Later _____ became a big business. _____ different plant
soapmaking, sold, claiming   Many, With, Washed

oils were _____ to be used in _____. Coconut oil,
planted, lard, imported   soapmaking, purchase, burning

palm oil, _____ cottonseed oil were added _____ improve the soap.
but, and, both   to, price, also

Today _____ large companies are our _____ soapmakers.
several, made, easier   ashes', tallow, country's

Each company makes _____ different kinds of soap, _____ as
but, cooking, many   such, improve, however

soap for doing _____, soap for dishwashing, soap _____ bathing, and
laundry, sell, oil   beside, grease, for

soap for _____. All the companies advertise _____ each
shampooing, into, carrying   but, and, imported

company says their _____ are the best. Millions of pounds of soap are
riverbanks, soaps, advertised

sold every year. What would great-grandmother think of that?

Maples

Over one hundred species of maple trees can be found in the northern hemisphere, including several which are native to North America. One of the most widely recognized North American varieties is the sugar maple.

The sugar maple was _____ surprise to colonists who _____ in the
                      a, sugar, but   boiled, location, settled

New England _____. They learned from native _____ how to obtain
            yellow, native, area   Americans, five, Lakes

sap _____ the tree and process _____ to produce sugar.
    with, rise, from   it, them, with

When _____ sent news of _____ process to England,
     they, prominent, she   eastern, this, learn

scientists _____ that a major discovery _____ been made.
           surmised, remained, foliage   did, native, had

The sugar _____ is a prominent part _____ the landscape,
          maple, widely, England   with, news, of

particularly in _____. The foliage turns a _____ yellow or
                Scientists, for, autumn   brilliant, hemisphere, several

orange flushed _____ red. Sugar maples can _____ found from the
               with, are, of   do, be, three

eastern _____ of the United States _____ Canada west through
        discovery, in, edge   but, and, prominent

Minnesota, _____ southward through northeastern Texas. _____ most
           then, with, when   The, By, Red

common location for _____ of sugar maples is _____ England, the
                    diameters, found, groves   One, Foliage, New

Appalachian mountains, _____ the Lakes states.
                       evaporate, and, from

Sugar _____ can range from sixty _____ eighty feet in
      maples, woody, States   to, location, for

height, _____ a diameter of two _____ three feet. Most maples _____ popular
        but, is with   with, sappy, to   go, are, for

as shade trees, _____ their wood is also _____ used in making
                but, in, tree   widely, easterly, keep

fine _____ and hardwood flooring.
     trees, recognize, furniture

Modern _____ has taken some of _____ romance out of
       colonist, equipment, locate   the, by, evaporated

the _____ process. However, _____ old-timers remain to keep
    sending, sugaring, are   enough, foliage, fresh

the _____ rhythmically dripping into old-fashioned _____ buckets.
    flooring, used, sap   brilliant, sugaring, above

The sap is then taken by sled to the boiling house where it is evaporated. The fragrance of wood smoke still rises from boiling houses, and some of the hot syrup is still poured onto fresh snow for a delicious instant taffy.

Indoor Plants

Many plants will grow indoors if the proper conditions exist. Plants must have the right soil, neither too acid nor too alkaline, and pots which permit them to grow. They must also have _____ light.
however, humid, adequate

Plants vary in _____ much light they require _____ what type of
how, children, other   *and, but, protect*

soil _____ prefer. Most plants thrive _____ located by a
you, they, with   *when, as, foliage*

window. _____ people use special fluorescent _____ to
Permit, Acid, Some   *climates, propagate, lights*

encourage their plants _____ grow.
to, inexpensive, for

Most plants that _____ grown indoors were originally _____ of the
is, special, are   *soils, natives, healthy*

jungle, and _____ are accustomed to warm, _____ climates. Sudden
if, they, we   *humid, frigid, breathe*

changes in _____ conditions are bad for _____ whether
inserting, jungle, growing   *plants, greenhouses, thrive*

they're use to _____ jungle or not. If _____ purchase a plant
a, in, common   *thrive, you, sails*

from _____ greenhouse, where it's been _____ a warm, humid
between, diseased, a   *in, redecorated, but*

environment, _____ transfer it to a _____ garage, it will
and, therefore, ingest   *lighted, provide, frigid*

certainly _____.
suffer, prefer, indoors

Plants in windowsills can _____ protected somewhat during
encourage, literally, be

the _____ weather by inserting newspaper _____ the plants and
condition, cold, adequate   *between, in, used*

the _____. Otherwise, plant leaves may _____ and drop off
garage, special, glass   *die, start, however*

from _____ cold temperatures.
extremely, cause, provided

There are _____ problems in raising houseplants. _____ are
neither, other, beside   *Insects, Easily, Windowsills*

attracted to them _____ can cause plant diseases. _____ common
hut, varieties, and   *Pat, Right, Some*

houseplants (for instance, _____) are poisonous and
diffenbachia, greenhouse, inserted

can _____ dangerous to pets or _____ if certain parts of _____
is, climates, be   *children, lights, therefore*   *very, the, on*

plant are ingested.

(Continued)

Like _____ plants, houseplants breathe in _____ dioxide and
human, all, diseases   extremely, drop, carbon

emit oxygen, _____ healthy houseplants can be _____ for people by
if, purchase, so   healthy, with, sudden

literally _____ good air to breathe. Houseplants are also a relatively
providing, whoever, cutting

inexpensive way to redecorate a room. Once started, many common varieties, such as

philodendron, can easily be propagated from cuttings.

MAZE ANSWERS

Level 1
My New Animal

1. tells, **spots**, DOORS
2. bad, **fur**, TAIL
3. **outdoors**, this, PARK
4. likes, HOUSE, **animal**
5. IS, **can**, to
6. **look**, LIKE, along
7. Let, **It**, I
8. a, **sun**, FOOD
9. **the**, OVER, happy
10. go, **to**, ON
11. **It**, THEY, With
12. a, DOORS, **food**
13. **Do**, HAS, Mother
14. car, DO, **is**

Level 2
The Country and the City

1. **wild**, LEFT, window
2. BUT, pink, **and**
3. NOBODY, Oh, **Many**
4. **You**, The, ALWAYS
5. **horses**, hurt, BALLOONS
6. ACROSS, **When**, Land
7. **flowers**, NUMBERS, there
8. ABOVE, band, **filled**
9. **animals**, NECKS, lots
10. DO, **are**, both
11. **many**, AFTER, table
12. THEY, see, **who**
13. CAN, pets, **are**
14. **is**, KNEW, hot
15. **are**, almost, WAKE
16. angry, **with**, ON
17. **to**, WITH, lots
18. LINE, **are**, things
19. **You**, COLOR, Act
20. **monkeys**, bedrooms, SLEEPS
21. DO, cake, **have**
22. **Dogs**, BAGS, Grows
23. **all**, TWO, breath
24. BLOW, **keep**, apple
25. **pets**, BANDS, tonight
26. Anything, LOUD, **When**
27. pretty, **city**, FLOOR
28. **gardens**, BUILDINGS, stay
29. **start**, RUN, baby
30. ASLEEP, but, **outdoors**
31. BUS, **wonderful**, cut
32. **and**, WITH, zoo
33. TREES, some, **people**
34. DOES, **have**, herself

Level 3
News

1. among, NEWSPAPERS, **who**
2. **They**, Extra, SQUIRRELS
3. **happening**, message, POINTING
4. CITY, **reporter**, that
5. DID, **can**, business
6. **and**, BUT, reporter
7. far, BOOKS, **wire**
8. write, **telephone**, COOKING
9. **over**, UNTIL, other
10. **news**, CITY, some
11. NEW, **same**, get
12. special, HAPPENS, **carries**
13. comic, **receive**, GO
14. **out**, BUT, call
15. everyone, LIVED, **wrote**
16. **to**, IN, other
17. **find**, WRITE, in
18. wire, FOR, **in**
19. **your**, DARK, with
20. MACHINE, **news**, around
21. **are**, CAN, story
22. can, THEY, **who**
23. **In**, BEFORE, news
24. some, FOR, **and**
25. **the**, AND, line
26. cities, **what**, EVERY
27. **events**, WIRES, pays
28. also, VOICES, **letters**
29. **newspaper**, TELEPHONE, and
30. SIGNALS, **them**, pays
31. early, ABOUT, **on**
32. same, IN, **the**
33. **the**, AND, call
34. LINE, **write**, paper
35. **strips**, TELEPHONES, answer
36. IN, wait, **so**
37. ALSO, button, **the**
38. **other**, LONG, carries
39. **the**, ON, everyone
40. in, AFTERNOONS, **movies**
41. **Some**, VOICES, Special
42. **begin**, bowls, GARDENING

240

MAZE ANSWERS

Level 4
The Kids in our Neighborhood

1. **could**, TOOK, never
2. being, ANIMAL, **our**
3. **It**, HE, also
4. SAID, **built**, with
5. **found**, COULD, junk
6. could, INTO, **a**
7. WALKED, **torn**, ahead
8. **of**, IF, aroma
9. **Finally**, ALWAYS, Atlas
10. answers, WERE, **met**
11. **couldn't**, there, ORGANIZED
12. with, **do**, GO
13. **that**, CLUBHOUSE, every
14. **to**, FOR, parents
15. WITH, **An**, Found
16. ARE, **would**, club
17. by, WERE, **could**
18. TO, Near, **The**
19. **we**, MEETINGS, roamed
20. IN, were, **to**
21. **It**, SHE, decided
22. **It**, HER, easy
23. ON, neighborhood, **the**
24. **Someone's**, VACATION, Lots
25. Summer, **take**, FIGURE
26. **need**, FINISH, warm
27. SAID, with, **might**
28. apologized, **overnight**, APPARENT
29. **Mary**, CLUBHOUSE, raining
30. **much**, EASY, over
31. BUT, everyone, **both**
32. IN, **the**, horn
33. **taken**, WARMED, under
34. easy, MIGHT, **had**
35. **to**, ON, beach
36. CLUBHOUSE, **someone**, figure
37. **about**, WITH, take
38. also, DID, **could**
39. **we**, IDEA, stay
40. ONTO, **the**, afternoon
41. **to**, IN, will
42. MONEY, **Everybody**, Decide
43. **And**, THE, Our
44. together, JUNK, **newsletters**

Level 5
Sheepdog

1. sheep, **left**, POISONED
2. LONG, are, **distance**
3. predators, **tried**, HEARD
4. **in**, BECAUSE, new
5. SHELTER, **coyotes**, well
6. SHEEP, go, **farmers**
7. hunt, FARMERS, **bait**
8. **poisoned**, GRAZING, around
9. to, **outlawed**, WALKED
10. **electric**, ROAMING, train
11. but, OFTEN, **out**
12. gone, ALSO, **expensive**
13. **think**, BAIT, year
14. COYOTES, help, **farmers**
15. **their**, because, USED
16. **a**, TO, new
17. SHELTERS, **dogs**, expensive
18. **and**, BUT, farm
19. move, **sheep**, WAYS
20. not, OVER, **to**
21. **countries**, DOGS, tries
22. BUT, now, **the**
23. **Herding**, PREDATOR, About
24. outlawed, SHEEP, **collies**
25. guard, **to**, BUT
26. now, **sheep**, FARMERS
27. **the**, away, AND
28. EXPENSIVE, lost, **usually**
29. **when**, but, NEAR
30. PUT, dog, **move**
31. BUT, **on**, new
32. method, BECAUSE, **with**
33. **time**, about, CONTROL
34. dog, **the**, AROUND
35. **control**, KEEP, bait
36. **are**, flock, DO
37. FARMER, uses, **Dog**
38. **Great**, control, OFTEN
39. also, **mountains**, ELECTRICITY
40. **are**, CAN, sheep
41. MOUNTAINS, over, **dogs**
42. SHELTERED, scientists, **floppy-eared**
43. AROUND, very, **a**
44. **hundred**, EXPENSIVE, but
45. **guard**, LOST, grow
46. WILL, **is**, never
47. AROUND, place, **with**

MAZE ANSWERS

Level 6
Soapmaking

1. NEAR, **just**, growing
2. FRANCE, old, **Rome**
3. BUT, **and**, almost
4. **the**, A, tell
5. IN, snow, **the**
6. BUT, wolves, **and**
7. were, HAD, never
8. **riverbank**, MOUNTAIN, talk
9. AUTOMOBILES, astounded, **clothes**
10. **claimed**, soapmaking, IMPORTED
11. TRANSFER, **get**, usually
12. **Several**, BUSINESS, About
13. were, DOWNHILL, **soap**
14. **sold**, PLANTED, easier
15. COULD, with, **had**
16. UNDER, **to**, bought
17. ANIMALS, **rich**, very
18. **the**, killed, IN
19. **used**, EATEN, clothes
20. BECAME, and, **used**
21. PASSING, only, **cooking**
22. **wood**, RIVER, bake
23. BECAUSE, Roman, **from**
24. WASHED, **found**, with
25. will, **homemade**, OUTSIDE
26. **soapmaking**, sold, CLAIMING
27. **Many**, With, WASHED
28. PLANTED, lard, **imported**
29. **soapmaking**, sold, CLAIMING
30. BUT, **and**, both
31. **to**, price, ALSO
32. **several**, made, EASIER
33. ASHES', tallow, **country's**
34. but, COOKING, **many**
35. **such**, improve, HOWEVER
36. **laundry**, sell, OIL
37. BESIDE, grease, **for**
38. **shampooing**, into, CARRYING
39. BUT, **and**, imported
40. RIVERBANKS, **soaps**, advertised

Level 7
Maples

1. **a**, sugar, BUT
2. BOILED, location, **settled**
3. YELLOW, native, **area**
4. **Americans**, five, LAKES
5. WITH, rise, **from**
6. **It**, THEM, with
7. **they**, prominent, SHE
9. EASTERN, **this**, learn
9. **surmised**, REMAINED, foliage
10. DID, native, **had**
11. **Maple**, widely, ENGLAND
12. WITH, news, **of**
13. SCIENTISTS, for, **Autumn**
14. **brilliant**, HEMISPHERE, several
15. **with**, are, OF
16. DO, **be**, three
17. DISCOVERY, in, **edge**
18. BUT, **and**, prominent
19. **then**, WITH, when
20. **The**, BY, Red
21. DIAMETERS, found, **groves**
22. ONE, Foliage, **New**
23. evaporate, **and**, FROM
24. **Maples**, woody, STATES
25. **to**, location, FOR
26. BUT, is, **with**
27. WITH, sappy, **to**
28. GO, **are**, for
29. **but**, IN, tree
30. **widely**, EASTERLY, keep
31. TREES, recognize, **furniture**
32. COLONIST, **equipment**, locate
33. **the**, BY, evaporated
34. SENDING, **sugaring**, are
35. **timers**, to, SYRUPS
36. FLOORING, used, **sap**
37. **fashioned**, houses, HUNDRED

Level 8
Indoor Plants

1. however, HUMID, **adequate**
2. **how**, children, OTHER
3. and, BUT, protect
4. YOU, **they**, with
5. **when**, AS, foliage
6. Permit, ACID, **Some**
7. CLIMATES, propagate, **lights**
8. **to**, inexpensive, FOR
9. IS, special, **are**
10. SOILS, **natives**, healthy
11. if, **they**, WE
12. **humid**, FRIGID, breathe
13. INSERTING, jungle, **growing**
14. **plants**, GREENHOUSES, thrive
15. **a**, IN, common
16. thrive, **you**, SAILS
17. BETWEEN, diseased, **a**
18. **in**, redecorated, BUT
19. **and**, THEREFORE, ingest
20. LIGHTED, provide, **frigid**
21. **suffer**, PREFER, indoors
22. ENCOURAGE, literally, **be**
23. condition, **cold**, ADEQUATE
24. **between**, IN, used
25. GARAGE, special, **glass**
26. **die**, START, however
27. **extremely**, cause, PROVIDED
28. NEITHER, **other**, beside
29. **Insects**, Easily, WINDOWSILLS
30. HUT, varieties, **and**
31. Pat, RIGHT, **Some**
32. **diffenbachia**, GREENHOUSE, inserted
33. IS, climates, **be**
34. **children**, LIGHTS, therefore
35. very, **the**, ON
36. HUMAN, **all**, diseases
37. EXTREMELY, drop, **carbon**
38. IF, purchase, **so**
39. **healthy**, with, SUDDEN
40. **providing**, whoever, CUTTING

242

Decoding Tests

This section contains eight reading passages. These are the ones students will read. You will need to make examiner copies for scoring. Do this by counting the words in the passage and writing the cumulative total at the end of each line. Next place a black triangle on each examiner passage to mark the 100th word in the passage. The triangle will make it easy to determine accuracy because, when the student reaches this mark, you only need to count the number of mistakes prior to it to obtain the proportion of errors. When you make scoring copies of the passages be sure to enlarge them so you will have room to write in the student's errors.

The passages were written using words identified at each grade level in five best selling basal reading series. However, because the concept of "grade level" is so impractical you may want to compare these passages to the text material your student needs to read. Another option is to select pages from classroom materials.

Exhibits 11.3*, 11.5*, 11.6*, 11.7* and 11.8* will be of great use when evaluating decoding. They are reproduced at the first of part B.

One Day a Mouse . . .

One day a mouse came to our house. She was in a box. That box was her home. She ate there and went to sleep there. She was a little mouse with a little house.

A cat lives at our house too. The cat saw the mouse. He sat still. He did not move. The mouse did not run. The cat looked hard at the mouse. "I will eat you mouse," the cat was thinking.

The mouse was thinking too. "I see you, cat, and you are bad news!"

I took the mouse to my room. No more cats for this mouse!

Party for Ben

Last Sunday afternoon, there was a party for Ben. First, Mom baked a big cake. She fixed something for us to drink and we put the food in a pretty basket. We put in some balloons too. Ben likes balloons. Then I got Ben and we were ready to go!

We walked to a place with big trees all around. It was a forest, I think. We looked and looked. At last, we found a nice spot with green grass. Ben rested and we fixed a place for the party.

Mom poured some milk for me. I blew up a big red balloon for Ben. We sang "Happy Birthday" with loud, funny voices. We ate white cake with dark icing and it was good! Then Mom asked some crazy riddles. I told her some riddles from school. We laughed and played some more games.

Then it was time for Ben's presents. Mom gave him a new blanket with soft insides. I gave him a new blue hat and lots of balloons. We both gave him birthday hugs.

We walked home happy. Ben was happy too, but he was tired. I put him on the bed upstairs. That bear had some birthday!

Cookies

Yesterday, we had just settled down to a good game of checkers. Then Pete said he was hungry for cookies. "Not just any cookies, good cookies," he said.

So there we were. I was just getting ready to do my famous triple jump and this guy gets hungry for cookies. "Okay," I said, "let's go look."

Looking for something to eat with Pete is an experience. You would normally look in a cookie jar or in a cupboard for cookies, right? Pete looks in the freezer first. I guess it makes sense. I mean, people usually freeze things in quantity. And Pete is a quantity eater.

Next, we looked in the oven. Pete always hopes that something will be left in the oven.

I suggested that we might take a look in the cupboard. If there's a pack of Fig Newtons or a box of graham crackers to be had, it's usually in the cupboard. A careful search revealed no cookies.

My family does not own a cookie jar, so that left us with no place to search next. Pete had that look in his eye. He was getting ready to say, "I'm going home to get something to eat." I could see my chance at a triple jump was ready to walk out the door.

"Wait," I yelled. Pete froze in his tracks. "Have you ever heard of applesauce wonders?" I asked. "They're just delicious!"

I ignored his funny look and grabbed the jar of applesauce.

"Makes my mouth water just to think about them," I said. I spread the applesauce on a handy soda cracker. I pushed a marshmallow on top of the whole thing and shoved. it into Pete's mouth. Now Pete asks for "applesauce wonders" everytime he comes to my house.

LEVEL 3

Chess

Chess was first played in China, India, and Persia. When armies invaded these countries, they learned the game of chess. They brought the game with them wherever their battles took them.

When the game finally reached Europe, the pieces were given the names they have today. The knight, the bishop, the king, the queen, and the rook (or castle) were all part of European life at that time. That's probably how the pieces got their names.

The object of the game is to win. All pieces are used to protect the king. If a player loses his king, he has lost the game.

Chess is played on a chess board which is set up in squares of two colors. Each piece is allowed to move a certain way. Some pieces can only move forward. Some pieces can only move diagonally. Pieces are moved in order to capture the other player's pieces. Or they can be used to protect a more valuable piece, like the king.

Each player has a full set of pieces. One player has the white pieces. One player has the black pieces. It doesn't matter how many pieces are captured. What matters is whether the king is lost.

Thinking ahead is the key to playing good chess. A player must know each piece and how it can move on the board.

Each player must study the way the other player moves. Then, if that player makes a mistake, the first player is ready to capture his king!

Olympic Games

In ancient times, the Greeks held a series of games every four years. These games tested athletic skill. They came to be known as the Olympic games. They were held at a place called Olympia.

The Olympic games were an important part of life in Greece. The Greeks said they wanted "a healthy mind in a healthy body."

Today these games attract athletes from all over the world. Having a modern version of the games was the idea of one man. His name was Baron Pierre de Coubertin and he was a French nobleman.

The site of the ancient games was discovered when he was a young man. It must have given him an idea that stayed with him a long time. He traveled all over the world. He noticed that young athletes were alike no matter what country they were from. So, in 1892, he presented a plan for the modern Olympic games to the Athletic Sports Union of France.

The idea was not accepted at first. But he did not give up. He wrote letters. He began to prepare for the International Athletic Congress meeting in 1894. He got countries like the United States and England and Sweden to back his plan. When it came time to hold the meeting, he was ready.

His plan was accepted. The first modern Olympic games were planned for 1896 in Athens, Greece. "A healthy mind in a healthy body" could be a goal for athletes all over the world.

Praying Mantis

The praying mantis is a strange insect. Some people say it looks funny or weird. Others say it's a terrifying monster. The mantis is different. A full-grown mantis looks like a pale green stick almost as big as your hand. It has goggle eyes and can swivel its head to watch something.

That something is usually the insect it's about to eat. The praying mantis eats other insects. Mantises even eat each other. If they're very hungry, they will even eat themselves. This habit of eating everything in sight has led some people to call them monsters.

Like all insects, the praying mantis has three pairs of legs. The two rear pairs are used only for walking. The front legs are also used as arms. They have sharp spines and hooks on them.

This insect is a great hunter. It attaches itself to a blade of grass or a twig. Then it waits patiently for some other insect to come into view. The mantis cannot hear and has no voice, but its eyesight is excellent. Once it sees its pray, it inches slowly toward its victim. Then it rears up on its hind legs and grabs the victim with its front legs.

After eating, the mantis wipes its claws and uses them to clean its face.

Adult mantises die each autumn. But hundreds of mantis eggs are left in special egg cases attached to rocks and twigs. In spring, the baby mantises start the cycle again.

Mantises can be helpful. Insect pests are always a problem for gardeners. Some gardeners do not like to use sprays to kill bugs, so they buy baby mantises to eat the bugs.

LEVEL 6

Bottle

Imagine there's a message for you in a bottle, bobbing about in the ocean. It's hard to figure the odds against that message ever reaching you. Scientists work with such odds every day. They dispatch many messages in special bottles as part of their study of ocean currents.

The water in the ocean follows certain pathways called currents. Generally, a ship following the currents will arrive at its destination much faster than a ship traveling in a straight line. In fact, that's how ocean currents were discovered.

More than two thousand years ago, the Greeks studied currents. They released bottles from their shoreline and tried to study where they went.

Centuries later, American Benjamin Franklin became interested in currents. After hearing sea captains tell of great "Rivers" within the ocean, Franklin began throwing bottles into the sea. He put messages inside with instructions for the finders to write and tell him where and when the bottles were found. Using this method, Franklin charted the Gulf Stream, one of the most powerful currents in the Atlantic Ocean.

Why do scientists still study currents? Changes in currents affect fishing activities and climate as well as shipping. Scientists prevent problems by tracking and predicting changes in currents. Many methods are used to study currents. Specially weighted and sealed bottles, like the mysterious message bottles of old, are just one method scientists use.

May

It is alleged that the merry month of May was named after Maia, the ancient Roman goddess of spring. The traditional celebration of May Day might well have originated in the Roman civilization.

During the Middle Ages, English villagers and townspeople celebrated May Day by erecting a Maypole. They attached gaily colored streamers to the Maypole, then proceeded to feast and dance around it. The English may also have established the tradition of crowning a pretty girl Queen of the May.

When colonists immigrated to America, they brought May Day customs with them. Some religious groups considered the May festival to be pagan and sinful, but the traditions survived; and today schoolchildren often create May baskets full of candy and seasonal flowers to leave at the doorsteps of their friends. In many contemporary towns and cities, attractive young women and men are still elected May royalty.

All this celebration of May occurs because the sun ascends higher and higher during May. Daytime temperatures will go up about ten degrees Fahrenheit in temperate latitudes. Even at high elevations, where snow can still be several feet deep, warmer temperatures cause melting and a few hardy plants poke through the snow and slush.

May is a period of changes, and the first day of May is a signal that those changes are about to commence. How will you choose a way to commemorate May?

You could consider talking with your parents, grandparents, and older friends to discuss how May was celebrated when they were younger. You can even investigate May customs in other cultures and foreign countries. Then create your own individual way to celebrate May!

Mathematics Tests

This section contains the following tests:

1. Addition facts

2. Subtraction facts

3. Multiplication facts

4. Division facts

5. Addition survey

6. Subtraction survey

7. Multiplication survey

8. Division survey

9. Fraction survey

10. Decimal/ratio/percent survey

11. Application survey

It also contains a sheet for determining the significance of computation errors.

The answers to these tests are found in the text on pages 343-351. The items are cross-referenced to the objectives and analysis grid in appendix C.

Exhibits 15.6*, 15.10*, 15.14* and 15.15*, which are used with these tests, are reproduced at the first of this part of the workbook.

Test 1

Add 1m

$$\begin{array}{r}16\\+2\\\hline\end{array}\qquad\begin{array}{r}8\\+4\\\hline\end{array}\qquad\begin{array}{r}8\\+11\\\hline\end{array}\qquad\begin{array}{r}7\\+13\\\hline\end{array}\qquad\begin{array}{r}8\\+5\\\hline\end{array}\qquad\begin{array}{r}10\\+10\\\hline\end{array}$$

$$\begin{array}{r}20\\+0\\\hline\end{array}\qquad\begin{array}{r}11\\+9\\\hline\end{array}\qquad\begin{array}{r}6\\+9\\\hline\end{array}\qquad\begin{array}{r}0\\+19\\\hline\end{array}\qquad\begin{array}{r}20\\+0\\\hline\end{array}\qquad\begin{array}{r}5\\+6\\\hline\end{array}$$

$$\begin{array}{r}7\\+2\\\hline\end{array}\qquad\begin{array}{r}15\\+4\\\hline\end{array}\qquad\begin{array}{r}14\\+5\\\hline\end{array}\qquad\begin{array}{r}5\\+1\\\hline\end{array}\qquad\begin{array}{r}3\\+15\\\hline\end{array}\qquad\begin{array}{r}18\\+2\\\hline\end{array}$$

$$\begin{array}{r}12\\+6\\\hline\end{array}\qquad\begin{array}{r}17\\+2\\\hline\end{array}\qquad\begin{array}{r}1\\+8\\\hline\end{array}\qquad\begin{array}{r}13\\+7\\\hline\end{array}\qquad\begin{array}{r}0\\+20\\\hline\end{array}\qquad\begin{array}{r}10\\+10\\\hline\end{array}\qquad\begin{array}{r}6\\+12\\\hline\end{array}$$

$$\begin{array}{r}9\\+1\\\hline\end{array}\qquad\begin{array}{r}8\\+5\\\hline\end{array}\qquad\begin{array}{r}2\\+4\\\hline\end{array}\qquad\begin{array}{r}3\\+17\\\hline\end{array}\qquad\begin{array}{r}1\\+13\\\hline\end{array}\qquad\begin{array}{r}9\\+1\\\hline\end{array}$$

$$\begin{array}{r}1\\+8\\\hline\end{array}\qquad\begin{array}{r}1\\+6\\\hline\end{array}\qquad\begin{array}{r}19\\+0\\\hline\end{array}\qquad\begin{array}{r}4\\+5\\\hline\end{array}\qquad\begin{array}{r}14\\+5\\\hline\end{array}\qquad\begin{array}{r}16\\+2\\\hline\end{array}$$

$$\begin{array}{r}2\\+18\\\hline\end{array}\qquad\begin{array}{r}3\\+17\\\hline\end{array}\qquad\begin{array}{r}1\\+6\\\hline\end{array}\qquad\begin{array}{r}1\\+8\\\hline\end{array}\qquad\begin{array}{r}18\\+1\\\hline\end{array}\qquad\begin{array}{r}8\\+0\\\hline\end{array}\qquad\begin{array}{r}7\\+11\\\hline\end{array}$$

$$\begin{array}{r}0\\+10\\\hline\end{array}\qquad\begin{array}{r}3\\+3\\\hline\end{array}\qquad\begin{array}{r}10\\+11\\\hline\end{array}\qquad\begin{array}{r}5\\+2\\\hline\end{array}\qquad\begin{array}{r}19\\+1\\\hline\end{array}\qquad\begin{array}{r}4\\+1\\\hline\end{array}$$

$$\begin{array}{r}15\\+5\\\hline\end{array}\qquad\begin{array}{r}4\\+16\\\hline\end{array}\qquad\begin{array}{r}4\\+7\\\hline\end{array}\qquad\begin{array}{r}2\\+3\\\hline\end{array}\qquad\begin{array}{r}19\\+5\\\hline\end{array}\qquad\begin{array}{r}2\\+17\\\hline\end{array}$$

$$\begin{array}{r}9\\+7\\\hline\end{array}\qquad\begin{array}{r}2\\+5\\\hline\end{array}\qquad\begin{array}{r}14\\+3\\\hline\end{array}\qquad\begin{array}{r}12\\+5\\\hline\end{array}\qquad\begin{array}{r}7\\+2\\\hline\end{array}\qquad\begin{array}{r}6\\+3\\\hline\end{array}$$

$$\begin{array}{r}3\\+6\\\hline\end{array}\qquad\begin{array}{r}10\\+10\\\hline\end{array}\qquad\begin{array}{r}14\\+3\\\hline\end{array}\qquad\begin{array}{r}9\\+0\\\hline\end{array}\qquad\begin{array}{r}12\\+4\\\hline\end{array}\qquad\begin{array}{r}0\\+9\\\hline\end{array}$$

$$\begin{array}{r}17\\+1\\\hline\end{array}\qquad\begin{array}{r}4\\+5\\\hline\end{array}\qquad\begin{array}{r}1\\+19\\\hline\end{array}\qquad\begin{array}{r}2\\+9\\\hline\end{array}\qquad\begin{array}{r}14\\+3\\\hline\end{array}$$

Subtraction problems (drill worksheet):

12 −10	2 −2	19 −5	6 −5	16 −7	3 −3	13 −6	1 −1	20 −9	10 −8	15 −9	4 −1	11 −8	0 −0
7 −3	17 −12	10 −9	15 −4	9 −6	13 −8	5 −2	19 −13	8 −1	14 −3	7 −5	13 −11	6 −5	14 −9
17 −14	1 −0	20 −8	0 −0	18 −11	9 −2	20 −10	4 −4	12 −10	2 −1	20 −16	3 −2	15 −13	8 −4
3 −1	18 −10	9 −2	13 −3	5 −2	11 −10	7 −2	15 −12	10 −6	17 −5	7 −7	12 −8	1 −1	19 −12
12 −8	2 −0	16 −12	3 −0	16 −4	4 −3	14 −3	0 −0	18 −10	5 −5	11 −7	6 −0	16 −9	8 −3
4 −1	15 −3	0 −0	20 −12	8 −4	17 −6	2 −1	18 −13	9 −6	19 −7	6 −2	14 −3	0 −0	11 −1
16 −9	5 −3	13 −2	10 −0	18 −6	9 −2	15 −3	7 −1	12 −2	6 −3	11 −0	5 −5	17 −2	2 −0

Subt 1m

Test 2

7 ×7	2 ×10	3 ×5	4 ×4	0 ×0	3 ×1
9 ×10	5 ×5	9 ×4	1 ×0	5 ×1	5 ×3
8 ×5	3 ×4	4 ×0	9 ×1	8 ×3	1 ×7
6 ×4	5 ×0	6 ×1	7 ×3	2 ×7	4 ×2
7 ×0	4 ×1	9 ×3	8 ×7	5 ×2	4 ×9
1 ×1	2 ×3	5 ×7	9 ×2	1 ×9	8 ×8
0 ×3	6 ×7	6 ×2	6 ×9	3 ×8	9 ×6
4 ×7	7 ×2	3 ×9	2 ×8	7 ×6	7 ×10
2 ×2	9 ×9	7 ×8	6 ×6	5 ×10	9 ×5
8 ×9	6 ×8	4 ×6	0 ×10	6 ×5	7 ×4
5 ×8	3 ×6	1 ×10	7 ×5	5 ×4	3 ×0
1 ×6	8 ×10	3 ×5	4 ×4	6 ×0	2 ×1

5)25	3)30	1)9	10)90	9)27	8)24	2)16	6)18	7)14	4)8
4)36	5)45	3)27	1)10	10)50	9)18	8)48	2)18	6)24	7)7
7)49	4)4	5)35	3)21	1)2	10)30	9)36	8)56	2)20	6)30
6)48	7)63	4)20	5)40	3)15	1)4	10)40	9)63	8)32	2)0
2)2	6)60	7)56	4)16	5)20	3)9	1)3	10)80	9)45	8)72
8)0	2)8	6)54	7)42	4)40	5)15	3)18	1)6	10)70	9)90
9)9	8)64	2)6	6)6	7)35	4)32	5)10	3)24	1)5	10)20
5)0	9)54	8)40	2)10	6)0	7)21	4)24	5)5	3)12	1)8
1)1	5)30	9)81	8)16	2)14	6)6	7)28	4)28	5)50	3)6

Div 1m

Test 4

$$\begin{array}{r} 0 \\ +3 \\ \hline \end{array}$$

$$\begin{array}{r} 1 \\ +0 \\ \hline \end{array}$$

$$\begin{array}{r} 5 \\ +6 \\ \hline \end{array}$$

$$\begin{array}{r} 13 \\ +6 \\ \hline \end{array}$$

$$\begin{array}{r} 8 \\ +7 \\ \hline \end{array}$$

$$\begin{array}{r} 32 \\ +8 \\ \hline \end{array}$$

$$\begin{array}{r} 43 \\ +5 \\ \hline \end{array}$$

$$\begin{array}{r} 64 \\ +2 \\ \hline \end{array}$$

$$\begin{array}{r} 9 \\ 3 \\ +4 \\ \hline \end{array}$$

$$\begin{array}{r} 7 \\ 2 \\ +2 \\ \hline \end{array}$$

$$\begin{array}{r} 18 \\ +96 \\ \hline \end{array}$$

$$\begin{array}{r} 22 \\ +53 \\ \hline \end{array}$$

$$\begin{array}{r} 70 \\ +19 \\ \hline \end{array}$$

$$\begin{array}{r} 31 \\ +24 \\ \hline \end{array}$$

$$\begin{array}{r} 47 \\ 9 \\ + \\ \hline \end{array}$$

$$\begin{array}{r} 283 \\ 21 \\ +2764 \\ \hline \end{array}$$

$$\begin{array}{r} 4020 \\ +689 \\ \hline \end{array}$$

$$\begin{array}{r} 569 \\ 201 \\ +877 \\ \hline \end{array}$$

$$\begin{array}{r} 48 \\ +37 \\ \hline \end{array}$$

$$\begin{array}{r} 95 \\ +25 \\ \hline \end{array}$$

257

$$\begin{array}{r} 19 \\ -\ 2 \\ \hline \end{array} \qquad \begin{array}{r} 14 \\ -\ 5 \\ \hline \end{array} \qquad \begin{array}{r} 10 \\ -\ 4 \\ \hline \end{array} \qquad \begin{array}{r} 16 \\ -\ 7 \\ \hline \end{array} \qquad \begin{array}{r} 3 \\ -2 \\ \hline \end{array}$$

$$\begin{array}{r} 80 \\ -\ 5 \\ \hline \end{array} \qquad \begin{array}{r} 60 \\ -60 \\ \hline \end{array} \qquad \begin{array}{r} 40 \\ -30 \\ \hline \end{array} \qquad \begin{array}{r} 50 \\ -10 \\ \hline \end{array} \qquad \begin{array}{r} 68 \\ -\ 5 \\ \hline \end{array}$$

$$\begin{array}{r} 46 \\ -13 \\ \hline \end{array} \qquad \begin{array}{r} 58 \\ -23 \\ \hline \end{array} \qquad \begin{array}{r} 93 \\ -61 \\ \hline \end{array} \qquad \begin{array}{r} 63 \\ -\ 9 \\ \hline \end{array} \qquad \begin{array}{r} 23 \\ -\ 6 \\ \hline \end{array}$$

$$\begin{array}{r} 5906 \\ -\ 248 \\ \hline \end{array} \qquad \begin{array}{r} 400 \\ -165 \\ \hline \end{array} \qquad \begin{array}{r} 8942 \\ -5961 \\ \hline \end{array} \qquad \begin{array}{r} 64 \\ -27 \\ \hline \end{array} \qquad \begin{array}{r} 53 \\ -29 \\ \hline \end{array}$$

$$2 \times 6$$

$$9 \times 5$$

$$\begin{array}{r} 8 \\ \times 3 \\ \hline \end{array}$$

$$\begin{array}{r} 64 \\ \times 7 \\ \hline \end{array}$$

$$\begin{array}{r} 24 \\ \times 3 \\ \hline \end{array}$$

$$\begin{array}{r} 91 \\ \times 1 \\ \hline \end{array}$$

$$\begin{array}{r} 18 \\ \times 9 \\ \hline \end{array}$$

$$\begin{array}{r} 22 \\ \times 86 \\ \hline \end{array}$$

$$\begin{array}{r} 85 \\ \times 63 \\ \hline \end{array}$$

$$194 \times 10 =$$

$$3 \times 1000 =$$

$$100 \times 74 =$$

$$\begin{array}{r} 102 \\ \times 40 \\ \hline \end{array}$$

$$\begin{array}{r} 40 \\ \times 31 \\ \hline \end{array}$$

$$\begin{array}{r} 7005 \\ \times 26 \\ \hline \end{array}$$

$$\begin{array}{r} 87 \\ \times 25 \\ \hline \end{array}$$

$$\begin{array}{r} 215 \\ \times 48 \\ \hline \end{array}$$

$$\begin{array}{r} 5684 \\ \times 39 \\ \hline \end{array}$$

$$5^2 =$$

$$12^2 =$$

259

$2\overline{)4}$

$7\overline{)56}$

$9\overline{)54}$

$8\overline{)32}$

$3\overline{)72}$

$5\overline{)80}$

$7\overline{)91}$

$5\overline{)23}$

$9\overline{)37}$

$7\overline{)169}$

$58\overline{)1209}$

$100\overline{)4200}$

$10\overline{)1260}$

$1\overline{)48}$

$8\overline{)8500}$

$31\overline{)1307}$

$15\overline{)306}$

$\sqrt{4}$

$\sqrt{121}$

$$1 = \frac{}{10}$$

$$\frac{2}{8} =$$

$$\frac{7}{3} =$$

$$\frac{1}{8} + \frac{3}{8} =$$

$$14\frac{8}{9} + 5\frac{5}{9} =$$

$$\frac{7}{12} + \frac{1}{3} =$$

$$\frac{3}{13} + \frac{1}{3} =$$

$$\frac{3}{4} - \frac{2}{11} =$$

$$\begin{array}{r} 1\frac{7}{10} \\ +2\frac{5}{6} \\ \hline \end{array}$$

$$\begin{array}{r} 4\frac{2}{7} \\ +6\frac{3}{5} \\ \hline \end{array}$$

$$\frac{5}{8} \times \frac{3}{4} =$$

$$\frac{2}{3} \times \frac{1}{6} =$$

$$\frac{3}{14} \times \frac{1}{1} =$$

$$12\frac{3}{8} \times 4\frac{5}{6} =$$

$$4\frac{1}{3} \times 7\frac{1}{2} =$$

$$\frac{2}{5} \div \frac{4}{9} =$$

$$\frac{3}{4} \div \frac{5}{7} =$$

$$11 \div \frac{1}{2} =$$

$$4 \div \frac{1}{7} =$$

$$8\frac{5}{8} \div 1\frac{1}{6} =$$

$$7\frac{1}{3} \div 2\frac{3}{4} =$$

Convert to %

$.016 =$ _____ %

Convert to %

$.7 =$ _____ %

Convert to %

$\dfrac{3}{5} =$ _____ %

$\dfrac{5}{8} = .$ _ _ _

Convert to %

$\dfrac{2}{8} =$ _____ %

$\begin{array}{r} 16.2 \\ \times\ .40 \\ \hline \end{array}$

$\begin{array}{r} 6.021 \\ +51.30 \\ \hline \end{array}$

$1.2\overline{)\,.72}$

Convert to fraction

$26\% =$ _____

$\begin{array}{r} 813 \\ -13.9 \\ \hline \end{array}$

$2.01\overline{)\,.603}$

Complete ratio

$2:8 = 4:$ _____

$\dfrac{4}{9} = .$ _ _ _

Convert to fraction

$40\% =$ _____

$\begin{array}{r} 90.5 \\ -1.68 \\ \hline \end{array}$

$\begin{array}{r} 2.96 \\ \times\ .06 \\ \hline \end{array}$

$\begin{array}{r} .042 \\ \times\ .306 \\ \hline \end{array}$

Complete ratio

_____ $:3 = 3:9$

Round to nearest tenth

$.5096 =$

Round to nearest hundredth

$.1694 =$

262

Practice Item A

Bud has 2 toy airplanes. Sis gives him 3 more. How many airplanes does Bud have all together?

a. $\begin{array}{r} 2 \\ -3 \\ \hline \end{array}$

b. $\begin{array}{r} 4 \\ \times 8 \\ \hline \end{array}$

c. $\begin{array}{r} 10 \\ \times 6 \\ \hline \end{array}$

d. $\begin{array}{r} 3 \\ +2 \\ \hline \end{array}$

Practice Item B

Jon has 10 comic books. Joe gives him 5 more. Jon sells 1. How many does Jon have left?

a. $\begin{array}{r} 10 \\ -1 \\ \hline \end{array}$ $\begin{array}{r} 5 \\ +1 \\ \hline \end{array}$

b. $\begin{array}{r} 10 \\ -5 \\ \hline \end{array}$

c. $\begin{array}{r} 10 \\ +5 \\ \hline \end{array}$ $\begin{array}{r} 15 \\ -1 \\ \hline \end{array}$

d. $\begin{array}{r} 10 \\ \times 5 \\ \hline \end{array}$ $1\overline{)50}$

Practice Item C

Ed has 8 toy cars. He gives 2 to Ray. How many does he have left?

a. 6

b. 16

c. 4

d. 10

Practice Item D

Kim has 6 music books. She gives 4 to Lori and 1 to Linda. How many does she have left?

a. 11

b. 1

c. 24

d. 3

1. There are 12 red apples and 2 green apples. How many apples are there all together?

   a. $2 - 12 =$

   b. $2 + 12 =$

   c. $12 \times 2 =$

   d. $12 \div 2 =$

2. 45 children are standing up. 9 children sit down. How many children are left standing?

   a. $45 \div 9 =$

   b. $45 + 9 =$

   c. $9 \times 45 =$

   d. $45 - 9 =$

3. There are ten rows of desks. There are seven desks in each row. How many desks are there all together?

   a. $\begin{array}{r} 10 \\ -7 \\ \hline \end{array}$

   b. $\begin{array}{r} 10 \\ +7 \\ \hline \end{array}$

   c. $\begin{array}{r} 10 \\ \times 7 \\ \hline \end{array}$

   d. $10 + 7$

4. 5 boxes contain 500 tacks. How many tacks are in each box?

   a. $500 \div 5$

   b. 500×5

   c. $500 - 5$

   d. $500 + 5$

263

264

5. There are 40 students. 25% of the students have blue eyes. How many have blue eyes?

a.
```
  40
+ .25
```

b.
```
    _____
.25 ) 40
```

c.
```
  40
- .25
```

d.
```
  40
× .25
```

6. Colleen has 2 crayfish and Gary has 4 crayfish for the science project. On Tuesday, Albert brings them three more. On Wednesday, Robin brings them 5. How many crayfish do they have?

a.
```
 2    6
+4   +5
```

b.
```
 4    8       ____
×2   ×5     3 ) 40
```

c.
```
 4    6
+2   -5
```

d.
```
 2    6    9
+4   +3   +5
```

7. There are 40 desks in the 4th grade classroom. 2 desks are loaned to the 3rd grade classroom, 5 desks are loaned to the 6th grade classroom. How many desks are left in the 4th grade classroom?

a.
```
 40   38
- 2   - 5
```

b.
```
 40   42
+ 2   + 5
```

c.
```
 40   36   34   29   24
- 4   - 2   - 3   - 5   - 6
```

d.
```
 40   36   33
- 4   - 3   - 6
```

8. There are 4 packages of pencils. Each package contains 5 pencils. There are 8 students, and three are boys. The pencils are to be divided equally among the girls. How many pencils will each girl get?

a.
```
 4    8       ____
×5   ×3    20 ) 24
```

b.
```
 4    8       ____
×5   -3     5 ) 20
```

c.
```
 5    8       ____
-4   +3     1 ) 11
```

d.
```
 5         ____
×4       8 ) 20
```

9. There are 30 pairs of scissors in the box. 10 are broken. Fifteen new pairs are given to the class. There are 5 art tables in the room. How many pairs of scissors that are not broken will each table get?

a.
```
 15    30     5        ____
-10   +15   +45     5 ) 50
```

b.
```
 30         ____
+10       5 ) 40
```

c.
```
 30    20    35
-10   +15   × 5
```

d.
```
 30    20       ____
-10   +15     5 ) 35
```

10. 2% of the students were absent on Tuesday. 20% of those present brought a sack lunch and 75% of those present bought a hot lunch. The rest of the students fixed a lunch in their classroom. What percent of the students in school fixed a lunch in their classroom?

a.
```
  20%   100%
+ 75%   - 95%
```

b.
```
   2%
  20%   100%
+ 75%   - 97%
```

c.
```
  .20    .20
× .02   × .75
```

d.
```
  75%   100%
× 20%   - 15%
```

11. There are 11 girls and 4 boys. How many *children* are there all together?

   a. 14

   b. 44

   c. 15

   d. 7

12. There are 42 pencils in a box. 7 pencils are given away. How many pencils are left?

   a. 49

   b. 6

   c. 294

   d. 35

13. There are 5 children on each team. There are 11 teams. How many children are there all together?

   a. 55

   b. 16

   c. 6

   d. 555

14. Students put the marbles from six packages into a jar. There were four hundred eighty marbles. How many marbles were there in each package?

   a. 486

   b. 474

   c. 80

   d. 2880

15. 1/3 of the 45 chairs are blue. How many blue chairs are there?

   a. 90

   b. 30

   c. 25

   d. 15

16. Herb had two pencils. Eleanor gave him 6 more pencils in the afternoon. The next day Jean gave him one pencil and Marilyn gave him two. How many pencils did Herb have?

   a. 11

   b. 6

   c. 8

   d. 5

265

266

17. There are 25 lemons and 30 apples. Ten of the apples are large. There are 5 people. How many small apples will each person get if the small apples are shared equally?

   a. 20

   b. 6

   c. 4

   d. 11

18. Jack drank 1 glass of milk at each meal for 5 meals. Kathy drank 2 glasses of milk at each meal for 6 meals. Maggie drank 4 glasses of milk at each meal for 5 meals. All together, how many more glasses of milk did Kathy drink than Jack?

   a. 7

   b. 12

   c. 2

   d. 37

19. There are 138 red pencils and 162 blue pencils. There are 6 packages of paper with 200 sheets in each package. If the pencils and paper are divided equally, how many pencils and how many sheets of paper will 150 students receive?

   a. 2 pencils, 1 sheet of paper

   b. 2 pencils, 8 sheets of paper

   c. 8 pencils, 2 sheets of paper

   d. 20 pencils, 80 sheets of paper

20. There are 60 students in the band. 10% of the students are in the drum section. 1/2 of the drummers need new drums. How many students need new drums?

   a. 6

   b. 30

   c. 20

   d. 3

21. Lizzie went to the feed-and-grain store to buy food for her goat. She bought 2 sacks of grain for fifteen dollars. What was the price of one sack of grain?

   a. $15.00
         + 2.

   b. $15.00
         × 2

   c. $15.00
         − 2.

   d.   2)$15.00

22. Chris borrowed a five dollar bill from Donald. On the way to the zoo, he bought two sandwiches and three drinks. The price of one drink was $.45. The price of one sandwich was $1.25. How much change did Chris receive from the five dollar bill?

   a. $1.25 $1.00
      + .45   + .80

   b. $.45 $1.25 $2.50 $5.00
     × 3   × 2   + 1.35   − 3.85

   c. $1.25 $5.00   3 $6.00
     + .45   − 1.70   ×2   − 3.30

   d. $.45 $1.25 $ .90 $5.00
     × 2   × 3   + 3.75   − 4.65

23. Margo needs $45.00 to fix her bicycle. She earned $20.00. How much more money does she need?

   a. $25.00

   b. $15.00

   c. $65.00

   d. $ 2.25

24. Kenneth has five dollars in change. It costs a quarter to play a video game. How many games can he play if he saves half of his money for lunch?

   a.   50

   b.   25

   c.   10

   d.   100

25. It was 27°C when Gabby got up in the morning. By the time she walked to school, it was 31°C. How many degrees warmer had it gotten?

   a.
$$\begin{array}{r} 27° \\ +31° \\ \hline \end{array}$$

   b.
$$\begin{array}{r} 31° \\ -27° \\ \hline \end{array}$$

   c.
$$\begin{array}{r} 27° \\ \times 31° \\ \hline \end{array}$$

   d. $27° \overline{)31°}$

26. It was 72°F when Gabby got up in the morning. By the time she walked to school, it was 91°F. How many degrees warmer had it gotten?

   a.
$$\begin{array}{r} 72° \\ +91° \\ \hline \end{array}$$

   b.
$$\begin{array}{r} 91° \\ -72° \\ \hline \end{array}$$

   c.
$$\begin{array}{r} 72° \\ \times 91° \\ \hline \end{array}$$

   d. $72° \overline{)91°}$

27. Kim writes 3 new songs in January. During the rest of the year, she writes 2 songs a month. How many songs does she write a year?

   a.
$$\begin{array}{r} 1 \\ \times 3 \\ \hline \end{array} \quad \begin{array}{r} 3 \\ \times 2 \\ \hline \end{array} \quad \begin{array}{r} 6 \\ +0 \\ \hline \end{array}$$

   b.
$$\begin{array}{r} 12 \\ -1 \\ \hline \end{array} \quad \begin{array}{r} 11 \\ \times 2 \\ \hline \end{array} \quad \begin{array}{r} 3 \\ +22 \\ \hline \end{array}$$

   c.
$$\begin{array}{r} 8 \\ -1 \\ \hline \end{array} \quad \begin{array}{r} 7 \\ +3 \\ \hline \end{array} \quad \begin{array}{r} 10 \\ +0 \\ \hline \end{array}$$

   d.
$$\begin{array}{r} 14 \\ -1 \\ \hline \end{array} \quad \begin{array}{r} 13 \\ \times 2 \\ \hline \end{array} \quad \begin{array}{r} 26 \\ +3 \\ \hline \end{array}$$

28. Fred and Paula hiked to the Sapphire Mine with the Scouts. It was 9:30 in the morning when they started. The hike took two hours. What time was it when they arrived?

   a.   7:30 A.M.

   b.   11:30 A.M.

   c.   11:30 P.M.

   d.   11:00 A.M.

267

29. Mary typed for 1 hr. and 30 min. on Thursday, 7 hrs. and 45 min. on Fri. and 4 hrs. and 45 min. on Sat. She rested for 20 minutes after she finished typing on Saturday. How many hours did she type?

a. 13 hr. 40 min.

b. 13 hr. 20 min.

c. 14 hr.

d. 12 hr. 140 min.

30. Eddie runs four kilometers each day. How many kilometers does he run in twelve days?

a. $\begin{array}{r} 12 \\ \times\ 4 \\ \hline \end{array}$

b. $4\overline{)12}$

c. $\begin{array}{r} 12 \\ -\ 4 \\ \hline \end{array}$

d. 1 km = $\begin{array}{r} 100 \\ \times\ 4 \\ \hline \end{array}$

31. Katie was teaching Cliff and John how to fish. They wanted to catch 20 kg of trout for dinner for their friends. Cliff caught a fish which weighed 1100 g. John caught a fish which weighed 896 g. How many more g. of fish do they need to catch?

a. $\begin{array}{r} 1100 \\ +\ 896 \\ \hline \end{array}$ 1 kg = $\begin{array}{r} 1000 \\ \times\ 20 \\ \hline \end{array}$ $\begin{array}{r} 20000 \\ -\ 1996 \\ \hline \end{array}$

b. $\begin{array}{r} 1100 \\ +\ 896 \\ \hline \end{array}$ $\begin{array}{r} 1996 \\ -\ 20 \\ \hline \end{array}$

c. $\begin{array}{r} 1100 \\ +\ 896 \\ \hline \end{array}$ $\begin{array}{r} 1996 \\ +\ 20 \\ \hline \end{array}$

d. $\begin{array}{r} 1100 \\ +\ 896 \\ \hline \end{array}$ 1 kg = $\begin{array}{r} 100 \\ \times\ 20 \\ \hline \end{array}$ $\begin{array}{r} 2000 \\ -\ 1996 \\ \hline \end{array}$

32. Kama had 45 centimeters of ribbon. She wanted to cut it into 3 equal lengths. How long would each length be?

a. 42 cm

b. 135 cm

c. 15 cm

d. 55 cm

33. It takes two liters of huckleberries to make a cobbler. Bobbi picked one liter of huckleberries in the morning. Amy picked 750 ml the same day. How much must Jennifer and Joy pick together before there is enough to make a cobbler?

a. $\begin{array}{r} 750\ ml \\ +\ 1 \\ \hline \end{array}$ $\begin{array}{r} 751\ ml \\ \times\ 2 \\ \hline \end{array}$

b. $\begin{array}{r} 750\ ml \\ \times\ 1 \\ \hline \end{array}$ $\begin{array}{r} 750\ ml \\ +\ 2 \\ \hline \end{array}$

c. 1 liter = $\begin{array}{r} 1000 \\ +\ 750 \\ \hline \end{array}$ 1000 ml × 2 = $\begin{array}{r} 2000 \\ -1750 \\ \hline \end{array}$

d. 1 liter = $\begin{array}{r} 100 \\ +\ 750 \\ \hline \end{array}$ 100 ml × 2 = $\begin{array}{r} 1750 \\ -\ 200 \\ \hline \end{array}$

34. Eddie runs four miles each day. How many miles does he run in twelve days?

a. $\begin{array}{r} 12 \\ \times\ 4 \\ \hline \end{array}$

b. $4\overline{)12}$

c. $\begin{array}{r} 12 \\ -\ 4 \\ \hline \end{array}$

d. 1 m = $\begin{array}{r} 5280 \\ \times\ 4 \\ \hline \end{array}$ $\begin{array}{r} 21120 \\ \times\ 12 \\ \hline \end{array}$

35. Katie was teaching Cliff and John how to fish. They wanted to catch 20 lb. of trout for dinner for their friends. Cliff caught a fish which weighed 110 oz. John caught a fish which weighed 89 oz. How many more oz. of fish do they have to catch?

a.
```
  110   1 lb = 16    320
+  89          ×20  -199
```

b.
```
  110        199
+  89    -    20
```

c.
```
  110        199
+  89    +    20
```

d.
```
  110   1 lb = 20    199
+  89          × 8  -160
```

36. Karna had 45 inches of ribbon. She wanted to cut it into 3 equal lengths. How long would each length be?

a. 42 in

b. 135 in

c. 15 in

d. 48 in

37. It takes two quarts of huckleberries to make a cobbler. Bobbi picked one quart of huckleberries in the morning. Amy picked one pt. the same day. How much must Jennifer and Joy pick together before there is enough to make a cobbler?

a. 4 pt.

b. 3 pt.

c. 1 pt.

d. 5 pt.

38. Connie Ann is marking the edges of a square field with chalk. Each of the four edges of this square field measures 32 meters. How many meters will Connie Ann walk if she marks each side?

a.
```
  32
+  4
```

b.
```
  32
×  4
```

c.
```
      ____
   4 )32
```

d.
```
  32
-  4
```

39. Ellen is buying carpet for the living room in her new house. The living room is 18 feet by 20 feet. The dining room is 8 feet by 12 feet. She knows that there are 9 square feet in one square yard. How many square yards of carpet does she need for the living room?

a.
```
  18   12    38
+20   + 8   +20
              ____
            9 )58
```

b.
```
  18   20    36
× 2   × 2   +40
              ____
            9 )76
```

c.
```
  18
+20
      ____
   9 )38
```

d.
```
  18
×20
      ____
   9 )360
```

40. Matthew and Randy varnished a floor that was 4 meters by 6 meters. They knew that the formula for surface area was length times width. What was the surface area they painted?

a. 10 square meters

b. 24 square meters

c. 20 square meters

d. 2 square meters

269

41. Howard is going to put a wire fence around a vegetable garden beside his house. He is putting another wire fence around a chicken yard behind his house. The vegetable garden is 3 meters by 2 meters and the chicken yard is 2 meters by 4 meters. The fence is sold by the meter. How many meters does he need?

a. 14

b. 48

c. 120

d. 22

42. Margaret and Mary Alice were going to fix a place for an ant colony to live. They decided to fill a glass tank with sand. The tank was 30 cm high, 20 cm wide and 40 centimeters long. They know that the formula for volume is length x width x height. What was the volume of the tank?

a. 1 m =   100 × 40 × 20 × 30 =

b. 30 + 20 + 40 =

c.   40   800
       ×20   × 30
       ————   ————   2400 ÷ 3 =

d. 40 × 20 × 30 =

43. Alvin and Joyce have 2 gardens which are shaped like a triangle. The base of each is 8 meters and the height is 10 meters. The fence is 2 meters high. What is the area of the two gardens?

a. $\frac{1}{2}$ × 8 × 2 =   8 × 10 =

b. $\frac{1}{2}$ × 8 × 10 =   40 × 2 =

c. 8 × 2 = $\frac{1}{2}$ (16) × 10 =

d. 8 × 2 =   2 × 16 × 10 =

44. Darin wanted to find the circumference of a circle. He knew that the formula for the circumference of a circle is π d. He found that the diameter of the circle was 10 cm and he knew that π = 3.14. What was the circumference of the circle?

a. 13.14 cm

b. 6.86 cm

c. 31.4 cm

d. 314.0 cm

45. A paper cone is twelve cm high and ten cm across the top. How many cubic cm of fruit flavored silvered ice would two cones contain if they were filled only to the top?

a. 3768 cubic centimeters

b. 314 cubic centimeters

c. 628 cubic centimeters

d. 60 cubic centimeters

270

Directions: All items on the survey tests are listed below. They are matched to objectives found in Appendix C of the text. The curriculum level at which each item is commonly taught is listed next to it (you will wish to change these if they are different at your school). If the student is currently assigned to a curriculum level at or above the level of a problem, then he/she is expected to pass it. Regardless of curriclum level, if the student has received instruction on an objective, he/she is also expected to pass it. Mark all items which you expect the student to pass with an X in the "Expected Pass" column before you give the test. Mark all items the student passed with an X in the "Pass" column. Mark any discrepancy between expected and actual performance with an X in the "Discrepancy" column. Total the discrepancies and transfer this total to the students IEP and/or record book. Specific-level testing may be required for objectives on which a discrepancy is noted.

DECIMALS, RATIOS, PERCENTS					
OBJECTIVE	ITEM	CURRICULUM LEVEL	EXPECTED PASS	PASS	DISCREPANCY
11a	20	8			
11a	19	8			
10a	18	8			
10a	17	8			
9a	16	7			
9a	15	7			
8a	14	7			
8a	13	7			
8a	12	7			
7a	11	7			
7a	10	7			
7a	9	7			
6a	8	8			
6a	7	8			
5a	6	8			
5a	5	8			
4a	4	8			
4a	3	8			
3a	2	7			
3a	1	7			

			FRACTIONS			
OBJECTIVE	ITEM	CURRICULUM LEVEL	EXPECTED PASS	PASS	DISCREPANCY
24a	21	6			
24a	20	6			
23a	19	6			
23a	18	6			
22a	17	6			
22a	16	6			
20a	15	6			
20a	14	6			
19a	13	6			
19a	12	6			
19a	11	6			
18a	10	6			
18a	9	6			
17a	8	6			
17a	7	6			
16a	6	6			
14a	5	6			
13a	4	5			
9a	3	5			
8a	2	5			
4a	1	5			

		DIVISION			
OBJECTIVE	ITEM	CURRICULUM LEVEL	EXPECTED PASS	PASS	DISCREPANCY
7a	20	8			
7a	19	8			
6a	18	5			
6a	17	5			
6a	16	5			
5a	15	5			
5a	14	5			
5a	13	5			
4a	12	5			
4a	11	4			
3a	10	4			
3a	9	4			
2a	8	4			
2a	7	4			
2a	6	4			
1a	5	4			
1a	4	4			
1a	3	4			
1a	2	4			
1a	1	4			

			MULTIPLICATION		
OBJECTIVE	ITEM	CURRICULUM LEVEL	EXPECTED PASS	PASS	DISCREPANCY
8a	20	8			
8a	19	8			
7a	18	5			
7a	17	4			
7a	16	4			
6a	15	5			
6a	14	4			
6a	13	4			
5a	12	5			
5a	11	5			
5a	10	5			
4a	9	4			
4a	8	4			
3a	7	4			
2a	6	4			
2a	5	4			
2a	4	4			
1a	3	4			
1a	2	4			
1a	1	4			

SUBTRACTION

OBJECTIVE	ITEM	CURRICULUM LEVEL	EXPECTED PASS	PASS	DISCREPANCY
7a	20	4			
7a	19	4			
7a	18	4			
6a	17	3			
6a	16	3			
5a	15	2			
5a	14	2			
5a	13	2			
4a	12	2			
4a	11	2			
4a	10	2			
3a	9	2			
3a	8	2			
3a	7	2			
2a	6	2			
1a	5	1			
1a	4	1			
1a	3	1			
1a	2	1			
1a	1	1			

ADDITION					
OBJECTIVE	ITEM	CURRICULUM LEVEL	EXPECTED PASS	PASS	DISCREPANCY
8a	20	4			
8a	19	4			
8a	18	3			
7a	17	3			
7a	16	3			
7a	15	3			
6a	14	2			
6a	13	2			
6a	12	2			
5a	11	2			
5a	10	2			
4a	9	2			
4a	8	2			
3a	7	2			
3a	6	2			
2a	5	1			
2a	4	1			
1a	3	1			
1a	2	1			
1a	1	1			

Content Vocabulary Tests

For Task-related Knowledge

These tests cover vocabulary from four domains. For every domain there are three tests at each of these levels: primary (grades 1 & 2), intermediate (grades 3-5), and advanced (grades 6-8). The primary tests are given individually and require the student to say the answer. The other tests are multiple-choice and the student marks the answers. The words on the tests were drawn from an analysis of textbooks. Words were selected if they appeared in several sources.

Performance criteria for these tests will have to be established locally, although a big difference in a student's score in one domain as opposed to the others may also be of interest.

All of the tests are supplied in the next few pages. The questions for the oral tests are presented first followed by the eight written tests, and then the answer key for the written tests. The correct answers for the oral tests are supplied with the questions.

Allow at least five minutes for each of the multiple choice tests.

Here are the written test numbers and what they sample:

	Primary	Intermediate	Advanced
Math/Science	oral	1	2
Social studies	oral	3	4
Language/Arts	oral	5	6
Everyday living	oral	7	8

Primary Level (grades 1, 2)
Content Vocabulary

Math/Science
Primary

Acceptable Responses

1. galaxy – **star system**
   Milky Way
   group of stars
2. pulse – **heartbeat**
   regular beat
   throb
3. vibrating – **shaking**
   moving back and forth
   unsteady motion
4. cycle – **repeating**
   time period
   regularly occurring
5. electricity – **electric current**
   power
   runs lamps, appliances
6. root – **part of a plant**
   under the ground
   feeds the plant
7. plus – **addition sign**
   add
   symbol used in arithmetic
8. equal – **having the same value**
   the same amount
   symbol used in arithmetic
9. height – **how tall**
   vertical side of a figure
   length of the vertical side
10. factor – **part of a product**
    reduce
    part of a multiplication problem

Acceptable Responses

11. minus – **subtraction sign**
    subtract
    comparison of two variables
12. quotient – **answer in division problem**
    how many times
    answer to ratio
13. angle – **slant**
    corner
    distance between diverging lines
14. average – **mean**
    add up and divide
    total score divided by number
    of scores
15. diameter – **width of a circle**
    length across a circle
    line which bisects a circle
16. graph – **chart**
    figure
    symbol used in arithmetic
17. melt – **change to liquid**
    dissolve
    turn into water
18. gravity – **having weight**
    pull of the earth
    center of gravity
19. liquid – **water**
    fluid
    pours freely
20. heat – **warmth**
    hot
    high temperature

Social Studies
Primary

Acceptable Responses

1. west – **direction**
   where the sun sets
   reference point
2. lake – **body of water**
   inland water
   pond
3. travel – **take a trip**
   go someplace
   journey
4. east – **direction**
   where the sun rises
   reference point
5. mayor – **elected official**
   head of the city
   chief of the city

Acceptable Responses

6. explorer – **discoverer**
   travels to faraway places
   seeks information
7. woodland – **forest**
   timberland
   covered with trees
8. trade – **exchange**
   swap
   business
9. transportation – **carrying goods**
   moving goods
   system of movement
10. climate – **weather**
    weather conditions over time
    region of the earth

Content Vocabulary Tests Instructions

278

11. goods – **things bought**
    things sold
    equipment, cloth, stuff
12. citizen – **member of society**
    lives in the town
    member of state
13. factory – **place where things are made**
    manufacturing facility
    building where things
    are made
14. frontier – **wild country**
    border
    unknown area
15. disaster – **sudden bad event**
    destruction
    terrible event

16. foreign – **another country**
    not from here
    outside the country
17. atlas – **map book**
    charts
    maps
18. communication – **message**
    sending and receiving
    messages
    exchange of information
19. harbor – **where ships load**
    protected body of water
    deep water close to shore
20. capital – **location of government**
    main city
    important place

Language/Music
Primary

1. props – **objects used in a play**
   scenery
   objects
2. parentheses – **curved lines**
   used to separate words
   contain an explanatory
   phrase
3. conversation – **talk**
   discussion
   exchange of ideas
4. vocabulary – **words you know**
   words you use
   list of word meanings
5. character – **person**
   someone in a story
   strange person
6. paragraph – **unit of writing**
   contains one idea
   begins on a new line
7. sentence – **a written statement**
   says one thing
   related group of words
8. dictionary – **book of words**
   explains words
   reference
9. plural – **more than one**
   many
   grammar form
10. synonyms – **same meaning**
    two words mean the same
    sometimes mean the same

11. poems – **verse**
    story that rhymes
    story in verse
12. rhymes – **sounds alike**
    same endings
    same sounds at the end
13. riddle – **puzzle**
    problem
    question
14. solo – **one voice**
    singing alone
    playing alone
15. chords – **musical notes**
    tone
    blended sounds
16. melody – **tune**
    arrangement of sounds
    nice music
17. stage – **platform**
    where the actors are
    theatre
18. actor – **man in a play**
    plays a character
    plays a part
19. author – **writes books**
    writer
    writes stories
20. audience – **those watching**
    those listening
    spectators

Content Vocabulary Tests Instructions

Everyday Living
Primary

Acceptable Responses

1. boy – **young man**
   male child
   school-age male
2. woman – **lady**
   adult female
   older girl
3. come – **get closer**
   get over here
   walk over
4. sit – **take a seat**
   take a chair
   stay still
5. water – **a liquid**
   drink it
   lake, river
6. year – **12 months**
   January to December
   from one birthday to the next
7. say – **tell**
   speak
   talk
8. follow – **go along**
   go behind
   obey directions
9. price – **cost**
   value
   how much
10. stop – **cease motion**
    prevent
    quit

Acceptable Responses

11. children – **kids**
    boys and girls
    young boys and girls
12. walk – **go by foot**
    path for walking
    sidewalk
13. boss – **person in charge**
    chief
    order around
14. save – **keep money**
    don't waste
    keep for later
15. tool – **utensil**
    for working with
    hammer, screwdriver
16. name – **what you're called**
    what something is called
    description
17. date of birth – **when you were born**
    birthday
    day and year of birth
18. age – **how old you are**
    time of life
    get older
19. left – **direction**
    opposite of right
    (indicates hand or points)
20. emergency – **need help**
    immediate action
    immediate need

280

Confident

1. membrane   a) unit of the body
              b) layer of tissue
              c) long bones

2. solar cell   a) three-dimensional mass
                b) produced during sunspot activity
                c) converts sunlight to electricity

3. nonconductor   a) does not allow transmission of current
                  b) goes against society
                  c) made out of hard metal

4. hibernate   a) period of dormancy
               b) go into seclusion
               c) foolishness

5. ecosystem   a) lawmaking group
               b) monetary policies
               c) environmental interrelationships

6. spore   a) boxing practice
           b) germ cell
           c) poisonous

7. reproduction   a) process giving rise to offspring
                  b) lengthy mining process
                  c) to start over again

8. reptile   a) type of floor covering
             b) to give information
             c) scaly, creeping animal

9. counterclockwise   a) right around the clock
                      b) left around the clock
                      c) regular dweller

10. fossil fuel   a) coal, oil, natural gas
                  b) petrified remains
                  c) oat, corn, barley

11. microorganism   a) a microscope
                    b) a microbe
                    c) a type of paper

12. ore   a) manually propel a boat
          b) narrow minded
          c) metal bearing mineral

13. circuit   a) electrical path
              b) travelling show
              c) point of crossing

14. tangent   a) a power hammer
              b) a juicy citrus fruit
              c) trigonometric function

15. negative number   a) an odd number
                      b) less than zero
                      c) no place value

16. circumference   a) percent of inside area
                    b) committee meeting
                    c) perimeter of a circle

17. cylinder   a) roller shaped object
               b) equal sided triangle
               c) a reference book

18. decimal   a) a fraction
              b) loudness of sound
              c) type of dessert

19. common factor   a) representing the same issue
                    b) divides evenly into two numbers
                    c) same size rectangles

20. mean   a) highest score
           b) average score
           c) combination of parts

281

1. abyss
   a) infected cyst
   b) bottomless pit
   c) road equipment

2. axis
   a) being able to reach something
   b) to keep changing one's mind
   c) straight line about which things revolve

3. condense
   a) to make more compact
   b) change from solid to liquid
   c) a general agreement

4. epicenter
   a) part of a continuing story
   b) earth's surface above the center of an earthquake
   c) inside concentric circle of a geometric form

5. diatom
   a) unicellular algae
   b) four-sided figure
   c) combination of proton and electron

6. saturation
   a) holding up to ridicule
   b) make a strong promise
   c) maximum concentration

7. solstice
   a) point of greatest distance from sun
   b) point of closest distance from sun
   c) electromagnetic switch

8. species
   a) one of a kind
   b) biological classification below genus
   c) a scale of values

9. blood pressure
   a) pressure exerted by the blood
   b) pressure at which the veins burst
   c) hemoglobin count

10. convex
    a) curved in
    b) curved out
    c) violent shaking

11. pasteurization
    a) soft, pale colors
    b) branching out from the center
    c) partial sterilization by heat

12. reflex
    a) related to the subject of the sentence
    b) type of blood vessel
    c) an inborn act

13. algorithm
    a) step-by-step procedure
    b) letters representing numbers
    c) musical composition

14. arc
    a) a scenic representation
    b) line from center of circle to perimeter
    c) curved line between two points

15. ellipse
    a) partial blocking of the sun
    b) a glowing fragment
    c) oval shape

16. equilateral
    a) having all angles equal
    b) having all sides equal
    c) many sided figure

17. exponent
    a) symbol indicating power of a number
    b) an integral part
    c) a structural form

18. median
    a) average score
    b) fortune teller
    c) middle score

19. pi
    a) 6.28
    b) 3.14
    c) 1/2 of 3.14

20. rational number
    a) number used only in equations
    b) divisible a finite number of times
    c) computer related

282

1. settler a) a type of dog
   b) a pioneer
   c) a highway

2. altitude a) height above sea level
   b) grassy farmland
   c) magnitude of an angle

3. liberty a) freedom
   b) growing up
   c) office building

4. colony a) sail-making factory
   b) disorder of the digestive system
   c) new settlement ruled by another country

5. assembly line a) waiting in line for a meeting
   b) each worker does one part over and over
   c) imaginary line of demarcation

6. income a) amount of money received
   b) a softball game
   c) immigrating to the U.S.

7. amendment a) the healing of broken bones
   b) ratified change in the Constitution
   c) a long dark alleyway

8. scab a) a strike breaker
   b) a bank branch
   c) a kind of spider

9. boycott a) a group of strangers
   b) a harbor-marking device
   c) refusal to buy a product

10. veto a) refuse to approve
    b) one who fought in the war
    c) a type of outer garment

11. civil a) war between nations
    b) to strain out impurities
    c) relating to citizens

12. textile a) a ceramic floor covering
    b) a woven cloth
    c) a chemical compound

13. executive branch a) part of the government
    b) longest limb on the tree
    c) a portion of the upper atmosphere

14. glacier a) a very smooth surface
    b) the flexible part of a shoe
    c) a large moving body of ice

15. fiscal year a) 12-month period used for accounting
    b) a year signifying sunspots
    c) relating to the Roman calendar

16. jury a) very thick forest or jungle
    b) gold rings and bracelets
    c) group of people appointed to give a verdict.

17. poverty a) being poor
    b) a holiday drink
    c) a large area of land

18. ballot a) a secret vote
    b) a poem set to music
    c) certain radio frequencies

19. lobbying a) waiting downstairs in a hotel
    b) planting a tree
    c) influencing lawmakers

20. strait a) a line that does not curve
    b) a narrow waterway
    c) special way of folding paper

283

1. archaeologist
   a) someone who designs buildings
   b) someone who studies old things
   c) an evil person

2. nationalism
   a) patriotic feeling
   b) chemical reaction
   c) all the citizens

3. monarchy
   a) structure in water
   b) multicolored butterfly
   c) country ruled by a king

4. immigrant
   a) one who comes to a country to live
   b) a small gland in the brain
   c) about to take place

5. bipartisan
   a) involving members of two parties
   b) wings above and below the fuselage
   c) without legal force

6. isolationist
   a) not rightly named
   b) having two equal sides
   c) believer in noninterference

7. caucuses
   a) prickly desert plant
   b) closed meetings to decide on policy
   c) hot red pepper

8. primary
   a) voting for election candidates
   b) mounted on horseback
   c) undercoat of paint

9. martial law
   a) a city law officer
   b) serious cattle disease
   c) military government

10. due process
    a) rotational axis
    b) calling in a loan
    c) adherence to proper procedure

11. featherbedding
    a) a quilt stuffed with down
    b) requiring more jobs than necessary
    c) adjacent to the forehead

12. constituents
    a) residents in an electoral district
    b) parts something is made of
    c) an area near the North Pole

13. annexation
    a) being next to
    b) incorporate within government domain
    c) reserved for the clergy

14. commonwealth
    a) a state or union of nations
    b) national treasury
    c) water-cooled pipe

15. summit meeting
    a) top of the mountain
    b) conference of high level officials
    c) divide into triangles

16. impeachment
    a) charge a public official with misconduct
    b) a skin infection found in children
    c) grove of fruit trees

17. ordinance
    a) weapons
    b) a law
    c) a bay window

18. revenue
    a) income
    b) worthless
    c) variety act

19. AFL-CIO
    a) football conference
    b) NATO
    c) labor organization

20. ratification
    a) random
    b) approval
    c) exterminate

1. biography a) harvesting machine
b) written history of a person's life
c) study of living tissue

2. pronunciation a) manner of saying words
b) part of speech referring to persons
c) a dangerous twig

3. byline a) farewell
b) piece of cloth
c) line indicating author's name

4. dialogue a) conversation between two or more persons
b) clock face
c) religious belief

5. primary colors a) navy uniforms
b) yellow, blue, red
c) mostly red colored

6. fantasy a) outer space
b) a safety platform
c) an imaginary happening

7. science fiction a) tale based on unproven extensions of current knowledge
b) the acquisition of knowledge through stories
c) a deep shovel for digging in soft soil

8. characterization a) a special feature
b) portrayal of a role
c) preserved foods

9. flashback a) return to earlier occurrence
b) unit of weight
c) waterproofing around chimney

10. abstract a) absent-minded
b) in poor condition
c) difficult to understand

11. novel a) fictional book
b) short story
c) combining of atoms

12. card catalog a) collection of greeting cards
b) list of books arranged systematically
c) loud, ringing sound

13. entertainment a) a steep grade
b) adventurous
c) a show

14. return address a) address of sender
b) reply address
c) controls electricity

15. essay a) to analyze ore
b) short piece of writing
c) tuba-like instrument

16. adjective a) modifier of a noun
b) mixing up
c) having a common border

17. present tense a) making a gift
b) expressive of present time
c) big reputation

18. harmony a) employed in industry
b) severe injury
c) melody arrangement

19. improvisation a) not decent
b) a kind of rhythm
c) unrehearsed act

20. volume a) surface area
b) loudness
c) paraffin

285

1. plot
   a) to fall flat
   b) plan of a story
   c) agreeable person

2. unabridged
   a) complete
   b) strange
   c) road washed out

3. abbreviation
   a) not present
   b) stream of charged particles
   c) shortened form of a word

4. subordinate clause
   a) dependent on another clause
   b) a legal document
   c) dependent child

5. interrogative
   a) shellfish
   b) question
   c) disrupt continuity

6. narration
   a) less than normal width
   b) a safety platform
   c) telling a story

7. index card
   a) found in card catalogue
   b) left side of a ship
   c) contains contents of book

8. outline
   a) contours
   b) plan
   c) treachery

9. script
   a) text of a play
   b) paper money
   c) a piece of wood

10. analogy
    a) skilled in analysis
    b) belief in yourself
    c) correspondence

11. edit
    a) give desired result
    b) prepare for publication
    c) command

12. drama
    a) story depicting serious events
    b) unit of measurement
    c) the space between things

13. thesis
    a) plural of this
    b) introductory statement
    c) main point in an essay

14. metaphor
    a) part of a poem
    b) figure of speech
    c) radioactive chemical

15. chronological
    a) according to the order of time
    b) high-quality sound
    c) instrument that tells time

16. ballad
    a) a voting slip
    b) a story song
    c) a clumsy fellow

17. ballet
    a) dance performance to convey story
    b) working only for money
    c) a travelling minstrel

18. overture
    a) an exaggeration
    b) a type of check
    c) orchestral introduction

19. hue
    a) a gardening implement
    b) gradation of color
    c) Greek letter

20. stage right
    a) use an opportunity
    b) to set up correctly
    c) position in the acting area

1. hazardous a) cloudy
           b) dangerous
           c) untrue

2. credit a) paying later
       b) business slump
       c) a small fish

3. employee a) hires people
          b) imaginary
          c) paid worker

4. maiden name a) nickname
             b) name before marriage
             c) military title

5. appointment a) a set time and day
            b) a sharp edge
            c) work done at home

6. full-time a) no time clock
         b) very thin
         c) work all day

7. investment a) outlay of money for profit
          b) type of special clothing
          c) interchange

8. personal property a) where you live
                 b) large tract of land
                 c) one's possessions

9. market value a) consumer interest in a product
             b) price agreeable to buyer and seller
             c) closeness to shopping area

10. interest a) fee for using money
         b) something unusual
         c) insurance

11. net proceeds a) amount taken in
            b) conduct estimate
            c) amount left after expenses

12. admission price a) discount price
               b) ticket cost
               c) confession

13. schedule a) timetable
          b) appointment
          c) division

14. fare a) unbiased
      b) ticket cost
      c) a long way

15. holiday a) day off from work
        b) sick day
        c) temporary

16. bank a) handkerchief
      b) save or borrow money
      c) school building

17. savings account a) safe-deposit box
                b) curved edge
                c) money in the bank

18. postal service a) process the mail
              b) bookkeeping office
              c) answering service

19. utility companies a) street paving
                  b) phone, electric, water, gas
                  c) landscaping

20. probation a) on-the-job trial period
           b) professional athlete
           c) pre-retirement period

1. FICA a) state retirement tax
          b) social security tax
          c) proceeds

2. exemption a) taxable at a higher rate
              b) argument over money
              c) portion not taxable

3. double time a) twice the hourly wage
                b) work twice as many hours
                c) two time clocks

4. commission a) hourly salary
               b) large agency
               c) percent of sales

5. collateral a) security for a loan
               b) investment
               c) applies only to bonds

6. depreciation a) nasty remarks
                 b) decrease in value over time
                 c) increase in taxes

7. estimate a) estate tax due
             b) statement of approximate cost
             c) hard to bear

8. dependents a) trustworthy
               b) all sources of income
               c) those needing another's support

9. employment history a) record of previous jobs
                       b) where you would like to work
                       c) government job

10. take-home pay a) pay that does not go in the bank
                   b) total pay including vacation pay
                   c) amount of pay left after all deductions

11. withholding a) deduction of taxes from pay
                 b) keeping information secret
                 c) profitable investment

12. qualifications a) skills related to a job
                    b) what you like to do
                    c) market value

13. punch in a) note departure time
              b) fight at work
              c) note arrival time

14. overtime a) working the night shift
              b) more than eight hours in one day
              c) getting to work late

15. finance charge a) fee for paperwork
                    b) applies only to credit cards
                    c) interest on purchase

16. safe-deposit box a) for night deposits
                      b) rented compartment in vault
                      c) box for overdue library books

17. express mail a) foreign mail delivery
                  b) next day delivery
                  c) shipped by freight

18. answering service a) service that answers personal letters
                       b) information directory
                       c) service that answers client's telephones

19. prime rate a) interest banks charge other banks
                b) long-term home mortgage interest
                c) interest banks pay to individuals

20. promissory note a) written loan application
                     b) written agreement to pay money
                     c) consolidation of bad debts

288

ANSWER KEY

Math/Science

Advanced (Obj. 12i)		Intermediate (Obj. 11i)	
1.	b	1.	b
2.	c	2.	c
3.	a	3.	a
4.	b	4.	a
5.	a	5.	c
6.	c	6.	b
7.	a	7.	a
8.	b	8.	c
9.	a	9.	b
10.	b	10.	a
11.	c	11.	b
12.	c	12.	c
13.	a	13.	a
14.	c	14.	c
15.	c	15.	b
16.	b	16.	c
17.	a	17.	a
18.	c	18.	a
19.	b	19.	b
20.	b	20.	b

Social Studies

Advanced (Obj. 9i)		Intermediate (Obj. 8i)	
1.	b	1.	b
2.	a	2.	a
3.	c	3.	a
4.	a	4.	c
5.	a	5.	b
6.	c	6.	a
7.	b	7.	b
8.	a	8.	a
9.	c	9.	c
10.	c	10.	a
11.	b	11.	c
12.	a	12.	b
13.	b	13.	a
14.	a	14.	c
15.	b	15.	a
16.	a	16.	c
17.	b	17.	a
18.	a	18.	a
19.	c	19.	c
20.	b	20.	b

Language/Music

Advanced (Obj. 6i)		Intermediate (Obj. 5i)	
1.	b	1.	b
2.	a	2.	a
3.	c	3.	c
4.	a	4.	a
5.	b	5.	b
6.	c	6.	c
7.	a	7.	a
8.	b	8.	b
9.	a	9.	a
10.	c	10.	c
11.	b	11.	a
12.	a	12.	b
13.	c	13.	c
14.	b	14.	a
15.	a	15.	b
16.	b	16.	a
17.	a	17.	b
18.	c	18.	c
19.	b	19.	c
20.	c	20.	b

Everyday Living

Advanced (Obj. 3i)		Intermediate (Obj. 2i)	
1.	b	1.	b
2.	c	2.	a
3.	a	3.	c
4.	c	4.	b
5.	a	5.	a
6.	b	6.	c
7.	b	7.	a
8.	c	8.	c
9.	a	9.	b
10.	c	10.	a
11.	a	11.	c
12.	a	12.	b
13.	c	13.	a
14.	b	14.	b
15.	c	15.	a
16.	b	16.	b
17.	b	17.	c
18.	c	18.	a
19.	a	19.	b
20.	b	20.	a